Nomad

Also by Ayaan Hirsi Ali

The Caged Virgin:
An Emancipation Proclamation for Women and Islam

Infidel

Nomad

FROM ISLAM
to AMERICA

*A Personal Journey
Through the Clash
of Civilizations*

Ayaan Hirsi Ali

SIMON &
SCHUSTER

London · New York · Sydney · Toronto

A CBS COMPANY

First published in Great Britain in 2010 by Simon & Schuster UK Ltd
A CBS COMPANY

Copyright © 2010 by Ayaan Hirsi Ali

1 3 5 7 9 10 8 6 4 2

Simon & Schuster UK Ltd
1st Floor
222 Gray's Inn Road
London
WC1X 8HB

www.simonandschuster.co.uk

Simon & Schuster Australia
Sydney

The names of many of the characters and locations in this book
have been changed, as have certain identifying characteristics.

A CIP catalogue copy for this book is available
from the British Library.

ISBN: 978-1-84737-664-0

Printed in the UK by CPI Mackays, Chatham ME5 8TD

To Chris DeMuth, my surrogate abeh—
a friend, a mentor, a guide to American life—
with respect and love

Narrated 'Imran bin Husain:

The Prophet said, "I looked at Paradise and found poor people forming the majority of its inhabitants; and I looked at Hell and saw that the majority of its inhabitants were women."
Hadith—Sahih Bukhari 4:464

Contents

PART III

SEX, MONEY, VIOLENCE

PART IV

REMEDIES

Introduction

All my life I have been a nomad. I have wandered, rootless. Every place I have settled in, I have been forced to flee; every certainty I have been taught, I have cast aside.

I was born in Mogadishu, Somalia, in 1969. When I was very small my father was jailed for his role in the political opposition to the brutal dictatorship. Then he escaped from prison and fled into exile. When I was eight my mother took my siblings and me to Saudi Arabia to live with him. A year later we were expelled from Saudi Arabia and moved to Ethiopia, where my father's opposition group was headquartered. After about eighteen months there, we moved again, to Kenya.

Every change of country threw me unprepared into whole new languages and sharply different habits of mind. Each time, I made a child's forlorn, often vain attempts to adapt. The one constant in my life was my mother's unbending attachment to Islam.

My father left Kenya, and us, when I was eleven. I didn't see him again until I was twenty-one. During his absence I had become a fervent and pious Muslim, under the influence of a schoolteacher. I also returned, for eight months, to Somalia, where I experienced the birth of the civil war and the chaos and brutality of the great exodus of 1991, when half the country was displaced and 350,000 people died.

When I was twenty-two my father ordered me to marry a relative, a stranger to me, who lived in Toronto, Canada. On my way from Kenya to Canada I was supposed to stop off in Germany, where I would pick up my visa to Canada and then continue my journey. Instead a kind of instinctive desperation prompted me to bolt. I took a train to Holland. This voyage was even more wrenching than the other journeys I had made, and my heart pounded with the implications of what I was doing and what my father and my clan would do when they discovered that I had run away.

In Holland I discovered the kindness of strangers. I was nothing to these people, and yet they fed and housed me, taught me their language, and allowed me to learn whatever I wanted to. Holland worked in a way that was different from any other country in which I had lived. It was peaceful, stable, prosperous, tolerant, generous, deeply good. As I learned Dutch I began to formulate an almost impossibly ambitious goal: I would study political science to find out why *this* society, although it appeared to me to be godless, *worked* when every society I had lived in, no matter how Muslim it claimed to be, was rotten with corruption, violence, and self-centered guile.

For a long time I teetered between the clear ideals of the Enlightenment that I learned about at university and my submission to the equally clear dictates of Allah that I feared to disobey. Working my way through university as a Dutch-Somali translator for the Dutch social services, I met many Muslims in difficult circumstances, in homes for battered women, prisons, special education classes. I never connected the dots—in fact I sought to avoid connecting the dots—so I could not see the connection between their belief in Islam and their poverty, between their religion and the oppression of women and the lack of free, individual choice.

It was, ironically, Osama bin Laden who freed me of those blinkers. After 9/11 I found it impossible to ignore his claims that the murderous destruction of innocent (if infidel) lives is consistent with the Quran. I looked in the Quran, and I found it to be so. To me this meant that I could no longer be a Muslim. In fact I realized then that I had not been a Muslim for a long time.

Speaking out about such matters, I began to receive death threats. I was also asked to run for the Dutch Parliament as a member of the free-market Liberal Party. When I became a member of Parliament, being young and black and female—and often accompanied by a bodyguard—I was very visible. But I was protected; my friends and colleagues were not. After the film director Theo van Gogh and I made a movie depicting how Islam crushes women, Theo was assassinated by a Muslim fanatic, a twenty-six-year-old man who had been born in Morocco and brought to Amsterdam by his parents.

I wrote a memoir, *Infidel,* about my experiences. I described how lucky I felt to have escaped places where people live in tribes and where the affairs of men are conducted according to the dictates and traditions of faith, how glad I was to live in a place where people of both sexes live equally as citizens. I related the random events that made my childhood so erratic; my mother's volatile temper; my father's absence; the caprices of dictators; how we coped with diseases, natural disasters, and wars. I described my arrival in Holland and my first impressions of life in a place where people are not the subjects of tyrants or governed by the dictates of the clan's bloodline but are citizens of governments they elect.

I touched on—but only touched on—my parallel and equally important mental journey. I described some of the questions that formed in my mind, the baby steps I took to make sense of the new world that I had entered, and the experiences that made me question my faith in Islam and the mores of my parents.

When I was writing *Infidel* I imagined that my travels were over. I thought that I was in Holland to stay, that I had taken root in its rich soil and would never have to uproot myself again. But I was wrong. I did have to leave. I came to America—like many before me—in search of an opportunity to build a life and a livelihood in freedom and in safety, a life that would be an ocean away from all the strife I had witnessed and the inner conflict I had suffered. This book, *Nomad,* explains why I chose America.

Readers of *Infidel* all over the world have offered me a great deal of support and encouragement. But they have also asked me a number of questions that I did not address in that book. They asked about the rest of my family. They asked about the experiences of other Muslim women. Time and again I heard the question: How typical was your experience? Are you in any way representative? *Nomad* answers that question. It is not only about my own life as a wanderer in the West; it is also about the lives of many immigrants to the West, the philosophical and very real difficulties of people, especially women, who live in a tightly closed traditional Muslim culture within a broadly open culture. It is about how Islamic ideals clash with Western ideals. It is about the clash of civilizations that I and millions of others have *lived* and continue to live.

When I moved to the United States and began again the process of anchoring myself in a new country, I was assailed by a new and intense homesickness that followed the death of my father in London. Reconnecting with my extended family—cousins and my own half sister—who live in the United States, the UK, and elsewhere, I found them tragically unsteady on their feet. One has AIDS, another has been indicted for attempting to murder her husband, and a third sends all the money he makes back home to Somalia to feed the clan. They all claim to be loyal to the values of our tribe and of Allah. They are permanent residents and citizens of the Western countries where they live, but their hearts and minds lie elsewhere. They dream of a time in Somalia that never existed: a time of peace, love, and harmony. Will they ever take root where they are? It seems unlikely. My discovery of their troubles is one of the subjects of *Nomad*.

So what, you may be thinking. Doesn't every culture have its dysfunctional families? Indeed, for filmmakers in Hollywood, dysfunctional Jewish and Christian families make for great entertainment. But I believe that the dysfunctional Muslim family constitutes a real threat to the very fabric of Western life.

The family is the crucible of human values. It is in the family that children are groomed to practice and promote the norms of their parents' culture. It is in the family that a cycle of loyalties is established and passed on to future generations. It is therefore of the utmost importance that we understand the dynamics of the Muslim family, for they hold the key to (among other things) the susceptibility of so many young Muslim men to Islamic radicalism. It is above all through families that conspiracy theories travel from the mosques and madrassas of Saudi Arabia and Egypt to the living rooms of homes in Holland, France, and America.

Many people in Europe and the United States dispute the thesis that we are living through a clash of civilizations between Islam and the West. But a radical minority of Muslims firmly believes that Islam is under siege. This minority is committed to winning the holy war it has declared against the West. It wants ultimately to restore a theocratic caliphate in Muslim countries and impose it on the rest of the world. A larger group of Muslims, most of them in Europe and America, believes that acts of terror committed by fellow Muslims will unleash a Western backlash against all Muslims indiscriminately. (There is in fact little evidence to suggest that such a backlash is happening, but despite this lack of evidence, the perception among Muslim immigrants persists and is fanned by radicals.) With this collective feeling of being persecuted, many Muslim families living in the West insulate themselves in ghettos of their own making. Within those ghettos the agents of radical Islam cultivate their message of hatred and seek foot soldiers to fight as martyrs for their distorted worldview. Unhappy, disoriented youths in dysfunctional immigrant families make perfect recruits to such a cause. With continuing immigration from the Muslim world and a significantly higher birth rate in Muslim families, this a phenomenon we ignore at our peril.

As an insider, I can illuminate the problem simply by relating the stories of my formative years, which include stories of my siblings and other relatives. In *Nomad* I try to describe how, in the most intimate sphere of family, my father and mother related or failed to relate to one another; the expectations they had of their children; their philosophy of parenting; the identity crisis they bequeathed to their children; their conflicted views toward sexuality, money, and violence; and above all, the role of religion in misshaping our family life.

There are times when I wonder what I would have done if my father had not left us in Kenya. If he had stayed, I would have been married off at a much earlier age and would never have had the courage or opportunity to flee in search of a better life. If my family had never left Somalia or if my mother had gotten her way and kept me at home instead of sending me to school, the seeds of my rebellion might not have taken root, seeds that inspired me to imagine a life for myself that was different from the one that I was accustomed to and different from the life my parents had in store for me. So many circumstances and decisions in my life were not in my control, and only in hindsight do I see the opportunities that allowed me to take control of my life.

out the hard way that lingering between the two value sys-
raddling the gap between the West and Islam, living a life of
guity—with an outward presentation of modernity and self-
ance and an inward clinging to tradition and dependence on the
clan—stunts the process of becoming one's own person. I felt great
mental anguish at the prospect of leaving my father to face the wrath
of our clan after I escaped; I was in a state of mental torture as I con-
templated the consequences of my leaving Islam, consequences that
would not fall on me but on my parents and other relatives. I suffered
many moments of weakness when I too entertained the idea of giving
up my needs and sacrificing my personal happiness for the peace of
mind of my parents, siblings, and clan.

My nomadic journey, in other words, has above all been mental—
even the last stage of that journey, from Holland to the United States. It
was a journey not just over thousands of miles, but a journey through
time, through hundreds of years. It was a journey from Africa, a place
where people are members of a tribe, to Europe and America, where
people are citizens (though they think of citizenship in quite distinct
ways from country to country). There were many misunderstandings,
expectations, and disappointments along the way, and I learned many
lessons. I learned that it is one thing to say farewell to tribal life; it is
quite another to practice the life of a citizen, which so many members
of my family have failed to do. And they are by no means alone.

Today close to a quarter of all people in the world identify themselves as Muslim, and the top ten refugee-producing nations in the
world are also Muslim. Most of those displaced peoples are heading
toward Europe and the United States. The scale of migration from
Muslim countries is almost certain to increase in the coming years
because the birth rate in those countries is so much higher than in the
West. The "problem family"—people like my relatives—will become
more and more common unless Western democracies understand
better how to integrate the newcomers into our societies: how to turn
them into citizens.

I see three main barriers to this process of integration, none of
them peculiar to my family. The first is Islam's treatment of women.
The will of little girls is stifled by Islam. By the time they menstruate they are rendered voiceless. They are reared to become submis-

sive robots who serve in the house as cleaners and cooks. They are required to comply with their father's choice of a mate, and after the wedding their lives are devoted to the sexual pleasures of their husband and to a life of childbearing. Their education is often cut short when they are still young girls, and thus as women they are wholly unable to prepare their own children to become successful citizens in modern, Western societies. Their daughters repeat the same pattern.

Some girls comply. Others lead a double life. Some run away and fall victim to prostitution and drugs. A few make their way on their own, as I did, and may even reconcile with their families. Each story is different, but the common factor is that Muslim women have to contend with much greater family control of their sexuality than women from other religious communities. This, in my view, is the biggest obstacle to the path of successful citizenship—not just for women, but also for the sons they rear and the men those sons become.

The second obstacle, which may seem trivial to some Western readers, is the difficulty many immigrants from Muslim countries have in dealing with money. Islamic attitudes toward credit and debt and the lack of education of Muslim women about financial matters means that most new immigrants arrive in the West wholly unprepared for the bewildering range of opportunities and obligations presented by a modern consumer society.

The third obstacle is the socialization of the Muslim mind. All Muslims are reared to believe that Muhammad, the founder of their religion, was perfectly virtuous and that the moral strictures he left behind should never be questioned. The Quran, as "revealed" to Muhammad, is considered infallible: it is the true word of Allah, and all its commands must be obeyed without question. This makes Muslims vulnerable to indoctrination in a way that followers of other faiths are not. Moreover, the violence that is endemic in so many Muslim societies, ranging from domestic violence to the incessant celebration of holy war, adds to the difficulty of turning people from that world into Western citizens.

I can sum up the three obstacles to the integration of people like my own family in three words: sex, money, and violence.

*   *   *

In the last part *of Nomad* I suggest some remedies. The West tends to respond to the social failures of Muslim immigrants with what can be called the racism of low expectations. This Western attitude is based on the idea that people of color must be exempted from "normal" standards of behavior. A well-meaning class of people holds that minorities should not share all of the obligations that the majority must meet. In liberal, democratic countries the majorities are white and most minorities are people of color. But most Muslims, like all other immigrants, migrate to the West not to be locked up in a minority, but to search for a better life, one that is safe and predictable and that holds the prospect of a better income and the opportunity of a good quality education for their children. To achieve this, I believe, they must learn to give up some of their habits, dogmas, and practices and acquire new ones.

There are many good men and women in the West who try to resettle refugees, scold their fellow citizens for not doing more, donate money to philanthropic organizations, and strive to eliminate discrimination. They lobby governments to exempt minorities from the standards of behavior of Western societies; they fight to help minorities preserve their cultures, and they excuse their religion from critical scrutiny. These people mean well, I have no doubt. But I believe that their well-intentioned activism is now a part of the very problem they seek to solve. To be blunt, their efforts to assist Muslims and other minorities are futile because, by postponing or at best prolonging the process of their transition to modernity—by creating the illusion that one can hold on to tribal norms and at the same time become a successful citizen—the proponents of multiculturalism lock subsequent generations born in the West into a no-man's-land of moral values. What comes packaged in a compassionate language of acceptance is really a cruel form of racism. And it is all the more cruel because it is expressed in sugary words of virtue.

I believe there are three institutions in Western society that could ease the transition into Western citizenship of these millions of nomads from the tribal cultures they are leaving. They are institutions that can compete with the agents of jihad for the hearts and minds of Muslims.

The first is public education. The European Enlightenment of the eighteenth century gave birth to schools and universities run on the principles of critical thinking. Education was aimed at helping the masses emancipate themselves from poverty, superstition, and tyranny through the development of their cognitive abilities. With the spread of democracy in the nineteenth and twentieth centuries, access to such reason-based institutions steadily expanded. Children from all social backgrounds were taught not only math, geography, science, and the arts, but also the social skills and the discipline required to achieve success in the world beyond the classroom. Literature expanded and challenged their imaginations so that they could empathize with characters from other times and places. This public education was geared toward grooming citizens, not preserving the separateness of tribe, the sanctity of the faith, or whatever happened to be the prejudice of the day.

Today, however, many schools and campuses in the West have opted to be more "considerate" of the faith, customs, and habits of the immigrant students they find in their classrooms. Out of a misguided politeness they refrain from openly challenging the beliefs of Muslim children and their parents. Textbooks gloss over the fundamentally unjust rules of Islam and present it as a peaceful religion. Institutions of reason must cast off these self-imposed blinkers and reinvest in developing the ability to think critically, no matter how impolite some people may find the results.

The second institution that can and must do more is the feminist movement. Western feminists should take on the plight of the Muslim woman and make it their own cause. Their aim should be to help the Muslim woman find her voice. Western feminists have a wealth of experience and resources at their disposal. There are three goals they must aspire to in helping their Muslim sisters. The first is to ensure that Muslim girls are free to complete their education; the second is to help them gain ownership of their own bodies and therefore their sexuality; and the third is to make sure that Muslim women have the opportunity not only to enter the workforce but also to stay in it. Unlike Muslim women in Muslim countries and Western women in the past, Muslim women in the West face specific constraints imposed on them by their families and communities. It is not enough to classify their problems as "domestic violence"; they are domestic in practice but legal and cultural in nature. There should be campaigns dedicated to exposing the special circumstances and restrictions of Muslim women and the dangers they face in the West; to educate Muslim men on the importance of women's emancipation and education and to punish them when they use violence; to protect Muslim women from physical harm.

The third and final institution I call on to rise to this challenge is the community of Christian churches. I myself have become an atheist, but I have encountered many Muslims who say they need a spiritual anchor in their lives. I have had the pleasure of meeting Christians whose concept of God is a far cry from Allah. Theirs is a reformed and partly secularized Christianity that could be a very useful ally in the battle against Islamic fanaticism. This modern Christian God is synonymous with love. His agents do not preach hatred, intolerance, and discord; this God is merciful, does not seek state power, and sees no competition with science. His followers view the Bible as a book full of parables, not direct commands to be obeyed. Right now, there are two extremes in Christianity, both of which are a liability to Western civilization. The first consists of those who damn the existence of other groups, They take the Bible literally and reject scientific explanations for the existence of man and nature in the name of "intelligent design." Such fundamentalist Christian groups invest a lot of time and energy in converting people. But much of what they preach is at odds with the core principles of the Enlightenment. At the other extreme are those who would appease Islam—like the spiritual head of the Church of England, the Archbishop of Canterbury, who holds that the implementation of Shari'a in the UK is inevitable. Those who adhere to a moderate, peaceful, reformed Christianity are not as active as the first group nor as vocal as the second. They should be. The Christianity of love and tolerance remains one of the West's most powerful antidotes to the Islam of hate and intolerance. Ex-Muslims find Jesus Christ to be a more attractive and humane figure than Muhammad, the founder of Islam.

My time as a nomad is coming to an end. My final destination has turned out to be the United States, as it has been for so many millions of wanderers for over two hundred years. America is now my home.

For better or worse, I share in the destiny of other Americans, and I would like to repay their generosity in welcoming me to their unique free society by sharing with them the insights I have gained through my years as a tribal Muslim nomad.

The message of *Nomad* is clear and can be stated at the outset: The West urgently needs to compete with the jihadis, the proponents of a holy war, for the hearts and minds of its own Muslim immigrant populations. It needs to provide education directed at breaking the spell of the infallible Prophet, to protect women from the oppressive dictates of the Quran, and to promote alternative sources of spirituality.

The contents of *Nomad,* like those of *Infidel,* are largely subjective. I make no claims to an exclusive possession of the one and only solution to becoming a successful citizen. Human nature, being what it is, does not lend itself to neat categories of "assimilable" and "unassimilable." There is no ready-made manual containing a recipe for an easy and hurdle-free reconciliation with modernity. Each individual is different and must contend with his or her unique set of opportunities and constraints. The same applies to families and communities faced with the twin challenges of adopting a new way of life while at the same time remaining true to the traditions of their forefathers and faiths.

In the end, then, this remains a very personal book, a kind of reckoning with my own roots. You might say the book is addressed to Sahra, the little sister I left behind in the world that I escaped. But it is also the conversation I would like to have had with my family, especially my father, who once understood and even propagated the modern life I now lead, before he fell back into a trance of submission to Allah. It is the conversation I would like to have had with my grandmother, who taught me to honor our bloodline, come what may.

While writing this book I constantly had in mind my brother's son, Jacob, growing up in Nairobi, and Sahra's baby daughter, Sagal, who was born in a bubble of Somalia in England. I hope that they will grow straight and strong and healthy—but also, above all, free.

PART I

A PROBLEM FAMILY

CHAPTER 1

My Father

When I walked into the Intensive Care Unit of the Royal London Hospital to see my father, I feared I might have come too late. He was sprawled across the hospital bed, his mouth eerily agape, and the machines that were attached to him were many and menacing. They beeped and ticked, and the lines that rapidly rose and fell on their monitors all seemed to be indicating a rapid countdown to his death.

"*Abeh*," I yelled at the top of my voice. "*Abeh*, it's me, Ayaan."

I squeezed his hand and anxiously kissed his forehead, and my father's eyes flew open. He smiled, and the warmth of his gaze and his smile radiated through the whole room. I put my palms over his right hand and he squeezed them and tried to speak, to force out at least a word or two. But he could only wheeze and gasp for breath. He strained to sit up, but he couldn't lift his body.

He was covered with white sheets, and it looked as if he were tied to the bed. Bald, he looked much smaller than I remembered. There was a terrible tube in his throat that was giving him oxygen through a ventilator; another led from his kidney to a dialysis machine, and yet another mess of tubes went into his wrist. I sat beside him and stroked his face and told him, "Abeh, Abeh, it's all right. Abeh, my poor Abeh, you're so sick."

He couldn't answer. Trying to speak, he would fall back, his chest pumping, and the machine that gave him oxygen would hiss and gasp for more air. Then, after resting for a moment or two, he would try again. He indicated with his right hand that he wanted a pen to write with, but he could hardly hold it; his muscles were too weak and he

3

made only scratches on the paper. He was struggling so hard to hold the pen that he began sliding off the bed.

The ward was large, and nurses were bustling about changing sheets and giving medication. I noticed that the doctor had an accent and for a moment thought that he was from Mexico. When I asked where he came from he told me that he was from Spain. The ward was run almost entirely by immigrants. I could not tell the nurses from the doctors, and as I looked around I tried to guess the origins of the members of the medical team, technicians, and cleaners: the Indian Peninsula, blacks who I thought were from East or West Africa, people who looked North African, a few women with headscarves over their medical uniforms. If there were any Somali employees in the ward I did not see them, and fortunately they did not see me.

One of the nurses unrolled a plastic smock, tied it around her waist, and asked me to step aside, but my father would not let go of me and I had to pry his fingers from around my hand. The nurse propped him up higher with pillows, staring at me oddly. One of the nurses told me that she had read an article about me in a magazine, so some of them knew who I was. I glanced away and noticed the chart on his bed; it listed my father as Hirsi Magan Abdirahman, although his name is Hirsi Magan Isse.

A young doctor told me that my father had leukemia. He could have lived another year had he not caught an infection, which had become septic. Now, although he was out of the coma that he had fallen into a few days earlier, only the machines were keeping him alive. I asked again and again if my father was in pain, but the doctor said no, he was uncomfortable, but there was no pain.

I asked the doctor if I could take a picture with my father. He refused. He said we needed to ask the permission of the patient, and the patient was not in any state to make that decision.

In 1992, when I left him in Nairobi, my father was a strong, vital man. He could be fierce, even frightening—a lion, a leader of men. When I was growing up he was my lord, my hero, someone whose absence was mysterious, whose presence I longed for, whose approval meant everything and whose wrath I feared.

Now so many disputes lay between us. I had offended him deeply in 1992 by running away from a Somali man he had chosen for me to marry. He had forgiven me for that; we had spoken together, stiffly, on the phone. A decade later I offended him again, when I declared myself an unbeliever and openly criticized Islam's treatment of women. Our last, and worst, conflict was after I made a film about the abuse and oppression of Muslim women, *Submission,* with Theo van Gogh in 2004. After that my father simply would not answer the phone; he would not talk to me. Sometime after Theo was killed, when I had to go into hiding and my phone was taken away from me, I stopped trying to call him. When people asked, I could say only that we were estranged.

I learned he was sick in June 2008, only a few weeks before his death. I had received a message from Marco, my ex-boyfriend in Holland, saying that my cousin Magool in England was looking for me urgently. Magool is not close to my father's family, but she is resourceful. When my half sister, Sahra, realized how sick my father was, she asked Magool to try to track me down, and Magool called Marco, the only person she knew to whom I had been close when she and I had last spoken, five years earlier.

I phoned my father at his apartment in a housing development in the East End of London. It was late in the evening where he was, a bright sunny afternoon on the East Coast of America where I was. I was shaking. When he came to the phone he sounded just like himself, strong and excited. At the sound of his voice I felt tears welling in my eyes and I said the only thing I wanted to convey, that I loved him, and I heard his smile, so powerful it seemed to come through the telephone.

"Of course you love me!" he burst out loudly. "And of course I love you! Haven't you seen how parents cuddle and connect with their children? Haven't you been out in nature where you see how animals pet and lick their young? Of course I love you. You are my child."

I told my father how much I wanted to see him, but I explained that it might be difficult to arrange security for a visit to his apartment, which is a mostly immigrant area and overwhelmingly Muslim. To visit such a place without protection would be like a very small insect risking a flight through a roomful of huge spiders' webs; the little bug might get through unnoticed, but if it gets caught the consequences are clear. On the other hand, if I went there *with* police, that would be bound to cause ill feeling, as if I could not trust my own family.

"Security!" my father cried. "What do you need security for? Allah will protect you against anyone who wants to harm you! No one in our community will lay a finger on you. And besides, our family has never had a reputation for being cowardly! In fact the other day one of our most prominent clan members said that he wanted to debate with you. If you want, I can ask them to put together a delegation and take you to Jeddah, so you can debate him in Saudi Arabia! Why don't you arrange a press conference and say that you are no longer an unbeliever? Tell them that you have returned to Islam and from now on you're a businesswoman!"

I laughed quietly at my father, and for a while I just enjoyed listening to him talk. Then I asked after his health. He said, "You must remember, Ayaan, that our health and our lives are in the hands of Allah. I am on my way to the hereafter. My dear child, what I want you to do is read just one chapter of the Quran. *Laa-uqsim Bi-yawmi-il-qiyaama.*"

He recited—in Arabic, of course, though we were speaking Somali—a chapter called "The Resurrection": "I do call to witness the resurrection day; and I do call to witness the self-reproaching spirit; Does man think that we cannot assemble his bones? Nay, we are able to put together in perfect order the very tips of his fingers. But man wishes to do wrong in the time in front of him; he questions, when is the day of resurrection?"

I told my father that I would not lie to him, and that I no longer believed in the example of the Prophet. He cut me off, and his tone became passionate, impatient, then retributive. He read me more verses of the Quran, translating them into Somali, and he listed many examples of people like me, who had left Islam but had come back to the faith. He talked about hordes of non-Muslims converting to Islam across the globe, and he told me about the one true god; he warned me not to risk my hereafter.

As I listened to him I told myself that this magisterial lecture was from a father expressing his love in the only way he knew. I wanted to believe that the very fact that he was lecturing me meant that, in some deeper sense, he had begun to forgive me for the person I had become. Possibly, however, it was not that. Possibly he was only doing his duty. Living as a Western woman meant I had shed my honor; I wore Western clothes, which to him was no better than if I walked around wearing no clothes at all. Worst of all, I had abjured Islam and written a book with the brazen, triumphant title *Infidel* to proclaim my apostasy. But my father knew that his life was coming to an end, and he wanted to make sure that all his children, despite their errors, were safe on a path to heaven.

I let him talk. I didn't make false promises to convert. If I had, that might have helped him leave in peace, but I couldn't do it, I couldn't lie to him about that. I managed to tell him gently that although I no longer agreed with Islam, I would read the Quran. I did not add that, every time I reread it, I became more critical of its messages.

He broke into a series of supplications: "May Allah protect you, may He bring you back to the straight path, may He take you to Heaven in the hereafter, may Allah bless you and keep you healthy." And at the end of every supplication I responded with the required formula: "*Amin,*" May it be so.

After a little while I told my father I had a flight to catch. He didn't ask where to, or why; I could tell that the details of terrestrial matters had little bearing for him now. Then I hung up, with so many more things left unsaid between us, and I almost missed the plane that was taking me to a conference in Brazil on multiculturalism.

At the end of June, after the conference in Brazil, I was scheduled to go to Australia for a colloquium on the Enlightenment. I planned to visit my father in London at the end of the summer. But in mid-August, on my way back from Australia, during a stopover in Los Angeles, I received another phone call from Marco. My father was in a coma.

I called my cousin Magool again, and she gave me the cell phone number of my half sister, Sahra. The last time I'd seen my father's youngest child, in 1992, Sahra was eight or nine years old, a wiry, energetic little kid. I had met her when stopping off in Ethiopia en route from my home in Kenya to Germany. From there, on my father's orders, I was supposed to go on to Canada, to join a man I barely knew, who was a distant cousin and who had become my husband. In those days Sahra lived in Addis Ababa with her mother, who, like my own mother, was still married to my father in spite of his absence. I had played with this little half sister of mine all afternoon, struggling to remember my childhood Amharic, which was the only language Sahra spoke back then and which I too had spoken when I was her age and still lived with my father.

Now, in the summer of 2008, Sahra was twenty-four. She was married and had her own four-month-old daughter. She lived with her mother, my father's third wife.

I didn't tell Sahra that I planned to visit our father in the hospital. It's a hideous thing to write, but I didn't really know if I could trust her with that information. I assume the closest members of my family don't actually want to kill me, but the truth is that I have shamed and hurt them; they have to deal with the outrage that my public statements cause, and undoubtedly some members of my clan do want to kill me for that.

Sahra volunteered the suggestion that if I did go to see Abeh, I should avoid visiting hours, when floods of Somalis would be going to the Royal London Hospital to seek a blessing from my father in order to improve their own chances of getting into heaven. For many, Abeh was a symbol of the battle against President Siad Barre's military regime, a man who had dedicated most of his adult life to overthrowing that regime. It would be the same in the East End of London as it was in Somalia: the many wives, the many children and grandchildren, the elders of the clan and the subclan and the brother subclans, scores and scores of relatives would come to my father to pay their respects. For many of those people I would not be welcome at my father's bedside because I was an unbeliever, an infidel, an avowed atheist, a filthy runaway, and worst of all, a traitor to the clan and to the faith. Some of them would certainly feel that I deserve to die, and to many more my presence would defile my father's deathbed and perhaps even cost him his place in the hereafter.

I felt no such rejection from Sahra, however. She was sweet and hushed, a little conspiratorial, as if by talking with her on the phone I had enrolled her in something clandestine and dangerous.

* * *

I needed to fly to London right away. Because this was an urgent, unplanned, purely personal trip, arranging security was going to be complicated, unlike attending a conference, for which everything is officially coordinated with the police weeks ahead of time. I knew it wouldn't be wise just to go, accompanied by the gentlemen who usually protect me in America. In Britain these men would not know their way around and would not be allowed to carry weapons. If I were rash in my planning I might put others as well as myself in danger.

I phoned a number of friends in Europe who I thought might be influential and asked them to try to help me arrange the protection I needed to make the trip. They spent many hours trying to help me, seemingly without success. One friend was told by a British official that as I was born in Somalia I should ask the Somali Embassy for help; they could approach the Foreign Office to seek security assistance for me. This absurd bureaucratic logic might have been comical in some circumstances, but not in the face of my need to get to London to see my dying father.

When my plane took off for London I still had no idea whether I would have any security protection when it landed. But that no longer mattered; after days of waiting I feared only that I might be too late. I knew that, if my father were to die, I would not be allowed to see his body. He would be whisked away by male relatives to be washed and prepared and buried within twenty-four hours. Women are not allowed to be present at the graveside during a Muslim burial ceremony. It is believed that their presence is disruptive; they might become hysterical, perhaps even hurl themselves into the grave to be with the corpse. It would be unseemly to try to attend.

My father had a contradictory attitude to women. He embraced some modern ideas on literacy, urged his first wife to attend university, and insisted that my sister Haweya and I go to school when my mother resisted the idea. He believed in women's strength and he repeatedly insisted that a woman's role was valuable and important. But as he aged he became more orthodox in his Islamic convictions that we must cover ourselves, marry, and submit to our husbands.

Despite his often eccentric views, even my father would not have tolerated seeing a woman at a funeral.

When I arrived at Heathrow Airport in London a large black car from the Dutch Embassy was there to greet me; another, smaller but even safer, held men from Scotland Yard. We drove straight to the hospital. Now, to my relief, my father lay alive before me. Poor Abeh. He was tied to a hospital bed, old, vulnerable, sick. He smiled deeply at me, and dozed, and then he would wake and gasp for air, trying again and again to speak, but nothing came out, only "Ash hah," gasping for breath. Then he would make kissing gestures to me with his lips and hold on to my hand as tightly as he could.

I felt heavy with the burden of everything I had never said to my father and the sheer waste of all the years we had been apart. The only words I could find were trite messages of love, and I said them over and over again. It was too late for anything else.

I hadn't gone to the hospital seeking absolution. I had ceased to believe in the idea that if I did the right thing, such as fulfill my duty to seek forgiveness from my parents and acquire their blessings, my sins would be washed away. Perhaps my presence did not even give him that much pleasure, since he could see that his daughter wore trousers and no headscarf. I went there just for the light in his eyes, for his acknowledgment of me, his love for me and mine for him—a mutual recognition that we had always been precious to each other.

He was using up his last reserves of strength in the effort to tell me something. I will never know what that was. For my father, God was the creator and the sustainer, but God was also ferocious and wrathful. Deep down I understood that on his deathbed my father was terrified that I risked the rage of Allah because I had rejected his faith. Father always taught us that those not forgiven by God will lead a miserable life on earth and eternal fire in the hereafter. But although our beliefs are not reconciled—and never will be, for they are worlds apart—my father did, I think, forgive me. He ultimately allowed his feelings of fatherly love to transcend his adherence to the demands of his unforgiving God.

*   *   *

Visiting hours were approaching. Soon the streams of Somalis that Sahra had warned me about would begin arriving to see my father, and I couldn't bear the idea of any kind of confrontation. So, painfully, I said good-bye to Abeh.

When the men from Scotland Yard escorted me out of the hospital I found myself standing on Whitechapel Road, the center of the largest Muslim population in Great Britain. A noisy, tarpaulin-covered street market was across the road, crowded with stalls selling lengths of saris, international phone cards, and spicy lamb sandwiches. On the pavement beside me, standing at the bus stop outside the hospital steps, was a collection of women wearing every variety of Muslim covering imaginable, from a pastel headscarf to the complete, thick black *niqaab* that covers you completely, with a veil of black cloth that blanks out your face, even your eyes. These were young, strong women, not doddering old ladies; some of them were pregnant, most of them had several small children, and they were out shopping for their families in the sunlight. Several wore a variation that was new to me: in addition to a long robe and headscarf they had an extra face veil fixed on with Velcro, with two thick black strips of cloth strapped so as to leave barely an inch or so uncovered, just skirting the eyelashes.

The phone booths and the signs for the London Underground were British, but I would not have thought I was in England. I smelled the lunchboxes of my schoolmates at the Muslim Girls' Secondary School in Nairobi, a heady clash of spices and food, and perfumed hair oils. Here again was the noisy bustle of the street and the mixture of people—Somalis and, I guess, Pakistanis and Bangladeshis—crowded at the market.

At the smells alone I felt a tug of longing for the innocence of youth. I don't know if in other cultures that sense of community is as strong, but for someone who has grown up within a clan, the feeling—the smell—of family is very powerful. Yet my longing was mixed with a dread of confrontation. What if somebody in this crowd recognized me, as people sometimes do, and decided to pick a fight? In the eyes of many of them, I am an infidel and a traitor, who goes about unpunished.

My bodyguards and I got back in the car and drove down Whitechapel

Road, slowly, in heavy traffic. Seated outside a *halal* fast-food shop was a small woman in a long black robe with a black embroidered beak of cloth tied over her nose and mouth, in the style of Algerian women. Two small children were crying in the buggy beside her, and she was trying to jiggle and comfort them while she lifted her cloth beak to try to eat her pastry modestly underneath it. Her older toddler was wearing a veil too. It was not a face veil, but it covered her hair and shoulders; it was white and lacy and elasticized so it fit snugly over her head. The child couldn't have been older than three.

Two shop fronts farther down was a huge mosque, the biggest mosque in London, my escorts told me. A small crowd of men stood outside it, all wearing loose clothing, long beards, and white skullcaps. All these people had left their countries of origin only to band together here, unwilling or unable to let go, where they enforce their culture more strongly even than in Nairobi. Here was the mosque, like a symbolic magnetic north, the force that moved their women to cover themselves so ferociously, the better to separate themselves from the dreadful influence of the culture and values of the country where they have chosen to live.

It was just a glimpse, and yet I felt an instant sense of panic and suffocation. I was right back in the heart of it all: inside the world of veils and blinkers, the world where women must hide their hair and their bodies, must cower to eat in public, and must follow a few steps behind their men on the street. A web of values—of honor and shame and religion—still entangled me together with all those women at the bus stop and almost every other woman along Whitechapel Road that morning. We were all very far from where we had been born, but only I had left behind that culture. They had brought their web of values with them, halfway across the world.

I felt as though I was the only true nomad.

CHAPTER 2

My Half Sister

Driving back to Heathrow Airport, I thought back to my first meeting with my half sister, Sahra, in Ethiopia in 1992, when she was eight years old and I was twenty-two and newly married, en route to Europe.

We had ended up speaking in sign language, smiling, holding hands, and misunderstanding one another. Sahra had been a charming little girl, with a bright child's curiosity and my father's way of being physically affectionate. She had sprinted about with the same kind of energy, enthusiasm, and playfulness as my sister Haweya. She was dressed that day in a sleeveless frock, torn and patched up in so many places that I could not help feeling a strong sense of shame that I did not bring her a new dress.

I was not sure whether the state of her frock was the result of poverty or simply acceptance of the Ethiopian approach to children. When we lived in Addis Ababa, most children were dressed in tatters and often seemed neglected by their parents. As a child I considered this Ethiopian neglect to be the epitome of freedom. I wanted to be left alone, to play as many hours of the day and night as I wanted to, rather than be put to work. Sahra's mother seemed as indulgent as mine had been rigid and forbidding.

But it was not only Sahra's frock that was tattered. The apartment was too. We were in a half room, separated from the other spaces by a thin cotton sheet that had once been white but now was stained by smoke and dust. The cement compound of the apartment building had once been smooth and even, but now, like many other shared compounds, it had cracks and large and small holes that were filled with little puddles of water. None of the tenants could afford to make repairs, and they did not work together to raise the money to maintain and clean the communal areas. By late afternoon fat mosquitoes zoomed and whined by my ears. I decided to marshal my best Arabic and Amharic to campaign for us to dry the puddles of water.

My stepmother had shrugged her shoulders in charming helplessness. "It is as Allah wills," she said. "The puddles will dry when it stops raining. Allah brings the rains and Allah makes the sun shine."

My father's third wife accepted her life as it came to her. Like my mother, she was passive, but her passiveness was different from my mother's. Both women were steeped in self-pity; both resigned themselves to their circumstances. But my mother cursed, scolded, screamed, demanded, and insulted those she blamed. Sahra's mom smiled and chided; she cast her eyes down and seemed to be content. Whatever the next day brought was Allah's choice, and she saw no point in defying events, her husband, or her God. Every sentence ended with *Inshallah,* "God willing." That was her method of survival.

I did not have the energy or the linguistic skill to suggest that although we could leave to Allah such things as making rain and making the sun shine, perhaps we could dry the puddles ourselves. I had had malaria twice as a child and learned in health education and science classes both in Juja Road and the Muslim Girls' Secondary School that the parasite that causes malaria lays its eggs in still water. To avoid getting sick we sprayed the mosquitoes and slept under nets, but we also had to dry out all the little puddles and pools of water that collected around our compound and even in the potholes in the streets around our house. We never succeeded in drying out the water in the neighborhood, of course, but as I grew up I dried our compound in Nairobi with a survivor's zeal and preached to Somali relatives about invisible animals that bred in the water.

Little Sahra and her mother lived a very communal life. Throughout the day people walked in and out of the building and its compound. There was a large stone water pitcher in a corner of the courtyard, and men would come in, scoop some water out in the large aluminum ladle, and drink straight from the ladle. Women used the same pitcher to make tea and fill their cooking pots. At one point that afternoon someone said something about hygiene: "Wash your hands before you use the pitcher. We all drink from it."

"What?" a young man responded with an awkward grin. "Wash hands with what? There is no water left." Indeed, the metal ladle hit the bottom of the stone pitcher with a clank, indicating that it was empty, and the older ladies began pleading and crying out for the younger women to fetch more water. Concern about hygiene was lost in the hubbub.

Everyone was talking, a friendly clamor of gossip and criticism of the *habash,* the Somali word for Ethiopians. Every sentence that everyone spoke was punctuated with "Allah willing" or "For the sake of Allah."

Sitting in the car that was driving me away from what was certainly the last time I would see my father, I thought about what had kept me away from my family, and from him, for so long: the rule that dictates that a man must command obedience from his women, from his wives and daughters—and they must submit to him. If a man's women stray from submission, they damage *him:* his good name, his authority, the sense that he is loyal and strong and true to his word. This belief is part of a larger one that individuals don't matter, that their choices and desires are meaningless, particularly if the individuals are women.

This sense of honor and male entitlement drastically restricts women's choices. A whole culture and its religion weigh down every Muslim, but the heaviest weight falls disproportionately on women's shoulders. We are bound to obey and bound to chastity and shame by Allah and the Prophet and by the fathers and husbands who are our guardians. The women along Whitechapel Road carry the burdens of all the obligations and religious rules that in Islam focus so obsessively on women, as surely as their counterparts in East Africa.

I still felt pained by the shame that I had cast on my father's good name. Because I was an apostate, an unbeliever, because I now lived as a Western woman, I had hurt him and harmed him, even defiled him by my rebellion. But I also knew that my rebellion was necessary, was vital.

Sahra had taken the contrary path. She did not rebel. Magool had told me that Sahra was deeply religious and that she wore the *jilbab,* a long black robe that covers your hair and all your body past your ankles and wrists, but not your face. Sahra's black shroud extended beyond the tips of her fingers and trailed on the ground; she sought with every word and gesture to express her submission to Allah's will and to the authority of men.

The Muslim veil, the different sorts of masks and beaks and *burkas*, are all gradations of mental slavery. You must ask permission to leave the house, and when you do go out you must always hide yourself behind thick drapery. Ashamed of your body, suppressing your desires—what small space in your life can you call your own?

The veil deliberately marks women as private and restricted property, nonpersons. The veil sets women apart from men and apart from the world; it restrains them, confines them, grooms them for docility. A mind can be cramped just as a body may be, and a Muslim veil blinkers both your vision and your destiny. It is the mark of a kind of apartheid, not the domination of a race but of a sex.

As we drove down Whitechapel Road I felt anger that this subjugation is silently tolerated, if not endorsed, not just by the British but by so many Western societies where the equality of the sexes is legally enshrined.

At the airport I phoned Sahra to tell her that I had come to see our father and was leaving again to go back the United States. "You are indeed the lucky one!" she said in Somali, laughing at her play on the meaning of my name, Ayaan, "fortunate." "Ever since you spoke to him on the phone weeks ago, he has not stopped talking about you."

We spoke a little about the family. I was careful not to say anything she might find offensive. I asked my sister why the hospital had registered my father under a false name, and she answered, "Oh, that's the name he used when he asked for asylum in Britain."

We talked about the hospital, and Sahra told me a funny story. When they took my father to the hospital, her mother told the nurses that she was his wife; then his first wife, Maryan Farah, had come, for she too now lived in England, and she told them that *she* was his wife. The whole staff seemed amused by the impossible number of people claiming to be his brothers and cousins. I chuckled. "They must think we're all crazy," Sahra said. I told her it was probably not the first time the hospital had seen such a thing.

Like her mother, every phrase Sahra spoke seemed to end with *Inshallah*, "If Allah wills it." At first it sounded well-behaved and highly civilized, but after so many sighs of acceptance and Allah willing and Sahra's showering me with Allah's blessings, I am ashamed to admit that it began to annoy me. I started to distrust her: she was no longer the skipping, happy child I met in 1992.

Now, before our first real conversation was over, Sahra too began trying to bring me back to Islam, to persuade me to give up my adopted way of life and join her in tradition and the dictates of Allah. As I listened, I pictured her, this little sister whom I had met only once, sixteen years ago, who was now sitting with her mother and her baby daughter in a flat in a housing project, dressed in layer upon layer of dark cloth.

Sahra has lived in England for years, but she did not take the road that I took, the one that released me from obedience and tradition and took me to Holland and the freedoms of the West. Though geographically she lives in a modern society, she has held on to the old, grim childhood values that place piety and submission to authority above all others. In doing so she has locked herself into poverty, squandering the opportunities that freedom offers her. If I had not bolted from my family, if I had married the man my father had contracted me to, I would probably now be living in the Canadian equivalent of Sahra's immigrant neighborhood. I might be living just like Sahra: conditioned to live in a prison within a society that is free.

"All you need to do is pray," Sahra was saying, warming to her task. "You'll see that Allah will open your heart, and your mind will follow."

I forced back the urge to share with my young half sister the merits of Enlightenment philosophy, the basis for Western freedom that for her was just a short walk away. I felt emotionally drained, physically tired from the long succession of planes, and I wasn't in London for a battle of ideas.

"Darling," I answered, "I'll think about it."

*   *   *

During the next few days I spoke with Sahra often. She came to seem like a strange kind of mirror, dressed in her *jilbab*, just as I had once worn a *jilbab* in Nairobi years ago. I could so easily have shared her life. The ideas that had shaped her had shaped me too, and sometimes I wondered whether one can ever truly escape such all-encompassing mental programming.

Of all his many children, Sahra was the child with whom my father spent the most time, to whom he paid the most attention. She still lives the *baarri* way, the way I was meant to live, as every good Somali girl must. She is obedient and submissive, but she is also conflicted; on the one hand, she wants the approval of our father, her mother, and the community, but on the other hand, she also, surely, wants to lead the life that is led by other girls her age who live in England.

This sense of being conflicted must leave her in limbo. She starts a vocational course but doesn't see it through; she begins English lessons but doesn't complete them. She does this because if she were to finish those studies and get a diploma, she could then find a job. But that would surely mean working outside the home; she would be gone for hours and might have to mix with men. She might even find herself tempted to put on makeup and participate in the social life of an office. Such a life is too dangerous: it would attack her basic sense of who she is. Yet by not getting a diploma Sahra has to live with her own dependence. In this renunciation of her mind and skills, however, she derives a bizarre reward of approval for being submissive.

I have shaken off my dependence on that sort of approval. No longer a Muslim, I am relieved of the fear of hell and can choose to indulge in the sins of the world. Sahra has the beautiful certainties of belonging and the terrible submission of self. I suffer the loneliness of gratifying my individualism; Sahra, that of self-denial and submission to the group.

The weight of Sahra's self-denial must be immense. These days in Britain, as all over Europe, Muslim women are demanding that they be allowed to wear the *hijab* at work. More and more wear the full *niqaab*, which covers even your face and eyes. These women believe that their own bodies are so powerfully toxic that even making eye contact with other people is a sin. The extent of self-loathing that this expresses is impossible to exaggerate, and it must be reawakened every time it meets the conflicting urge to work, to go out of the home, to encounter the outside world.

Sahra told me that she wanted to become a lawyer. How on earth did she think that would be possible? In England women lawyers are chic and powerfully feminine, unafraid to confront men. The British legal system in itself is blasphemy to a convinced Muslim, for it seeks to replace Allah's laws with man-made ones. She also mentioned an interest in psychology. I wondered how she would fare with Freud while remaining loyal to Muhammad.

Learning the infidel language was surely sinful enough. I remembered a scene in a mosque in 1990, when my sister Haweya and I were briefly living in Mogadishu. It was during Ramadan, and we had joined the Taraweh prayers, a very long series of prayer followed by supplications. In the Mogadishu heat, sitting on hard sisal mats in the women's section, Haweya and I were speaking to each other in English in between the supplications. The women around us expressed genuine shock that we would bring into such a holy place the language of the devil himself. They told us that our prayers did not mean a thing and would gain us no rewards in heaven, for by forcing them to listen to us speak the devil's language we were affecting their own piety.

Our two worlds, Sahra's and mine, coexist in the same city streets, but one is framed above all by the oppression of individuals, especially women, and the other glorifies individuality. Can those two sets of values ever be reconciled within Sahra, between her and her daughter, or on the streets of European cities? Will she ever understand that home is where she is, instead of an imagined past in a Somalia that is no longer even a whole country, riven as it is by war? For how long will Western societies, whose roots drink from the rational sources of the Enlightenment, continue to tolerate the spread of Sahra's way of life, like ivy on their trunks, an alien and possibly lethal growth?

Perhaps Sahra had been there, among the crowd of women standing at the bus stop outside the hospital. She would have been under her *jilbab*, so I would never have recognized her.

Sahra's baby daughter, Sagal, was born in England. She may grow up to be a successful, self-reliant career woman. With luck, good schools, patient educators, and personal resourcefulness and determination, this is possible—but not, I think, very likely.

How old will Sagal be when she puts on her first veil to walk down the city streets of the UK, and will she be "cut"—will her genitals be mutilated and sewn when she is five or six years old, like those of almost every Somali girl child? Our father had been against this barbaric practice, but my maternal grandmother had insisted on it for my sister and me. The threat to Sagal's body and health from this practice might come from Sahra and her own grandmother rather than from the men of our family. Genital mutilation occurs in Britain (although it is illegal), just as it occurs abroad. In itself, it does not prevent a woman from developing an independent mind. But the scar may be a constant reminder of the punishments in store for the rebellious.

Sahra may choose to enroll Sagal in a Muslim school, where she will be isolated from the values that underlie success in Britain. Most of her fellow students will come from homes where English is a second language. Some of her teachers will have been selected more for their piety than their ability as educators, others for their willingness to cooperate with the norms of the Muslim school. Some teachers will have applied out of a strong sense of idealism; others will have been motivated by a combination of some or all of these factors. Education will be by rote learning and submission, not inquiry and an open mind.

Or Sagal may be sent to one of the local state schools. Given the ethnic mix of her immigrant neighborhood, these schools are likely to be made up of children from immigrant families, often polygamous or single-parent families, where English is unlikely to be spoken at home. These schools are often in areas that are unsafe for children, with drug dealers and menacing teenage boys on street corners, random and frightening violence. In such neighborhoods you see teenage girls tattooed and pierced, in clothing so scanty you sometimes wonder if they forgot their skirt or pants, and cheek by jowl with them, girls shrouded in black *burkas* that conceal their faces and eyes so that they look like a cross between Darth Vader and the Teenage

Mutant Ninja Turtles. If any sort of school can be worse than a Muslim school it is these schools in deprived inner-city areas. Teachers are beaten down into exhaustion and indifference by the discipline problems they face. Kids are either bullies or they are bullied; they take the initiative to be violent, or they suffer. Graffiti is the art, hip-hop the music, zealotry the faith. Kids who grow up in this environment are likely to have permanent language problems; they may be regarded as unemployable because they do not have a middle-class work ethic.

It is no wonder, therefore, that the immigrant community looks to religious schools in such areas; disgusted by state schools, where their kids drop out after receiving a substandard education, they seek an alternative and comfortable system of beliefs and morals that they understand. Yet the Muslim schools are easily as bad, for there the kids are brainwashed into a way of life that diminishes their chances of success even further. Such children will be altogether cut off from the society in which their parents have chosen to live.

It may be that Sahra and Sagal will manage to inch their way into the ranks of the British middle classes. A temporary job, a helpful friend, a scholarship—these things are possible. I think I could help. But I know that my offers of help will be rejected as un-Islamic, infidel and heinous. For is it not true that Allah will reward those who suffer in his name, those who endure pain and shame and mocking because they choose to serve him?

After all, entering the middle class of Britain or any other Western democracy is such a lowly goal compared with entering heaven, with its rivers, springs, and cascading brooks, and fruits and wines that are a thousand times better than those made on earth. Wrapped in her shroud-like *jilbab,* Sahra believes staunchly, just as my father did, that her suffering in this life will be richly rewarded in the hereafter. Her daughter may have to pay the price on earth. I only hope she finds a little window of escape, as I did.

CHAPTER 3

My Mother

My father died a week after I went to see him at the hospital. Just before he died, he slipped back into unconsciousness. The machines kept him alive until the doctors pulled the plug. I knew it was going to happen, and yet when I found out I still felt a pain that was primeval in its intensity.

I would have to stay away from the funeral. All day long I imagined the scene in his apartment: all the women of the clan coming by, sitting on the floor, drinking tea, telling stories, consoling each other, wailing, and waiting for the men to return from the cemetery where they buried him.

I found myself walking around my apartment in America, obsessively cleaning, trying not to think. I could have gone to see my father earlier; I couldn't ignore the choice I had made. I could have canceled my trip to Brazil or my trip to Australia and just flown to him after that first phone call in June. I could easily have called and canceled my commitments, but I didn't go to see him because it wasn't *convenient,* because my sense of belonging had shifted away from my duty to my father, away from the smells of Somalia and Nairobi, to a new tribe.

I had made a selfish choice. I did not go because I could count on my hands the number of times I had spoken to my father since I had wriggled out of his grasp sixteen years before, and every time the conversation was the same: a sermon that was not just monotonous, but dismaying.

Even after I fled from my father and his plans for me, I had still looked up to him as a leader, as someone who had acted against the injustice and tyranny in Somalia, who had fought to bring his family, tribe, and nation into a democratic, modern system of governance.

The first cracks of my disenchantment came in 2000, when I met him in Germany, where he had gone for an eye operation. It was the first time I had seen him after eight years of exile. I was still studying at the University of Leiden, bursting with all kinds of ideas, longing to see him again yet afraid of what he would say to me. Even so, when my father began talking about Islamic law, making what seemed to me weak, even silly arguments, I was almost speechless. This was my father. He was still a brilliant thinker and leader, invincible and strong, so I made excuses: this couldn't possibly be the real man. After that meeting, however, every conversation ended the same way; even when we last spoke on the phone, before I had gone to Brazil, I had wanted to stop myself feeling disappointed at how inconsistent his ideas and beliefs were, how irrational.

Just as I had lied about my identity when I sought asylum in Holland, my father too, it seemed, had lied to cheat the asylum system so that he could live in Britain. The tribal hero, the preserver of the culture of Islam and the clan, took handouts from the unbelievers on a false pretext, with a fake passport, though, unlike me, he had nothing but contempt for their values and way of life. Before he died he had even applied for and received British citizenship, not because he wanted to be a British subject but because of the instrumental benefits of free housing and health care. At the same time, he continued to lecture me never to be loyal to a secular state; he repeatedly urged me to return to the true faith. If I had stayed with him for a week he would have trapped me in a week-long lecture. He would have asked me to reunite with the family—his wives, their daughters, some of whom probably think I should be put to death and who certainly consider me a whore.

We who are born into Islam don't talk much about the pain, the tensions and ambiguities of polygamy. (Polygamy, of course, predates Islam, but the Prophet Muhammad elevated it and sanctioned it into law, just as he did child marriage.) It is in fact very difficult for all the wives and children of one man to pretend to live happily, in union. Polygamy creates a context of uncertainty, distrust, envy, and jealousy. There are plots. How much is the other wife getting? Who is the favored child? Who will he marry next, and how can we manipulate him most efficiently? Rival wives and their children plot and are often said to cast spells on each other. If security, safety, and predictability are the recipe for a healthy and happy family, then polygamy is everything a happy family is not. It is about conflict, uncertainty, and the constant struggle for power.

My grandmother, a second wife herself, used to say that our family was too noble to feel jealousy. Nobility in Somali nomadic culture is synonymous with self-restraint, with resilience. A higher-status clan is more self-conscious, hence more stoic. Expressions of jealousy or any other kind of emotion are frowned upon. My grandmother said she was lucky, and people called her spoiled, because after her older cowife died her husband didn't take another wife for many years, until my grandmother had had nine children. Even then, he only married again because eight of those children were girls.

My grandmother had thought her position was safe, because even though she had given birth to daughter after daughter, for years her husband did not marry another wife. And then he did marry again. And that third wife, to my grandmother's enduring shame, gave birth to three boys. My grandfather had a total of thirteen children.

There was nothing my grandmother could do and nothing she wished to say, so she did not protest. But after that, the worst in her came to the fore: she became mean and petty, exploding with temper at her children, who took the brunt of her anger.

Long after I was an adult, I realized that it was jealousy that finally drove my grandmother to walk away from her husband. After my grandfather's new wife had her second son, my grandmother could no longer contain her shame and envy, and she left their home in the desert, ostensibly to look after her adult children, which included my mother.

My mother's story was similar. Even though she was my father's second wife, from the day she learned that my father had married a third woman and had another child, Sahra, my mother became erratic, sometimes exploding with grief and pain and violence. She had fainting episodes and skin diseases, symptoms caused by suppressed jealousy. From being a strong, accomplished woman she became a wreck, and we, her children, bore the brunt of her misery.

Of my father's six children who made it to adulthood, three have suffered mental illnesses so severe that they can barely function. My sister Haweya died after three years of depression and psychotic attacks; my brother Mahad is a manic-depressive, unable to hold down a job; one of our half sisters has had psychotic episodes since she was eighteen. Aunts and uncles on both sides of my family have cases of *Waalli*, or generic "madness," as they call all mental problems in Somali.

Perhaps polygamy invites madness, or perhaps it is the clash between aspiration and reality. All my relatives desperately wanted to be modern. They yearned for freedom, but once they found it they were bewildered and broken by it. Obviously mental instability has biological factors too, but it is also affected by the culture we mature in, the tactics and strategies of survival we develop, the relationships we have with others, and the unbearable dissonance between the world we are told to see and the world in which we actually live.

As I spoke with Magool after my father's death, it occurred to me that the message that Abeh had tried so desperately to tell me on his deathbed was probably that I should look after his wives: his first wife, who also lives in England; his second wife, my mother, who lives in Somalia; his third wife, Sahra's mother; and his fourth wife, a woman whom he married in Somalia after Sahra was born and with whom he had no children. I had almost forgotten about the fourth wife's existence.

I pondered this for some time, something I had never permitted myself to do while he was alive. My father had hurt so many people, as he married women and fathered children and then left them behind, more or less untended. Judging my father by my adoptive Western standards, I found that he had failed in his duties toward his wives and children.

I have never condemned my father or allowed myself to feel real anger toward him. But if I had gone to his side and spoken truthfully to him before he died, I might have had to open an emotional closet I have nailed shut. Now that he was dead I felt contempt for myself, and I was filled with regret for everything he and I might have done differently.

*   *   *

I grew closer to Magool in the weeks after my father's death. My young cousin had grown up smart, independent, a free spirit, tough and yet compassionate, with a no-nonsense attitude toward life. Now she was the suddenly my only precious link to my extended family. Magool had lived with me for over six months in the Netherlands in the early 1990s. Unlike Sahra, she adopted the Western values of individual responsibility in matters of life, love, and family. Because everyone in her environment had tried to convert her back to Islam, she knew how annoying the process was and never tried to convert me. Magool was also my connection to the Somali bloodline to which, whether I liked it or not, I still belonged.

One day I asked Magool for news of my mother, and she told me a story that surprised and pleased me.

All those long years after my father had left my mother alone in Kenya with three children, Ma had refused to say more than a word or two to him. Her mute, awful anger lay between them even before he left us; her silence filled our house on Park Road in Nairobi, until he could no longer bear it. When he came back to Kenya ten years later, she turned away from his outstretched arms and ignored his endearments, even in the presence of family and friends.

After I fled my family and my father moved to London, Ma followed the news about him closely, Magool told me. When she learned that he was dying and suffering, she believed it was because his soul was not being allowed to depart quietly and in peace. My father's kidneys failed, then started functioning again; he would breathe on his own for a while and then had to be hooked up to the ventilator again. Ma saw all this not as the effects of leukemia or the septic infection that was raging through his body and killing his organs but as a sign of, a prelude to, the explicit tortures of the grave that loom so large in Islamic teaching.

In the hell described in the Quran, flames lick the flesh of the sinful; burning embers will be placed under their feet, their scalps will be scalded and their brains boiled. These tortures are endless, for as their skin is burned it is replaced and burned again. In the suffering of my father on his deathbed, my mother believed, Allah and his angels were giving him a taste of the punishments to come for his wrongdoings.

I imagined my mother must have asked herself whom my father

could have wronged more than he had wronged her. Who else had he abandoned, cheated on, dragged to foreign countries? Who but she had gone hungry and watched her fatherless children fall away and betray her after he departed? Who could possibly have suffered more than she because of the sins of Hirsi Magan Isse? My mother felt she held the keys to my father's last chance for salvation before the grave, so she resolved to act.

Perhaps she thought that by doing good she might be forgiven for her own sins. Or perhaps it was because she truly loved him. (This is what I tell myself.) Maybe her sense of ethics and justice, of being the daughter of a respected judge among the nomads, never deserted her, or maybe her act was all about power. Whatever her reasoning, my mother decided to register at my father's deathbed like his other wives. Her presence was different from theirs, however. She cajoled Magool, the daughter of her younger sister, into going to the hospital on her behalf to deliver a message.

I am not sure how, but Magool had grown friendly with my half sister, Sahra. She found out from Sahra that my father was in the Royal London Hospital in Whitechapel, and also found out which ward he was in. Then she went to see him with a message from my mother. Unlike me, she did not talk at first, but hovered quietly for a few minutes, until she felt comfortable enough to whisper his name. Magool said that he opened his eyes and raised his head to see who she was. Making eye contact with him, she then delivered the message my mother had made her memorize:

> Dear Uncle Hirsi,
>
> I am here on behalf of Asha Artan Umar, the mother of your children. She wanted me to convey to you that she forgives you for any ill will that has come to pass between the two of you. She seeks forgiveness from you for any wrongdoing on her part and she wishes you an easy passage to the hereafter. She prays fervently for your admission into paradise and for Allah's mercy on you between now and when you meet Him.

When Magool related this story to me, I asked her how Abeh had responded. "I don't know if he heard me," she answered. "He lifted up his head for a second, and then his head fell back on the pillows. He closed his eyes briefly and then opened them again. I am assuming he heard. At least that is what I told your Ma."

"What did you tell her, exactly?"

"I told her that he heard me, that I could see he understood. I'm not sure he really did, but she is old and lonely and it will do her good to know that the father of her children got her message."

I don't remember my mother being in a forgiving mood too often, but I knew how much this would mean to her, and it made me feel better too. Regardless of her motivation, my mother's message to my father was gracious and timely, and it surely brought her some peace.

One afternoon, less than a week after my father had passed away, Magool phoned me. "Ayaan, *Abaayo*," she said, using an endearment that is best translated as "dear sister."

"Yes, *Abaayo*, dear, what is it?" *Is there more bad news?* I wondered.

"*Abaayo*, Ayaan . . ."

"Uhhhmm, *Abaayo* Magool."

"*Abaayo* Ayaan."

"*Abbbaaayyo.* Yessss." I tried to contain my irritation but failed.

"Will you do me a favor, *Abaayo*, please, *Abaayo*?" Magool asked me. "Just this once?"

"*Abaayo,* what is it?"

"Please, *Abaayo,* just say yes first?"

I hesitated. I had no idea what Magool would ask for, and I didn't want to commit to something I could never deliver. From the old days I knew that Somali relatives ask—no, *demand*—money, immigration papers, the smuggling of people and goods; they request to be allowed to camp in your home for three days only, which stretch into forever. All this is preceded by floods of endearments of "dear sister" and "dear cousin" and all the special Somali words for every inflexion of relationship that lies beyond and in between.

"It depends, *Abaayo*," I responded. "I will say yes if what you ask won't compromise my safety, if it is legal, and if I can afford it."

Magool laughed. "No problem, *Abaayo*."

I was now more intrigued than irritated. "So?"

"*Abaayo,* phone your mother."

I was silent for a few seconds, taking the time to find the right response, and when I spoke again my voice was so soft that she asked me to repeat what I said. "Magool, I don't know if Ma wants to talk to me anymore."

"*Abaayo*"—the compassion in Magool's voice was plainly audible now—"I will give you her phone number. Yes, she wants to talk to you. She is all alone now. My ma was with her until a few months ago. Now my mother has gone to Tanzania with my brother. Your mother is all by herself and she asks after you all the time. Please, call her. Promise me you will call her."

At first I felt a jolt of childlike excitement. Then I felt fear; I dreaded the confrontation that would be bound to occur as soon as I spoke with my mother. But that was soon overcome by the sense of duty she had inculcated in me, and the guilt of having neglected her. My father had just passed away. What if my mother was taken ill? Would I ever see her again? I knew the answer: my mother is in Somalia and I am an infidel who would be killed instantly on arrival. I would not be present at her bedside.

But at least I could talk to her. And so I tried the number Magool gave me. I got an out-of-order signal, a busy signal, a recorded female voice telling me in English and Spanish, "All circuits are busy now. Please try your call again later." Magool had warned me that getting through to Somalia was hard and advised me to keep trying; I called so often, whenever I had a little free time, that it became a habit. I had almost come to believe that Magool had deluded me and the line would never work when finally, one afternoon, in the front seat of the Land Rover of a friend of mine who was driving me out of town to buy furniture for an apartment I had just rented, I connected to the phone line in my mother's dirt-floor house in Las Anod, a place located between Somaliland and Puntland, two autonomous regions in what was once Somalia.

"Hello," said a soft voice on the other end. (This greeting came to us Somalis when the British introduced the telephone to our country; ever since, Somalis say *hello* when they pick up a phone.)

"Hello, *hooyo,* Ma. It is me, Ayaan." I held my breath, certain she would curse and hang up on me.

"Hello, did you say Ayaan?" Now I was certain it was my mother. I hadn't recognized her voice at first.

"*Hooyo*, mother, mother. Yes, it is Ayaan. It is me. Please don't hang up."

"Allah has brought you back to me. I am not going to hang up."

"Mother, how are you? Do you know that Father just passed away?"

"I know that. You must know, my daughter, that death is the only thing that is certain. We are all going to die. What credit for the here-after have you built for yourself?"

I sighed. My ma had not changed. It was as though the five years in which she and I hadn't spoken had never been. Her voice was the same, with its echoes of her Dhulbahante clan, and so were her con-stant references to death, to the hereafter, and her expectations and demands, her evident, manifest disappointment in me, her oldest daughter. I made an attempt to change the subject: "Ma, I think it was gracious of you to send Magool to forgive him on your behalf."

"Did she pass on my message?" she asked me eagerly. "What did he say?" My mother was desperate to know how Magool had handled it; she must have heard gossip about Magool's ungodly life, for she also wanted to know whether her messenger to his hospital bed was appropriately dressed.

"Ma," I replied, "Magool is a responsible and honorable young woman. She did exactly as you said. She told me that Abeh responded, that he understood her, and I am sure you can be comfortable that it was not too late."

"Ayaan, did you go and see him?"

"Yes, Ma, I did. I am happy I did. It was tough."

Our conversation went on like this, stiff and tense, almost like strangers speaking, but with ripples of unspoken meanings and fears. Ma filled me in on the details of my grandmother's death, in 2006, "around the time that Saddam Hussein was tried and executed," as Magool had said. Grandmother had become deaf, Ma told me, and she grew smaller and more immobile, until one day that mighty, fear-some force of will stopped breathing.

She told me a little about her own life since then. She was liv-ing alone in Sool, a district in what was once the land of the Dhul-bahante, her nomad clan of camel herders. I paused for a moment to imagine it: a little hamlet of cinderblock buildings, unpaved roads, thorn bushes, and endless dust. She would have to fetch wood to make charcoal for the brazier. Perhaps she was comforted by being among her ancestral people.

Then my mother turned the conversation back to what I was doing to invest in my hereafter. "Do you pray and fast, and read the Quran, my daughter?"

It took me so long to think of a good answer that she asked if I was still there. I decided to tell her the truth. "Ma, I don't pray or fast, and I read the Quran occasionally. What I find in the Quran does not appeal to me."

As soon as I said the words I regretted it. Predictably, she flew into a rage. "Infidel!" she cried. "You have abandoned God and all that is good, and you have abandoned your mother. You are lost!"

Then she hung up on me.

I was shaking and trying not to cry. To my friend Linda, who had been sitting beside me in the driver's seat, the whole conversation had been a series of weird emotional noises in the strange sounds of the Somali language. Now, baffled, she looked on as I raged and tried not to cry in her front seat.

"My mother never listens and she never did listen to me," I burst out. "Should I lie to her? Why does she want me to deceive her? Isn't that just self-deception? What will she gain from my telling her that I pray and fast? You know, listening to her trying to frighten me into believing that dead people will all stand up on just one day and traipse around and be tried in a giant tribunal, and separated into the good ones and the bad ones—it's just insanity!" On and on I went, sounding pretty much like my mother, ranting.

Linda, clutching the steering wheel with one hand and trying to calm me down with the other, implored me to listen to her. "Ayaan, please, try to empathize with your mother. She's all alone . . ."

"My mother is scared. It's worse than being alone: she's frightened," I said. "She believes in a God who has her paralyzed in fear. She is worried that her God is going to torture *me* in my grave and burn me in *my* afterlife. These are not fairy tales to her, she believes them to be as real and true as the red lights we are approaching now, and it is the only thing that matters to her. She will never give up on it."

Linda slowed down and pulled over, and then she let me have it. She told me that, as a mother, she could feel my mother's pain. She told me that even though *she* had hung up on *me*, I should call my ma right back.

So I did.

I was almost certain the call wouldn't get through, and that if it did, Ma wouldn't answer. I thought she would be seething, feeling sorry for herself and cursing me. But she answered the phone, and before she had a chance to berate me I yelled at the top of my voice, fearful that she would interrupt me or cut me off, "*Hooyo*, I am sorry I hurt you—I am sorry that I don't pray and fast—I promise I will work hard at attempting to let it all in—I will go into the Quran with an open mind. Please forgive me . . ."

"Stop rambling and listen," Ma broke in, louder. "I want you to listen."

I caught my breath and asked her one more time not to hang up.

"I am not going to hang up," she told me. "*You* are the one who disappeared for all these years, who left me alone with only your poor brother Mahad, who, you know, is sick. Your sister died, your father left me, and my mother passed away. You are all I have. I am not going to hang up on you."

"Ma, I am really sorry," I stammered. "I want to help. I have some money for you. I want to send it to you. How do I do that? I don't know of any *Hawala* enterprises here in the U.S. who can transport money safely to Somalia. Besides, many of them are being investigated by the U.S. government for helping al Qaeda . . ."

"I don't want to talk about money," my mother said. "Allah is the giver and taker of life and of nourishment. I want to talk to you about Allah. He sustains me; he sustained me all the time you were gone. I want you to listen. Are you listening?"

Dutifully, I answered that I was listening, though I pursed my lips.

"I am displeased that you gave up your faith in Allah. Do you remember when we were in Somalia, you got a fever, you had malaria. I thought I was going to lose you. I had lost Quman, your youngest sister, a few months before. I was desperate, so desperate to keep you, and I begged Allah, and he let you live.

"Do you remember the airport in Jeddah, when your father did not show up? You children were too young to understand it then, but the Saudis almost put us on a plane back to Somalia, where our escape would have been discovered, and all of us might have been put behind bars. I prayed to Allah, prayed for his mercy. I understood that he was testing me and I never lost faith in him."

I wanted to say that it was thanks to the inefficient if terrifying Saudi bureaucracy, plus sheer luck, that we made it out of Somalia. All those secular factors combined had saved us from being caught, not her one-sided conversation with Allah. But all I did was purse my lips some more and say, "Hmmm, yes, Mother."

"Do you remember our lives in Ethiopia? You and Mahad got lost one day and all the Somalis were predicting the Ethiopians would bring you back cut into little pieces. I prayed all night and you were both brought back to me healthy and alive. Throughout those low hours of desolation I never lost faith in him."

I remembered, acutely, Ma's prejudice against Ethiopians, how even after they brought us back safely she never lost that narrow-mindedness. *Do please get to the point,* I thought.

"I gave birth in Ethiopia to a dead baby. I wept and wept and went through it all without once losing faith in the creator and sustainer."

"Hm." *Because you are a survivor, Ma. And your belief contributed to your survival, no doubt about it. You derived strength from your belief in Allah, but it also blinded you to options you had, and never took.*

"I was dumped with the three of you in Kenya. Your father left me in a strange place with nothing. I took on all the humiliation his absence exposed me to. I watched your brother drop out of school. I listened to the news from my home and relatives in Somalia who were massacred by Siad Barre. I fell ill, I endured losing my home, I watched my youngest daughter lose her mind and I dealt with the shame she brought on me. I endured your distance and silence and now I'm sitting here with nothing. My only son is no support. All of you have abandoned me. There are open wounds on my leg, there's fluid coming out of them that is neither blood nor water. I itch. I can't sleep. And not once have I lost faith in Allah."

I wanted to say, *Ma, Abeh left because the two of you were incompatible. You mollycoddled Mahad into a spineless mommy's boy; he grew up frightened by Abeh, and you beat and cursed Haweya systematically. You were dogmatic* and incurious. *And faith in Allah has nothing to do with it. You made choices that made your life miserable and blamed others.* I was surprised at my own anger, my inward blasphemy. But I said only, "Yes, Mother."

"We will all face our maker," my mother told me. "You will die too."

"Yes, mother," I said, thinking of the words of the British philosopher Bertrand Russell: "When I die I shall rot."

"So tell me," she asked, and I knew she was fighting back tears— I had grown up with her eternal sense of abandonment and self-pity. "What is it that makes you question the Almighty? Why are you so feeble in faith? What are you committed to, then? What happened to you? Are you bewitched? How can you doubt him? I can bear everything, but I can't bear the thought of you forsaking Allah and inviting his wrath. You are my child and I can't bear the thought of you in hell."

I thought, *I am feeble in faith because Allah is full of misogyny. He is arbitrary and incoherent. Faith in him demands that I relinquish my responsibility, become a member of a herd. He denies me pleasure, the adventure of learning, friendships. I am feeble in faith, Mother, because faith in Allah has reduced you to a terrified old woman—because I don't want to be like you.* What I said was "When I die I will rot."

I instantly regretted it. It was like torturing her to say such things, even though it is what I believe to be true. Ma was not interested in my thoughts or my answers. Her queries didn't seek affirmation, only obedience. She wanted me to lie to her.

So I again said I was sorry. "Mother, I will try, I promise to try my best," I murmured. This was hypocritical, and I knew it.

At first I called my mother every day, then once every two days, and then every weekend. My conversations with her grew ever more unbearably depressing. Eventually I ended up calling her perhaps once a month.

Our talks were always strained. Ma wanted forgiveness from God. I wanted forgiveness from her. She wanted forgiveness for herself because, since I had strayed, God might want her to pay in the hereafter for doing a poor job of teaching me his commandments. As long as we talked, we served each other by soothing our own images of ourselves, preserving each other's pride. I couldn't bring myself to tell her any details of my life; everything I said would be interpreted by her as irreligious, blasphemous, or immoral. I would try to avoid the subject of religion, but that is not easy in the Somali language, where all greetings and farewells are beset with Allah's will, mercy, and blessings. In every conversation my mother deployed every kind of tactic she could to try to persuade me to return to her strategy for survival—belief in Islam—even though to me it was the root cause that had made her life so miserable in the first place.

I found myself falling back into my old habit of punctuating her sentences with appropriate noises that would convey that I was listening, though in fact I zoned out until I could interrupt her with a question. After a while, a typical phone conversation with her would go like this:

"Hello, Ma. It is Ayaan."

"Assalaamu-alaika." (May Allah bless you.)

"How are you, Mother? Did you sleep well?"

"Allah is merciful. He takes care of me. I sleep well and eat well because the Almighty desires so. And you, Ayaan, are you praying?"

"Not yet, mother."

"You have abandoned your mother and you have abandoned God. Does it not matter to you? Please, just wash, just stand on the mat, bow your head. Who knows what Allah will inspire."

I would feel shame and guilt, and anger at my own shame and guilt. How easily I fell back into the habit of seeking to assuage my mother's anger. So I would try to deflect the conversation: Had she received my latest bank order to pay for medicine and food? Then I would try to race away. "Mother, I just called to greet you, I have to run, I will call you when I have more time."

"What are you pursuing? What is chasing you? Remember to pray and thank Allah . . ."

"Ma, I have to go." Talking to her, I always find myself implicitly obeying the Somali rule that a child cannot end the conversation. I can't just hang up. I have to wait for her to indicate that I can go.

"Haste is bad. Why did you call me if you have no time? You have distanced yourself from Allah and from us, you are on the edge, you must come back, you must pray . . ."

"Ma, I have to run, to work, please let me go."

"Go then, my child, may Allah bless you and protect you from the *jinn* and from Satan."

"*Amin, amin, amin*, you too. 'Bye." I would hang up feeling inadequate, a failure.

I felt like a failure because talking to her stirred in me the dormant feelings of guilt and duty to serve and obey my parents. As long as I was not in direct contact with Ma or other relatives, or people from our culture, I could suppress these sentiments. But having heard her voice and learning of her plight in her remote village in Somalia, I felt the pangs of guilt cut through my soul. Ma also knew how to work me, from when I was a little girl. As she continued to complain about how she had been abandoned and neglected by my father, Mahad, and Haweya, about the civil war, about her skin ailment, her age and general malaise, I tormented myself with "What if" questions. What if I had been resourceful enough to send her money, called her, sent her pictures, just let her know that I cared, that I was her daughter?

I wondered if I had been "good." Duty was the most basic virtue I was indoctrinated with as a child. But I knew the answer. It was clear to me that from the perspective of my upbringing, by her own standards, I had failed my mother.

It was difficult to contain the flood of nostalgia that overwhelmed me after my father died. My memory, mysteriously, marks the colors of places for me, so that recalling even just those colors can be soothing. My mind still harks back to colors, long after forgetting the stories and the streets and even the people.

I remember the off-white sand in front of our house in Mogadishu and the blue of the cloudless sky, the houses painted white with shutters that were sometimes blue but mainly green, a whole spectrum of weather-beaten green paints. The bougainvillea were an explosion of purple, pink, crimson, and all the shades in between, in the bright, hot, and unrelenting sun. I remember the yellow-green of the papaya tree and the brown blotches on the flanks of the white goats, and how you could tell them from sheep, even across a great distance, because the sheep's heads were black and their bodies white. I remember the cobalt blue of my first school uniform and the yellow of the shirts of the boys who terrified me. The bright colors of the shawls and draped garments worn by the women and the darker hues of gray and green of the sarongs worn by the men are as fresh in my mind as if I had seen them only yesterday. I remember the stark palette of grays, whites, and blacks in Saudi Arabia, then the suddenly clanging, clashing colors when we moved to Kenya. My memories of Holland are a series of dim but lovely harmonies, muted cream-colored stone and mild green fields and gray skies.

In the weeks and months that followed my father's death, it was the season that in America they so poetically call fall. Outside my window in the house I was visiting in upstate New York, tall trees, which I was told were oaks and maples, filled the landscape. Almost as I watched them, their large leaves seemed to shift color, some maroon, some yellow and red. Then they fell so that the ground became a vast, beautiful carpet, embroidered with designs in gold, brown, and deep oxblood.

The sky is of a different blue in America, not as sharply bright as the one above Mogadishu and not as dim and gray as the sky above Leiden. I yearned for the warmth of a fireplace where I could stare at the flames that so resemble the beauty outdoors, where I could warm my toes and think about what it would be like if I were still encircled by my family.

When my sister Haweya died in 1998 I wanted to die too. I felt that all the compromise solutions that I had patched together to enable me to negotiate a successful life in a modern country alongside the ancient values we had been taught made me a worthless, spineless person. I thought that the best of us had been taken, and that I didn't deserve life if she could not have it.

When my father died I did not so much miss him as I missed the illusion of certainty, the childish feeling that I was beloved. I longed for a structured, stable life, one in which my goals and the behavior required of me were consistent. In a way, I understood fully what Sahra and others saw in religion, which is the chance to be like a child again, protected, taken by the arm and told what is right and what is wrong, what to do and what not to do—to take a break from thinking.

*   *   *

I felt remorse at my alienation from Sahra and the rest of my family. Sahra may be downtrodden from an objective standpoint (or, at any rate, from mine), but she doesn't feel that way. She has a daughter and a husband; she is protected from loneliness. She *belongs*. She has the certainty, the strength, the clear goals that stem from belief. She was with my father through his old age and death. I was not.

I was thirty-eight years old and I was only beginning to truly understand why people want to belong somewhere, and to understand how difficult it is to sever all ties with the culture and religion in which you are born. Outwardly I was a success. People wrote articles about me, they asked me what books I was reading and what I thought of Barack Obama. My speeches received standing ovations. But my personal life was a mess. I had escaped from my family and gone to Europe because I hadn't wanted to be trapped in marriage to a virtual stranger I didn't like. Now, in America, I felt rootless, lost. To be a nomad, always wandering, had always sounded romantic. In practice, to be homeless and living out of a suitcase was a little foretaste of hell.

I stared at the black-and-white photograph of my grandmother that hangs on my living-room wall. I felt a stab of pain and avoided her piercing eyes, but her words had jabbed their way into my mind: *The world outside the clan is rough, and you are alone in it.*

CHAPTER 4

My Brother's Story

Ma told me that my brother Mahad, who lived in Nairobi, was bad-gering her for my phone number. She hadn't given it to him. She warned me that if she did, he would ask me to help him get a visa to Europe or America, and she begged me not to do it. She had a terrible fear of losing him to the infidel countries, which, in her mind, had driven Haweya to madness and death, and me to far worse: to apostasy, immorality, immortal doom. The West had taken her daughters, and Mahad was all she had left. She asked me to send him money so that he could come live with her in northern Somalia.

I wondered what complex and conflicting emotions Mahad felt when he heard that Abeh had died. When my little sister Haweya and I were small, our brother seemed to us to have the key to a privileged connection with our father. When Abeh had languished in a prison in Mogadishu, Mahad had visited him. Ma always took her eldest son to places she would never allow her daughters to venture to.

Then Abeh escaped, and we girls were at last allowed to participate in the adventure. We fled Somalia and moved to Saudi Arabia when Mahad was ten, I was eight, and Haweya six and a half. In Saudi Arabia we would at last meet our father, Ma said. But when we begged Mahad for details about Abeh, he assumed a pompous, professorial tone and described a figure of mythical proportions: hugely tall, infinitely strong, impossibly understanding and good.

I wondered out loud whether Abeh walked or floated. Mahad said I was foolish. Mahad always told me how foolish I was. He used the word *doqon*—"gullible, dupe"—and it hurt. But I was too excited by the prospect of meeting Abeh to dwell for too long on bad feelings.

"Oh, Mahad," little Haweya interrupted, "will he lift me up on his neck, like our uncle?"

"He might," Mahad replied. "Come here, little one, let me lift you on my neck." He bent down, and clumsy Haweya clambered onto his back, tugging his hair. Mahad began yelling.

Ma came in; we were making too much noise, again. The two-bedroom flat in Mecca was hot, far too hot, and too small for us. We were used to a house in Mogadishu, with a yard to run in and a talal tree to climb. Ma was afraid that we would annoy the neighbors so much that we'd be evicted from the apartment. She used to order Mahad to take charge of his younger sisters and keep us quiet. Now Haweya had pulled his hair a little too hard and *he* was making the noise. She let him have it. "You're letting me down again," she cried. "I am on my own. Must I look for food to keep you from howling at night, or must I keep you from behaving like animals? You tell me."

Mahad entreated, "But she pulled my hair."

"How did she reach your head?" Ma snapped.

"She wanted to know if Abeh would put her on his neck."

Ma screamed as if there was fire throughout the building, "You *wa'al* bastard child. All three of you are cursed—monsters, cursed! I hope death finds you in lumps. May the ancestors tear you to pieces!"

Mahad, his voice shrill and desperate, pleaded, "Ma, this one wanted to know if Abeh walks on air and this one wanted to climb on my neck. What do you want me to do?"

Kicking off her shoe, Ma hurled it at his head and raced toward him menacingly. "What I want from you is to be a man, you traitor. I want you to be a man. You are such a weakling, defeated by two girls! How will you ever stand up to men? How will you wrestle? How will you honor your forefathers, fight a lion, earn your share of she-camels? It is my tragedy, my unfortunate fate that I have but one son and he is incapable of even keeping his sisters under control. How will you ever lead an army? Control a battalion? Rule a people? You can't manage two little girls—what are you good for?"

Mahad ran off to the bathroom, fighting tears.

Neither Mahad nor Haweya nor I had ever seen a lion. I had seen camels, also cows, goats, sheep, lizards, and a reptile called *abbeso* that terrified me into such a fit that to this day the thought of it keeps me from looking up what it might be called in English. But I certainly didn't know the difference between he-camels and she-camels. Mahad may have had an inkling, but I doubt that he ever got close enough to a camel to tell its sex.

For a rare moment I felt grateful to be a girl. I would never have to wrestle lions, real or imagined.

Mahad, having more freedom than we did, was exposed to all sorts of adventures, but he also had to face much worse trials than we did. In Saudi Arabia the law requires women to hide and never step outside without being escorted by a male guardian. Our mother leaned on Mahad, her ten-year-old, to act as that legal male guardian for her whenever our father was away, which turned out to be most of the time. She indulged him with luxuries she would not have wasted on girls, but she also ordered him to take responsibility not only for his behavior but also for Haweya's and mine. He acted as Ma's interpreter from Arabic, which we learned in school, to Somali. He was expected to decipher the world for her, to protect her and us, though he was only ten. Sometimes he heard the Saudi men say lewd and ugly things to Ma. Sometimes they called her *abda* (slave) and other times *aswad* (black). Mahad would pretend not to hear them; he never translated those words.

It would be an understatement to call Mahad's relationship with Abeh troubled. But from the instant Abeh finally arrived in Saudi Arabia, my father adored me, indulged me, forgave me my mistakes, cuddled me and stroked my hair. He let Haweya climb on his neck, tug his hair, and sprint back and forth in the tiny flat, screaming the ancient battle cries that our grandmother had taught us. Abeh's attitude to Mahad was just the opposite of this indulgence. He showed little physical affection. He ordered Mahad to stand up and raise his chin and look him in the eye. He expected Mahad to be impeccable in manners, in dress, in prayers, in helping Ma.

Mahad could never fill Abeh's shoes. When he failed to meet our father's lofty and often vague demands, Abeh would glare at him. Abeh humiliated Mahad and often slapped him across the face.

When we moved to the Saudi capital, Riyadh, one of my father's relatives came to visit us. He drove a white Toyota pickup. He left his key in the ignition to greet my parents before seeking a parking space. When we saw him coming into the house with extended arms, Mahad slipped past him and ran to the pickup. He started the engine and hit the accelerator, then the brake, knocking his head on the steering wheel. The car responded to Mahad's handling with screeching noises that attracted the attention of the adults, who were engaged in elaborate exchanges of greetings. Ma stepped outside without her black *hijab* and screamed in shock. She yelled that Mahad had hit his head. My father strode out of the house, opened the door of the truck, pulled Mahad out, lifted him with both hands, and threw him on the ground. Then he kicked Mahad. He removed his belt with one clean swing and started lashing my brother, now helpless on the ground.

As always when Abeh hit Mahad, Ma threw herself at our father, screaming curses, begging Allah to make him barren, and appealing to our ancestors to paralyze him. She started beating my father on his back and shoulders, first using her hands, then throwing her shoes at him. Father hurled a few words of contempt at Mahad—something about honor—and then went back into the house to attend to his relative.

Mahad was writhing in pain, doubly humiliated because not only we, the girls, were watching, but so were the little boys from the neighboring homes. He did all he could not to cry, then gave up and howled like an animal.

Every evening Abeh would order us to wash, brush our teeth, put on our nightclothes, pray, and go to bed. Haweya and I would usually obey, but Mahad used this routine to try Abeh's patience in silent mutiny. He would go into the bathroom, lock the door, and stay in there for hours. My mother would listen for the sound of running water and hear none. No one knew what Mahad did in there, but he would not turn on the shower. Meanwhile our bedtime was being delayed. Ma would stop my father from breaking down the door. After what seemed like hours, Mahad would emerge as dry as when he went in, dressed just as before. My father and mother would argue loudly; Ma would call my father names, and Abeh would retaliate by calling Mahad names. They were disgraceful names: comparing Mahad to a girl, calling him a coward, threatening to whip him with the belt, saying he was not his son.

Sometimes, just before prayer time, if Abeh was home he would spit at Mahad, "You filthy boy—or maybe I should call you a girl—did you do your ablutions?"

Mahad would look down and press out of his lips, "Yes, Father."

Abeh would shout, "Look at me, look me in the eye!"

Mahad would turn up his chin, find a spot on my father's forehead, and glare.

"Did you do your ablutions?" Father would growl. Ma would position herself between her son and her husband.

"Yes, Father," Mahad would say, his voice trembling.

"But you are dry. Where is the wetness?"

"I dry fast," Mahad would stammer.

Abeh would raise his voice: "Liar! Liar! Little, filthy liar, you will never be a man. You don't have what it takes. Get away from me! Right behind your mother's skirt—that's where you belong."

Mahad's tears would glide out of his eyes and down his cheeks. He would stand and watch my father turn away and leave the room. The next morning Abeh would shake Mahad awake and drag him to the bathroom sink, where he would tower over him as Mahad did his ablutions. Or Abeh would demonstrate how to go about it quickly. Wash your hands, clean your mouth by gargling three times, then your nose. Abeh cupped his hand, filled it with water, and carried it quickly to his nostrils, then inhaled deeply—an act that, when Mahad tried it, had him sputtering, coughing and sneezing like a drowning lamb.

After a series of scoldings and insults, Mahad would be led to the prayer mat, where Haweya and I would be waiting for him. Then we would all steal back into bed; prayer was at 5 a.m. and we didn't have to leave for school until 7. At that time, again, my father would have to shake Mahad awake, order him to brush his teeth, wash his face, put on his uniform, and get ready, and to do it all quickly. Mahad never did. Just as we'd be about to leave for school, Father would catch sight of Mahad on a wooden stool, half dressed, clutching both socks in his hands and dozing off, mouth slightly open, eyes closed, head tilted to one side and looking like it would drop off his neck.

Abeh would sneak up, put his face on the same level as Mahad's droopy one, slap him, and order him, "Wake up, woman!" He'd catch

Mahad's breath and shout, "The smell of your mouth is foul, you didn't brush your teeth. You are not my son, you are indeed a *wa'al*, a bastard child."

As Abeh pulled Mahad from the stool, Ma would intervene. She would somehow find her way between the two, and after Abeh gave in she would help Mahad put on his socks.

When Abeh was absent for weeks on end, I would pine for him. Haweya would ask loudly for him. Ma would cry that she was alone and let down by her husband. But Mahad never asked for our father. He ran around with the boys on the block. Whenever Ma announced that Abeh was on his way home, I pranced and jumped about in joy. Mahad's face fell into a brooding scowl, a look that didn't leave his face until Abeh's departure.

Other than school, Quran school, and a few visits to relatives, Haweya and I virtually never left the house. We were not allowed to dress up and go out. We were stuck inside, bored senseless in the hot, small flat in Mecca, and later in the much roomier house in Riyadh. But Mahad would dress up and go out with my father to manly locations, such as the mosque or the souk or to some formal Somali lunch or dinner.

The Friday prayer was another source of sibling rivalry. Every Thursday night that our father spent with us, Ma ironed my father's and Mahad's *thaubs*, the long, white shirt-like robe that Saudi men wear. She set out their *imamah* headscarves and black *igal* cords, and during dinner Abeh would instruct Mahad on how to behave and whom he should greet. Ma would call Mahad her prince and tell him that how he behaved would reflect on Abeh's good name and our own.

Haweya and I begged to go with Abeh to the beautiful mosque, to listen as the men gathered outside to talk politics and tribal affairs and washed at the communal taps and bent in unison. We vowed that we would put on our best faces and not bring shame to the family. The answer was always the same: a girl's honor was best preserved at home.

Every Friday morning we watched Mahad and Abeh leave and felt deprived of the world outside the door that shut in our faces. The world outside was for men. We were born girls. It was Allah's choice.

Our role—or mine really, for Haweya was too small—was to help prepare the elaborate Friday lunch. We would serve it after the men filed out of the mosque and walked to the tribunal of justice, known as Chop-chop Square. There men and boys would take their seats and watch the sinners being punished with stonings, floggings, amputations, or beheadings. Abeh rarely lingered there, but Mahad, in passing, saw enough.

Mahad never had an appetite for lunch on Fridays. He was not cheerful or excited when he returned from the weekly visit to the mosque and Chop-chop Square. He became more silent and brooding. His behavior toward Abeh grew steadily worse. It was as if he deliberately sabotaged every simple instruction. He also became more violent to me, and even to Haweya, for whom he had always had a soft and protective spot. He would beat us. As small children we had often fought, but now his kicks and punches were much crueler, and he had even begun throwing things. It was as if he had lost all sense of restraint.

Other little boys whom we met while growing up were just as terrified of their fathers as Mahad was of Abeh. The sons of Somali relatives who came to visit us, and those whom we visited, were full of awe for their fathers and older men in general. Our Saudi and Palestinian neighbors in Riyadh and Jeddah were the same. The boys would go out in packs and play on the streets until a father showed up. Then they would all freeze and glide back into their homes with drooping heads. A father's authority was established through physical violence and harsh scorn for any mistakes his son made. Alternately, the boy would be praised—mainly by the women, but sometimes also by the fathers—in terms that seemed, even to us, unrealistic and overblown.

For instance, Abeh would tell Mahad, "You will rule a people. You will undo the oppression in Somalia. You will be a just ruler." Mother would call him a prince and refer to him as the Chosen One. She told him that her father had been a judge and that his grandfather had conquered lands and people, so Mahad's destiny was to be a great leader.

Mahad would respond with excitement. He could imagine becoming a prince. The Palestinian ten- and eleven-year-old boys that he played with, refugees from the Israeli conflict, were also told that they would be heroes who would more or less single-handedly drive the evil Jews out of their land. When the boys went outside they played a game of war, driving out evil Jews, until they were called in to lunch or to prayer or told to make less noise.

At school, Mahad's reports were outstanding, but his Saudi teachers said that he chose to stand apart and did not care to join in group games. At first Mahad used to tell us girls to explain to Mother that in school he was called "black slave." Abeh's response was, "You must give the boy who calls you *abid* a good reason never to do it again." He would tell Mahad that he, Abeh, had personally defeated large numbers of men in combat, and he would try to teach Mahad how to fight. He would head-butt Mahad, and Mahad was not allowed to show pain or cry even when Abeh butted his little head with his own heavy one.

After a time Mahad stopped telling our parents what was going on at school. When we were eating he would pick up his plate and throw it across the room, accompanied by a gut-wrenching cry. He would beat his fists on the table repeatedly. He would pick fights with other boys. His academic results remained excellent, but his brooding was interspersed with violent rage that he mostly took out on me. Then for months he would be so passive that he had to be physically carried out of bed, and only after a great deal of prodding and scolding would he do anything at all.

We left for Ethiopia, where there was no suffocating Saudi segregation of men and women. In Ethiopia men and women mixed freely, as did boys and girls at school, and this made us much happier. The happiest person of us all was our father. Abeh was completely in his element. The building where his Somali opposition movement was headquartered was huge. There were hundreds of rooms, some for soldiers, others for politicians and intellectuals who contributed to the exile radio station that they used in order to lure more men out of Somalia to join our cause. Father was at the top of that hierarchy. He spent hours in meetings discussing strategy, finding resources, keeping up the morale of the soldiers. He also composed stories called "The Source of Healing," which he broadcast on the radio every week.

The least happy person in the whole of Ethiopia was my mother. To her the Ethiopians were sinners (because they were not Muslims), and they were of inferior class and heritage. They were also at war with Somalia. (Abeh was also at war with Somalia, but somehow this did not amount to the same thing. He was opposing a dictator, according to her, while the lowly Ethiopians were our nation's most ancient enemy.)

Mahad, Haweya, and I were really quite happy with the change. Mahad in particular could mix with Somali men of our clan, who looked like him, who spoke our language and did not call him *abid.* Being the son of my father, he was treated respectfully by them. They were kind and indulgent. My mother put a lot of effort into feeding those young men food that they hadn't had for a long time—lamb, rice, various kinds of spaghetti, spices like coriander and ginger— which reminded them of home.

Most of these young men chewed *qat*, a drug. They would sit together in a circle, drinking dark tea with lots of sugar, holding twigs and sorting the leaves, throwing away the dry ones and slipping the softer, juicy ones into their mouths. They made pouches in their cheeks, quite openly sucking in the juice of this drug. Certainly Mahad, and often Haweya and I too, were present to witness these gatherings.

Ma reproached our father: "Look what you've done! You have exposed your only son to addiction. He is going to copy these men. He is going to get addicted to *qat*."

Abeh would attempt to calm her. "Mahad is my son. He is a Magan. Don't underestimate my son. He will never do anything like that. In the entire Magan family, no one chews *qat*."

Ma would list the Magan offspring who did, in fact, chew *qat*. She would plead to return to Saudi Arabia, for it was clear we could not return to Somalia. "Our name, the traditions of our ancestors, no longer protect us from these evils," she would remind Abeh. "I sought protection in the house of God. I wanted us to live in Mecca, where we are reminded to pray five times a day, where we can stay pure. You brought us to an evil land. These people never wash. Did you see yesterday, I was walking with my mother and this woman suddenly crawled on the sidewalk and she urinated! She did it before us! In this country, they drink alcohol and they fornicate more than Faadumo Artan's he-goats. Mahad is our only son. He is going to be corrupted here. This place is too big. I run after him, but he outruns me. He's almost twelve; soon he will be taller than I am."

Mahad now had a choice of more than ten bathrooms to hide out in. The buildings were very long, with lots of rooms. When he was ordered to take a shower, he would say, "Yes, I will go to the one in so-and-so's room." Ma would be exhausted and Abeh would be at some late-night meeting, so Mahad would run out and he wouldn't get back until we were all asleep, or perhaps not until morning, sleeping wherever he liked. Ma was torn between involving my father and dreading the severity of his punishment of Mahad. Most of the time she elected not to involve Abeh. In the morning a driver would arrive in the Land Rover that took us to school, and Mahad would be in the front seat, still wearing the same uniform he had worn for days, looking as if he hadn't even taken it off to sleep. His eyes were red, encrusted with sleep, there'd be stains on his cheeks from where his drool had dried. His hair, which he refused to have cut, had now grown to a huge afro, and because he slept on one side his bed-head made it appear that he had sloppy cotton candy where a nice, round afro should have been. He often lost his shoelaces or his schoolbag; his breath was truly vile.

All of this disorder reflected badly not only on Mahad but very much on my father. The driver, Haile Gorgeus, would look at Mahad with contempt, occasionally forbidding him to enter his car in such a state. Ma would come, balancing lunch boxes, and catching sight of Mahad would scream at the top of her lungs. He would cry and beg, "Please, please, don't tell Father." Ma would beg the driver to wait while she rushed Mahad back into our rooms, where she and my grandmother would strip him and scrub him themselves, though he howled in pain and shame. My grandmother would hold him by his hair and brush his teeth until his gums bled.

The three of them wove a conspiracy to conceal these events from Abeh. Haweya would wander off, driving Haile Gorgeus crazy, and immaculate little me, goody-two-shoes, would prattle to whoever would listen, "We shall be late to school."

Mahad would reemerge clean, red-eyed, and grouchy as hell. He would demand total silence in the car. It was complete tyranny. And we were, indeed, often late to school, but none of us told Abeh. We were all part of the conspiracy to protect the prince, our older brother.

Mahad bonded with some of the young soldiers of Abeh's exile army before they were sent into combat on the Ethiopia-Somalia border. Some of them didn't come back; others returned missing a leg, or both legs, or an eye. Some lived only a short while before dying from their wounds. Haweya and I were not allowed to go to funerals, but Mahad was obliged to attend. When Haweya and I grew up, we would become wives and mothers; when Mahad grew up, he would have to go to the front lines of battle. If his destiny was to be a leader, he would send his men to their deaths. But no one starts as a leader; everyone starts as an ordinary soldier, and Mahad didn't seem to be able to accept this idea.

Mahad's academic reports remained perfect. He was by far the brightest of us children. He picked up the Amharic language with ease. His speech, his writing, his grammar, his handwriting, his grades in math, geography, sciences—all were excellent. But his teachers in Ethiopia, like his teachers in Saudi Arabia, complained that he was silent and brooding.

When my mom gave birth to a stillborn baby, the house was engulfed in sadness. My mother's unhappiness grew until it filled the entire household with a silent, bitter hostility. Finally Abeh gave in and agreed to move us out of Ethiopia.

When we moved to Kenya, Mahad was a month shy of his twelfth birthday. I was ten. Abeh was absent most of the time. He would walk out of the house after the morning prayer, at sunrise, and rarely returned before we were all in bed again. Sometimes he left on trips for a week at a time. His relationship with Mahad continued to deteriorate; his relationship with Ma was even worse.

Abeh wanted us all to attend the Nairobi Muslim Girls' Primary School, a misnomer, because the primary section of that school was coed. It cost a huge amount of money, and you had to pass an admission exam and an interview to get in. Abeh took all three of us to take the exam. Only Mahad passed. He obtained not only excellent marks but compliments on his behavior during the oral interview. Haweya was told that she was promising; she could come back and take the exam again next year. I failed utterly, having performed poorly in every subject. On the morning we received the results, Ma whacked me on the head and scolded me with the insults I had long ago become used to. But Abeh's behavior toward me did not change. He hugged me, stroked me, and called me his "only son." He played chess with Haweya and me. He took us out on a boat. His behavior to Mahad also did not change; he told him that although he did well on the exam, he could have done better. According to my father, Mahad stood in the wrong way, made the wrong eye contact, held his pencil wrong. Nothing Mahad could do was worthy of being Abeh's only son.

Abeh began to visit Ethiopia for longer periods. On the rare occasions he was with us, he never wasted a moment to tell Mahad that he must be the man of the house. "You are in charge. Your sisters will soon become women. If they shame the family, it's your responsibility. They will take away your honor. If your mother spends one unhappy night in her bed, it's your responsibility. Be there for her. Listen to her. Obey her. Do not bring her undue trouble." Mahad nodded and nodded and nodded. If he didn't understand what Father was asking of him, he didn't express it. If he felt it was unfair that Father made huge, adult demands on him, he didn't express it. He just kept nodding and saying, "Yes, Abeh. Yes, Abeh. Yes, Abeh." Mahad was obliged by Father to stand in a sort of military pose as these conversations occurred: feet shoulder-width apart, hands folded quietly in front of him, eyes up, staring blankly between Abeh's eyes. It was unclear to me whether Mahad even registered what Father was asking of him. Every time we saw Abeh, he drilled Mahad in this way. Finally, after a last, terrible row with my mother, Abeh left for Ethiopia. Mahad was almost thirteen.

Abeh didn't return for ten years. After he left, Mahad's problems with authority became far more visible. One day he came home in a brooding frame of mind, head down, kicking stones, and threw himself on the mattress, arms and legs wide, which my grandmother, who had come with us to Kenya, considered to be very disrespectful. She chased him off the mattress. He went into a corner and pulled out a novel and started reading it. On the cover of the novel was a long-haired white woman in a bikini with her legs wide open; her face was held by a man, also white, who was staring deep into her eyes. This picture offended my grandmother even more than Mahad's pose on the mattress, and she went screaming for my mother.

After Abeh left, the quarrels between Mahad and Mother and Grandmother became a constant part of our lives, as irritating and inevitable as the dust in the streets of Nairobi.

After the usual scolding and shouting and name-calling, Mother offered Mahad food that he refused to eat.

MA: What's the matter? What happened?
MAHAD: I think I'm going to be expelled from school.
MA: Why? What have you done?
MAHAD: I got ninety-seven percent on my math test.
MA: Surely you're not going to be expelled for getting ninety-seven percent on your math test? You've done much poorer in the past. (Ma had no idea what school grades meant. To her, any mistakes meant you were doing badly.)
MAHAD: It's different this time. I burned the school.

Ma threw shoes. She called upon her ancestors. She lamented her fate. "Your father left me! May the ancestors curse him! May they curse you! May Allah paralyze you!" She picked up the plate of food she had been trying to cajole Mahad into eating and launched it across the room. I watched, dreading the mess I would later have to clean up. On the other hand, I was entranced with the idea of burning the school. What did it feel like? What was it like, to be expelled from school? It was the most horrible thing that could happen, I thought. My ears burned to hear more. But beyond all the drama, I knew I was witness to a tragic fact: Ma now had no authority at all over Mahad. Abeh was gone and, if this expulsion meant Mahad would not go to school anymore, then he was going to grow up on the streets like a vagabond.

Ma retrieved her shoes and set off to get the relatives. The next few weeks were spent talking to the school authorities and collecting money to compensate for the classroom that Mahad had set alight. Mahad wasn't allowed to come back to class, but all the persuading and the bribing resulted in a compromise: he would be allowed to take his final exams, the important passageway to a good secondary school.

When my mother's anger and disappointment over the incident subsided, it became apparent why Mahad had set the school on fire. His math teacher, a woman, had scheduled a mock exam in preparation for the finals. This teacher had suffered many disputes with Mahad. He would not listen to her; he would talk during class; he was surly and disrespectful. When he got his mock exam results and found that he had received a score of 67 percent, he walked up to her desk and demanded that she adjust his marks. The teacher sent him away. Mahad persisted in trying to show her that his sums were correct. She refused to look at them and ordered him to go away. He went to his favorite teacher, a man with a great reputation; this teacher looked at the numbers and told Mahad he was right, he had actually earned 97 percent on the test.

Mahad showed the headmistress the discrepancy between his sums and the marks he received. The next day the headmistress told him, "I do not have the authority to intervene. You have to work this out with your teacher." Mahad then went back to his math teacher, who again sent him away, scolding him for being disrespectful and disobedient. The day after, he conspired with another student who, just like Mahad, had problems with authority in general, particularly in having a female teacher boss him around. One day, when the lessons were over, they forced open the teacher's closet in their classroom and set everyone's exam papers on fire.

When the time came for his final exams, once again Mahad performed an academic miracle. Thousands of Kenyan children took the exam, but although Mahad had been speaking English for only two years—and for three months had not attended school or done any kind of schoolwork—he emerged among the top ten students in the nation.

Because Mahad's results were so good he applied to the best schools and was accepted into most of them. My mother settled on Starehe Boys' Center and School, a school that was started by an Englishman for children who lived in the streets; to cover the operating costs, smart children from wealthy families were also admitted. Kids like Mahad from low-income families but who had very high academic scores were allowed to pay less tuition.

All our relatives, my mother, and our religious leaders kept reminding Mahad, *Whatever happens, don't give up our culture and the glorious, millennial customs of our ancestors.* Meanwhile the Kenyan educational authorities were "Africanizing" the school curriculum. Mahad's reading list shifted from English classics, like Dickens and Trollope, to African writers like Chinua Achebe. These authors were obsessed with the awful manner in which British colonialism had disrupted the lives of their ancestors. Ironically, however, Mahad read about Achebe's tribe and ancient customs in English, the language of the imperialist oppressor whom we were supposed to condemn. Mahad routinely achieved top marks in English. He was drilled to wear a school uniform (with a tie), obey the school prefects, and play cricket and rounders, foreign sports. Everything he did and excelled at earned him a paradox of extreme praise for academic achievement and extreme contempt for betraying his tribal customs and religious dogmas.

At first Mahad was a day student, but because he was always late to school, our mother, together with the headmaster, decided to make him a boarder. Then he began cutting school for days at a time, though my mother thought he was attending. His teachers didn't notice his absences at first. He had joined some other kids who were playing truant. No word ever reached me of their doing anything particularly bad; I think they spent their days just hanging out, talking about girls and plotting how to get into discos. At home Mahad berated and lectured Haweya and me: we must maintain strict morality, we must remain virgins. When we asked him why he spent time with bad girls, he said, "That's just how it is. Some girls are bad for us boys to amuse ourselves. Some girls are honorable and they get married."

Ma wanted three things from Mahad. First, she wanted him to help her discipline Haweya and me. This cooperation was most often expressed in tying us up and beating us. I hated him for the pain he was causing me, but watching him hurt Haweya was unbearable. Haweya was always being punished for going outside the house, staying up late reading novels, and coming home late from school. As she grew older, she also developed an interest in going to discos. Ma induced Mahad to hunt her down and bring her home, where he would call her a whore and tie her down and beat her. I would be punished for neglecting to complete the housework, the cooking, cleaning, tidying up, washing the clothes, and doing the grocery shopping. I was also punished for annoying Grandmother. I memorized her lines of curses and lamentations and I would stand in front of her, wiggle my bottom, and pretend to be her, repeating her verses. I also hung out with my friends in school, then came home late and lied that I had been in the mosque.

The second thing Ma wanted from Mahad was to stay in school. She told him the worst thing that could happen to *her* was for him to drop out. It would mean she was a complete failure, as a mother and as a woman. Only his destiny was significant—not hers, and certainly not Haweya's or my own. She tried to indulge Mahad by making him good food, sometimes by bribing him with a bit of money. Unfortunately none of that helped. Mahad skipped class so often that his headmaster called Ma to school and said he had no choice but to expel him.

Ma began spending days and nights searching for Mahad in dark alleys, on the streets. She went knocking on the doors of boys she thought were his friends, asking to search their houses for her son. Sometimes she solicited the help of male Somali relatives. For days all we did was look for Mahad. When he emerged from these long hiding periods, Ma would get him into the house and put huge padlocks on the door so he was unable to leave. Then, when she wasn't paying attention, he would climb over the wall, despite the shards of glass that were fixed to the top to deter thieves.

In one incident, Ma caught him right on our driveway as he was sneaking out. She threw herself at him. Mahad, now fifteen and almost as tall as a man, kept pushing forward. Ma threw herself on the ground, clutched at his ankle, cried and screamed; she would not let him go. Stiff with embarrassment as the neighbors came out to watch what was happening, Mahad conceded and went back into the house. He stayed as long as Ma played watchman, but in a few days he left again.

The third thing Ma wanted from Mahad was to be pious: to read the Quran, pray, and one day perhaps even become a religious leader. I was beginning to be attracted to the teachings of Sister Aziza, an Islamic studies teacher at my school. I was covering myself in a *hijab* and praying more; looking back, I see that slowly but surely I was subscribing to the tenets of the Muslim Brotherhood, a jihadi movement. But Mahad was more attracted to the lures of the street. He became a chain smoker; there were rumors that he drank beer and perhaps even hard liquor. (At the time I didn't know the difference.) There were also rumors that he was chewing *qat*.

It was common knowledge that boys like Mahad, who had dropped out, whose fathers were absent, and whose mothers had no authority over them, grew up to be men with no jobs, no wives, no children. Sometimes they were lucky and their parents arranged a marriage for them, to keep them clothed and housed and fed and off the streets. But the marriages always broke down. There were hordes of such lost young Somali men in Eastleigh, a neighborhood in Nairobi. They spent most of their days sleeping in cramped rented rooms and their evenings chewing *qat*. Then, with borrowed money, they looked for prostitutes. Some of them were involved in crime; they made the streets unsafe.

Some of these young men later repented and joined the Muslim Brotherhood. They would go to Saudi Arabia on Islamic scholarships and come back as preachers of what we would now call radical Islam. Their own story was compelling, for they had been saved from evil, Westernized behavior when Allah showed them the straight path. My mother actively tried to bring Mahad in contact with these agents. But nothing seemed to work.

As Mahad sank deeper into the mire, Ma's next strategy was to mobilize the clansmen one more time and have him sent to Somalia. At the age of about seventeen he set off to meet our paternal uncles and aunts, and even traveled to Ayl, on the northern coast, which had just been captured by my father's opposition army. He wasn't just Mahad any more: he was Hirsi Magan's son—if not a prince, then at least a man with a long and honorable bloodline and a lofty destiny. He deserved to rule. Surely he wouldn't betray the clan and himself by remaining a street boy.

While in Somalia Mahad regularly sent my mother letters written in beautiful English. I read them to her, translating them as I went. I ached with sadness that he had dropped out of school. Mahad was so gifted; he could have become a writer. Unfortunately no one had prepared him to set realistic goals and work for them. From his early days, his head was filled with vague notions of honor, wrestling lions, and conquering peoples, goals that bore no relationship to his reality and that only confused his sense of himself.

Then Haweya also dropped out of school, and in 1990 she and I were sent to Somalia too. When I saw Mahad again he was tall and handsome, with a new air of confidence about him. He had enrolled as a student at a Somali-American business school, which I think was paid for by the United Nations, because we were refugees. He said he was thinking of starting a business with some of our relatives. But although I saw him talking to a lot of different people, I never saw him actually do any business; we certainly saw no sign that he was making money.

Both Haweya and I had done secretarial training, and we found employment with the United Nations within a month of our arrival in Mogadishu. We were hired to type, take shorthand, and answer the phone. Our jobs paid relatively well. Mahad neither sought nor found a job with any local or international organization. He didn't know how to type or take shorthand or file, and he refused to learn, believing that the work we did was beneath him. It was also beneath him to do any kind of manual labor. He had chosen the path of business, but he didn't want to become a lowly apprentice. Many of our relatives were in the transport business, but no one had started out as an executive; most of them had begun as long-distance drivers or mechanics. Mahad didn't want to do any of that. As bright as he was, he would have learned fast, but emotionally he was unprepared and undisciplined. His sense of self was both terribly fragile and completely grandiose. He felt, I think, that he could not risk taking a servile position as an apprentice. A prince doesn't do that.

We make our sons. This is the tragedy of the tribal Muslim man, and especially the firstborn son: the overblown expectations, the ruinous vanity, the unstable sense of self that relies on the oppression of one group of people—women—to maintain the other group's self-image. Instead of learning from experience, instead of working, Mahad engaged in a variety of defense mechanisms involving arrogance, self-delusion, and scapegoating. His problems were always somebody else's fault.

Trouble was brewing in Somalia: the civil war was about to erupt.

In November 1990 my mother, who was still in Nairobi, demanded that Haweya and I return, because she had heard so much about girls being raped by gangs of militia. Mahad played the part of guardian very well. He arranged for meetings with our male relatives and successfully raised enough money to send Haweya and me to Kenya by road. He found a male relative, our nephew, to act as our guardian en route. About a month after we arrived in Nairobi, Mahad showed up too, and right after him came a whole stream of refugees.

One of them was our uncle, and he wanted Mahad to take him to the border between Somalia and Kenya to look for his family. That was a clansman's duty. But Mahad dragged his feet, said "Tomorrow." Because I could no longer stand his procrastination, I volunteered. When my uncle accepted my offer, to Mahad it was like being kicked in the gut. It reminded me of my father calling him a girl, telling him to hide behind his mother's skirts, where he belonged. When our uncle and I were out on the border, searching for his wife and children, Mahad showed up. He had been driven to come by the obligation of honor and the shame that would be heaped upon him by the gossiping tongues of the Osman Mohammud clan if he didn't fulfill his duty.

A few months later my father came to Nairobi. Haweya and I had not seen him in ten years, and I, for one, was overjoyed that he was back. But the tension between him and Mahad was palpable. Mahad always boasted that he would stand up to Abeh, but when push came to shove, he yielded without a word. Father would wake us up at five to pray. Mahad had always lain in bed until noon; he never got around to doing anything until four or five in the afternoon, and even though Ma prodded and begged and pleaded with him every single day to pray, he never did. But when Abeh sang the call to prayer at dawn, Mahad jumped up as though he had been stung by a wasp, rushed to the bathroom, performed his ablutions, and stood on the prayer mat alongside our father, just like when he was a very young boy. And, just like Abeh, he sat down for about an hour and read from the Quran before he went to bed.

To avoid these rituals, Mahad developed the habit of sleeping in hotels and sometimes in the homes of his Kenyan friends. But he never stood up to my father. He never told him, "No, I'm not going to pray" or "Leave me alone, I'm going to sleep in." He did not dare.

Another time, Mahad encountered Abeh near the large mosque in the city center of Nairobi. Mahad was walking with one of his friends, a Kenyan, and apparently both of them were smoking. As soon as Mahad saw Abeh, he folded the burning cigarette in his hand, shoved it quickly into his pocket, and as it burned a hole through his trousers, he stood in front of my father with a stoic expression.

My father never tired of telling this anecdote, and every time he did he called Mahad a coward and demanded to know why he did not just face up to him like a man. If a man is doing something he knows he shouldn't do, he should be brave enough to stand up and defend himself.

When my father arranged my marriage to a distant relative who lived in Canada, Mahad saw how unhappy I was. He talked about how he was going to stand up to Father and convince him to change his mind. I believed him; I was so desperate that I thought Mahad truly would help me convince Father that this marriage was wrong for me. But when the occasion presented itself, Mahad said absolutely nothing. He wouldn't even bring up the subject. My father would then go on and on about what a wonderful match he had made, and Mahad would just nod.

So I left. I made my own life in Holland. I learned from the sporadic letters Haweya sent that Mahad had found and secretly married a good woman, Suban, who was tall, beautiful, of a prominent clan. She was a refugee. Her family had been wealthy in the past, but now, because of the civil war, they were destitute. This was fortunate for Mahad, for it meant that he wouldn't have to pay a very high bride price, perhaps even none. Haweya hinted that Abeh approved of the marriage, but she said Ma was opposed: the girl wasn't good enough. I think Ma hated her because she felt Suban had taken Mahad away. Ma always wanted her son to marry a girl of the Dhulbahante clan. But perhaps, like some mothers all over the world, she would have hated any woman who married her son.

Mahad postponed disclosing the marriage to my mother until Suban was pregnant.

CHAPTER 5

My Brother's Son

I didn't see Mahad again until after Haweya died in 1998. I was living with my Dutch boyfriend, attending the University of Leiden, working toward a master's degree in political science; I had a job as a translator and had applied for Dutch citizenship. Mahad was still in Nairobi. Although his wife, Suban, was expecting a child at any moment, he was living in my mother's apartment.

Haweya was buried while I was in midair between Amsterdam and Nairobi. Mahad's son was born ten days after she died, barely a week after I arrived back in Kenya.

When Mahad came home and told my mother, "Ma, Suban has given birth," my mother's face was stone cold. She did not move a muscle.

"Ma, I have a boy, I have a little boy," Mahad said.

Ma turned her face away; her eyes filled with tears and her lips quivered. She told Mahad, "He is not yours, he is a bastard child."

Mahad did not know whether Ma was sad, angry, and confused because of Haweya's death, or whether she was just being her usual difficult self.

When I went to visit the new baby, he was barely three days old. Suban was trying to soothe him by holding him to her breast, but he curled his little red, wrinkled face away from her nipple; he squinted and cried.

My visit to Suban was a secret of sorts. When I mentioned to Ma and Mahad that I wanted to see his baby and meet his wife, Ma erupted. "Did you say you wanted to betray me, like Haweya betrayed me? Like your absolutely good-for-nothing brother betrayed me?"

I knew that Ma did not approve of Mahad's choice of wife; Haweya had told me that. But I thought it was natural for a woman to welcome her grandchild, a grand*son,* into the world. Instead Ma pouted on her mattress, draped in her *garbasaar* robes, crestfallen and gaunt. She had always been thin, but now she looked so emaciated that every time I looked at her I was overcome with pity and guilt.

But her attitude toward the new baby made me feel confused and angry. Ma had just lost a child; Mahad and I a sister. Why would she be upset about the arrival of a new life?

"As always, off you'll go to air my shame to other women," she ranted.

I protested; all I wanted to do was to see my brother's baby. But Ma cut me off. "That boy is a *wa'al,* a bastard, he is not Mahad's child. The harlot gives herself to any man who throws her a shilling."

Mahad broke in. "Stop it, Ma, please, Ma, I beg you."

"May the almighty Allah take you both!" she cried, shaking. "He took away Haweya to protect me from her shame."

I was aghast. This was a jolt back into reality, hearing Ma curse and writhe in self-pity like this. I had been gone for over five years. I had forgotten or repressed the memory of her vindictiveness, her resentment, her ranting, which when we were young had usually been directed at me. Clearly she had found a new scapegoat: Mahad's wife, Suban.

Mahad had suggested that I should sneak off to see Suban and the baby, so as not to upset our mother while she was mourning the death of her daughter. I thought it ironic and bizarre that he felt he could not celebrate the birth of his son.

Now, as I sat on a mattress across from Suban, watching her lament her fate in a raised voice that had her newborn squinting with displeasure on her lap, I marveled at the similarity between Ma and my sister-in-law: both tall and thin; both burning with resentment. It must be difficult to cope with having a baby for the first time, particularly in such circumstances. But the sense of despair Suban felt at being let down by my brother caused in her the same anger and confusion that my mother felt when my father neglected his responsibilities to her and his children. And her response was the same: placing the responsibility for her own destiny on external factors.

"Ayaan, I hold you and your family responsible for abandoning me," she began. "You are here now in Nairobi, not for me, not for your only male heir—you are here because your sister died. And what have you brought me? What have you brought for your nephew? You came from a rich country and yet you come here empty-handed.

"Do you know how your mother treats me?" she continued. "Do you know of her campaign to separate me from your brother? She thinks she hurts me, but she's hurting your nephew, your bloodline. Allah the Almighty is my witness, I shall always tell this boy, my son, about your mother's machinations."

Her voice grew louder as she explored the possibilities of revenge she had in store for the Magan family. "I have on my lap the only male who carries on the name of Hirsi Magan," she screamed. The baby wriggled and twisted his head from side to side. Still glaring at me, she tried to pop her nipple into his mouth. He cried even more loudly.

The room was dimly lit with a *feynoos*, the paraffin lantern most commonly used by Somalis. There was a switch and a lightbulb fastened to a wire hanging from the roof, but I surmised that the electricity had been turned off. In the flickering light I could see that the paint was peeling from the walls in some places. The floor between Suban's mattress and the mattress I sat on was cement, painted in red; this paint too was peeling in some places. In one corner of the room was an iron charcoal brazier with a pot of tea on it, and to keep the odors of food and diapers suppressed Suban had set up a *dab-qaad,* or fire-carrier, a domed piece of pottery pierced with air holes that held embers of frankincense.

The room was tiny, almost a closet, with one minuscule window; the ceilings were blackened from the cooking smoke. There was no need at all to shout; in that small space, I could hear her very well.

Suban caught my eye as I glanced around the room. "I grew up in a villa in Mogadishu," she said, sounding suddenly desperately pathetic. "If any of you Magans ever came to us, my father would honor you, treat you like kings. Look at this miserable room where your brother and mother have put me. I would not put animals here. I gave your brother my honor, my womb, I bore him a son. And you—my cousin, my sister-in-law—you are rich. I know the story. You drive around in a fancy car; you make money from the misery of the refugees in Holland, translating for the infidels. And yet you did not bother to bring the little boy anything. You are rich and you do not share a penny."

Sitting across from Suban, I thought of the reports I translated for the parents of Somali children living in Holland. These reports were compiled by Dutch psychologists and pediatricians working for the social services to analyze children with developmental problems. Some had motor difficulties because their harassed mothers penned them into cribs or harnessed them to prams and buggies for far too long. Others were understimulated in their cognitive and social development, particularly their faculty of language. Many of these children had first been introduced to toys and writing and drawing implements when they arrived in school at the age of four or five. They had not been groomed to take on the challenges of living in a modern world. Their parents had failed to provide proper tools.

How would my tiny nephew fare under his mother's care? Her complaints of my mother and Mahad's neglect were justifiable. Suban was barely literate, but seemed strong, resilient, able to cope. But like my mother, Suban did not speak any language except Somali, and like Ma she despised the Kenyans. Where would this baby go to school? Suban had grown up with servants, Somali Bantus, known as *Sab,* who commonly worked almost as slaves for the higher clans. Would she be able to care for her son? And how would he fare in Nairobi, without a proper father? It was not likely that Mahad would be much of a protector and guide.

Mahad and Suban disagreed on everything, from whose fault it was that she got pregnant to the name of their child. Mahad had chosen the name Ya'qub; Suban wanted to call the baby Abdullahi, slave of Allah. She had my mother's fanatical religiosity and adherence to Arabic names and all things Arab-related.

As I held my wriggling nephew in my arms, it came to me for the first time that, viewed from the perspective of many generations, my family was hurtling backward instead of progressing. My grandfather Magan had earned his nickname, *The Protector of Those He Vanquished,* by conquering and annexing land that belonged to other clans. My father, his son, was able to adapt from the life of a legendary Somali warlord to that of a modern leader. He read Italian in Rome and

English in America and went back to Somalia to contribute to building a nation. But his only son, Mahad, was a dropout from school, unable to earn a living. Mahad's own son would be brought up in this tiny, cell-like room in a Somali enclave of Nairobi, where the roads seemed to have dissolved, leaving large potholes filled with dust in dry weather and mud in the rain.

In the past none of this would have struck me as unusual. Now, though, to my newly Dutch eyes, the whole neighborhood was a festering cauldron of disease and poverty. I returned to Ma's house on foot. Eastleigh was bursting with new inhabitants, refugees who were still pouring out of Somalia or the huge refugee camps along the border. They brought lice, scabies, and tuberculosis.

The night after I visited Suban, Mahad had told me that he was going to divorce her. I asked him why. I thought he was going to tell me, "I don't love her, I hate her, I don't want to be with her." I expected him to say, "She's a bad woman, spiteful and malicious and I can't bear her." Instead he said, "She promised not to get pregnant, and she got pregnant."

I was shocked. "What do you mean?" I asked.

"I told her how to count the menstrual cycles," he said. "I told her the day they came, the day they ended, and when she could get pregnant. And she promised me, she was going to observe this. She betrayed me."

I found it difficult to control my rage at Mahad's attitude. I told him how irresponsible he was being, that he had a healthy baby boy with a woman who was of our clan. I said, "You just wanted to have a good time with her. Now, as always, you don't want to take responsibility—you are letting that poor girl down and you are letting your baby down."

Mahad was clenching his fists and his jaw. The last time he hit me was in 1986, before he went to Somalia. I thought he might hit me again. He did not; he just walked away.

This was not the right time for a fight. I had to avoid trouble. Mahad and my mother could take away my passport if they wanted to. They could keep me in this terrible place to teach me a lesson, and without my passport I might never be able to go back to my life of freedom in Holland.

*   *   *

After a few weeks in Nairobi I returned to Holland, to my job translating for Somali refugees and immigrants interacting with the Dutch
social services. I saw many Somali mothers with babies who looked
just like Mahad's son, who had been abandoned by men just like my
brother. They were tormented by mothers-in-law just like my mother,
and like my family they were all focused backward, to a mythical past of
life as nomads in the Somali desert. They would tell their little children
about Somalia's heroes, about milking camels, and to hate other clans.
They would emotionally blackmail their children not to become "too
Dutch," to speak Somali instead of Dutch and not give up their culture.

These children performed poorly in school. As part of their evalu-
ations they were given puzzles to work out; they were required to say
"please" and "thank you" and to behave properly at the dinner table.
In Holland these are important indicators that children are well-
adjusted. But all the Somali children I translated for, who in their
homes certainly ate on the floor, with their hands, flatly failed these
tests. That meant they would not go to a normal school; they would
go to a "special school" for "remedial learning." The Dutch government would spend a lot of money on coaching them to catch up.

There seemed to be a pattern of such disconnects between the
expectations of the parents and the reality of the children in many
immigrant families in Holland—not just Somalis, but also families
from Morocco, Turkey, Iraq, Afghanistan, and the former Yugosla-
via. I was amazed that officials in so many different institutions—
social workers, schoolteachers, the police, child protection services,
domestic violence agencies—all assumed that there was some deep
cultural puzzle that they did not understand. In itself that was not a
bad assumption, but then they proceeded to *protect* these puzzling cultural norms. This was the advice they received from anthropologists,
Arabists, Islamologists, cultural experts, and ethnic organizations, all
of whom insisted that these behaviors were something special and
unique and worth preserving in these homes.

I worried about my brother's child. How could he ever become
successful in the modern world with the familial strife around him?

After a short interval, just as he had led me to expect, Mahad divorced Suban. With all his notions of noble upbringing and family honor, with all his lofty illusions of becoming a prince, he couldn't even act with integrity in his own personal life.

I decided to convince my mother to go back to Somalia. She had always complained that my father had deprived her of the company of her family and forced her to live among foreigners. She wanted to go home, so I told her I would pay for her to go. She would be with her brother and his children, her sisters and their children. She would go back to the sounds and smells of the Dhulbahante lands where she was born.

Even though I encouraged Ma to return to her place of birth, which lies far removed from the constant unrest in Mogadishu, I worried about this move. Ma was used to the luxury of living in a large city. Nairobi is not the best city in the world, but there you are protected from the worst of the weather and, most of the time, you have electricity and running water. There are doctors. You buy milk in packs; you do not milk the cows yourself. You do not have to slaughter animals for meat; you buy it. To get to my mother's apartment in Nairobi, you had to walk up four flights of stairs, without an elevator. But there was no threat from wild animals, like snakes and scorpions and other reptiles. She had a toilet and a bathroom.

I said all of this to Ma. She told me, "I want to go back. I am alone, lonely. I want to be with my family."

So in 1998 I paid for her to make the long journey to Las Anod with an escort, and she left. Suban and Mahad were already divorced; according to Shari'a law, all Mahad had to do was get a couple of his buddies and pronounce the *talaq,* the declaration "I divorce thee, and Allah is my witness." But now, at least, Suban could not complain that Ma was interfering between her and Mahad, and Mahad could not complain that was he was being held hostage by our mother. I thought I had fixed the problem.

During this period Mahad and I corresponded a little. He would phone or write lists of demands specifying the consignment of clothes I should send him and the business contacts I should make. He was imperious, ranting; his temper seemed always on the brink of explosion. He would explain at length that he was planning to get together a militia to defend the Somali coast from polluters. At five guilders a minute, these were expensive calls, and I remember them well. Although his pride was based on no visible achievement, Mahad often used the term *honor*. "Think about our name," he would scold me, telling me that I was obliged to help him in the name of family honor.

A few months after my mother left for Puntland I received a phone call from my father, who was in another part of Puntland at the time. His voice was sad. "Ayaan, my child, this time I am calling about Mahad."

I felt the tears shoot to my eyes and a sensation of total helplessness. I thought Abeh was telling me that Mahad had died. Instead he said, "Mahad has lost his mind. It is worse than being dead. He is tied up in ropes. I have prayed to Allah to make him well again."

From what my father told me in further telephone conversations, it appeared that Mahad was suffering from manic depression.

Of the three of us siblings, it was Mahad who should have succeeded in life. He was the brightest; he had by far the most opportunities; above all, he had the right to succeed. He was continually encouraged to think of himself as the biggest, best, most incredible being. Even as a child, Mahad was always highly sensitive to the requirements of honor. He would brood about the misdeeds of his sisters, and beat us. But as soon as a visitor showed up, whether a Kenyan or the most noble of our clan, he would be charming, reserved, and go to great lengths to demonstrate our family's refinement and superiority.

After the Somali civil war, however, Mahad saw that our father's aspirations for Somalia's future had become irrelevant. Our mother was abandoned and bitter; our sister had gone mad and died after multiple abortions; and I was living out of wedlock with an infidel. Having always aspired to greatness and wealth without ever developing any skills or holding down a job that would have enabled him to achieve them, Mahad must have seen all this as the failure of our family. Our family honor was in ruins. And since everyone had always told Mahad that it was up to him, the only boy, to uphold and defend the family's honor, perhaps he believed that this failure was ultimately his fault, that he couldn't live up to the aspirations and the duties of a good Muslim son.

My nephew's life was going to be in the hands of his mother. I thought that I had fixed the problems between the adults responsible for this young boy, but now Mahad would not be in any position to help his son. There seemed to be nothing I could do, at least not from Holland.

I continued to maintain sporadic telephone contact with my father and my mother. Despite my fears, Ma seemed to be thriving in her village in Puntland. The money I sent her was enough to pay for her upkeep and her food. Sometimes she shared it with her relatives. Her nieces brought her water, carrying it in pails and jerry cans from nearby wells. They also swept her front yard, fetched her charcoal, and cooked for her. She said she was never alone. At night she sat with her brother and sisters and their children, and they talked about their childhood and the different directions that their lives had gone, about the civil war and the things that had brought them back to their place of birth. All around them was desert, scrub, sheep, and stretches of unpaved roads on which merchants traveled in trucks, bringing in sugar, rice, and other staples.

Ma told me that Mahad was sick because he was bewitched by Suban. Sometimes she said he was bewitched by my father's first wife. Mahad spent long periods in the hospital, and longer periods holed up in a room in Eastleigh, barely supporting himself, let alone his child. Abeh said Suban was angry and lonely and that she had sent the little boy, hardly two years old, to Qardo, near the northern tip of Somalia, where Abeh was living. The little boy first responded to the name Abdullahi, but after he was put in my father's hands he was called Ya'qub. I decided to call him Jacob. I begged Father to send him back to Nairobi so that he could go to a proper school. After a while Abeh persuaded Suban to take the boy back.

Between 2001 and 2006 my family broke off all contact with me. I had no idea how Mahad's young son was faring, no idea whether he was even attending school. In 2006 I reestablished contact with Mahad, who was still living in Eastleigh, the Somali neighborhood in Nairobi. His health and state of mind were precarious. Some days he seemed fine, and at other times he would be delirious, saying he heard voices. At such times he would rarely leave his bed. Although they were divorced, Suban visited him regularly, washing his clothes, cooking his food, calling relatives when Mahad became ill.

After Abeh died, I got back in contact with Mahad. His voice wasn't the same; it was slurred and slow, as if his tongue were too large for his mouth. The first conversation was one long monologue: I had abandoned him; I didn't care about him; this is what success does, it estranges you from family; it alienates you from religion—a long list of accusations. The two concrete things he wanted from me were money (which I sent) and a visa for resettlement in America (which I didn't send).

Mahad refused to acknowledge his mental illness. I asked him if he were seeing a doctor. I begged him to go and get medicine. But he insisted there was nothing wrong with him. "I just talk to myself, that's all," he said. "I lie down and rest a lot. But they read the Quran over me and it makes me feel better."

I knew the procedure. A group of people read passages from the Quran and spit into a pail of water and sprinkle it on the patient. Or they spit on his bedcovers after every few passages. Not large drops but little lines of saliva, with the tongue quickly returning to the mouth after letting a little drop fall, a very particular kind of gesture.

I asked for news of Jacob. He was doing well in school, Mahad said; he was fine, healthy and cheerful. I tried to visualize him, ten years old, just a bit older than the son of some friends of mine. I saw him as tall like his father and strong-boned like his mother. I suppose I fantasized that Jacob was the one who would be able to break apart the restrictive shackles of our family and faith and attain the successes that his father and grandfather had not.

But Jacob would soon be a teenager. And I remembered all too well how tragically twisted Mahad had become during his teenage years in Nairobi, how he had squandered years that he should have spent studying in high school. I knew that nowadays radical Islamic cells were rife in Eastleigh, preying on the disadvantaged and disaffected, far more than when Mahad and I were young.

I found comfort in a conversation I had with Suban one day. As usual, she asked me for money, but she also asked me to send her clothes. When I asked her to describe what kind of clothes she wanted, she said skirts and blouses. This gave me hope, for I thought that if she were attracted to shrouding herself in a *jilbab* she would not ask for such clothes.

I began sending money to Mahad, and also to Suban. When Jacob left primary school I made arrangements for a friend to go to Nairobi to find a really good school for him, a school with a library and laboratories and good teachers. I offered to pay the fees. This went very well, and Jacob has been attending that school ever since. On the days when Mahad is not too depressed or too manic, he shows some interest in his son. Mahad told me that the boy is doing very well in school, that his reading, his English, his social skills are all excellent.

It's important to me that Jacob get an easier initiation into modernity than Mahad had. I can't influence his home situation. I can only imagine what it is like: confusing assignments, the nostalgic dreams of nomadic life, warlords as heroes, and a strong dose of Islam. He's probably been taught how to do his ablutions, stand on a mat, face Mecca and pray five times a day. He's been taught the ideas of sin, hell, and the hereafter.

I have no real strategy for protecting Jacob. I have tried, and failed, to persuade Suban to send him to me, so that I can bring him up in a Western environment. I fix my hopes for him on his schooling. I hope that they will teach him to have faith in life as it is now, on Earth, and help him develop coping skills that embrace modernity. I want him to discover thinkers and writers who will teach him how complex life is, that it's full of predicaments, and that the art of living is finding your way through these predicaments. Life is not about projecting onto others your inability to cope, nurturing hatred and then going off either to self-destruction or to annihilate those who have been more successful than you.

I have hope in Jacob's future—a future that is modest and that may contain fewer heroes and more loneliness than the future my brother had been led to aspire to, but one that is more humane.

CHAPTER 6

My Cousins

In the months following my father's death, with news of my mother and Mahad swirling about me, I found myself actively seeking out more news of members of my extended family through my cousin Magool. I was not just going through the motions of politeness when I begged for updates. I had made a journey, physical and mental, from the tribal framework to that of the West, but now it was as if a door had reopened to the world beyond the looking glass where I came from. I needed to look back and discover what had become of my relatives—and perhaps also to make sense of what my family roots had made of me.

Magool told me first about another of our cousins, Ladan, a year younger than I. My grandmother used to single her out as the most evil child she had ever known, and warned me to stay away from her, never play with her, and most of all never copy her waywardness.

After what Somalis call simply *Qabta*, "The Apocalypse," when the civil war broke out and the great Somali exodus began in December 1990, Ladan and her mother fled to Kismayo and then to Kenya, where Ladan got into trouble. Pregnant, she didn't know where to find a clandestine abortion clinic and she didn't have money to go to a proper hospital. At just about that time, worried that her pregnancy would show, she got an opportunity to travel on a false passport to the UK, where, like everyone else, she asked for refugee status. A few months after her arrival she gave birth to a girl.

I knew of this through the normal Somali gossip network, just as I had already heard that Ladan chewed *qat,* the mildly intoxicating leafy narcotic about which my mother was so concerned when we lived in Ethiopia. In 1998, when I too was living in Europe, I went to visit Ladan. She told me the most shocking stories about her life. I learned about an industry housed in the hidden corners of some Mogadishu neighborhoods where, if a girl had misstepped and had the cash, women would sew her vagina closed. These same women, for a fee, would also cut open a bride whose scar from her childhood mutilation was too thick to be opened forcibly by her husband. (Often, just as no anesthetic is used in the mutilation, none is used to reopen the woman.) They also secretly carry out abortions and deliver babies who are known to be *wa'al*, bastards. Those children and their unwed mothers endure a truly terrible life.

When I visited her, Ladan was single and her daughter, Su'ad, was about five. Su'ad was overweight, she lisped and could not seem to walk straight, and she had a look of constant terror in her eyes. Ladan yelled at her, cursed her, and sometimes hit her. Su'ad was lonely; she told me that she had no friends and that the kids in school refused to play with her and giggled behind her back, calling her fat. The teachers ignored her. Ladan either hadn't noticed any of this or didn't think it was important.

Now, in 2008, Su'ad was a teenager, Magool told me, and Ladan was pregnant again, by another man. Given what I knew about Ladan, I asked if she was ready for another child; she was still on welfare. Magool is younger than I, but her reply sounded as though it came from the lips of a world-weary old woman. "Planning is not something Ladan is good at," she said.

Magool said that Ladan was now completely addicted to *qat,* and Su'ad was growing up amid addiction, abuse, and emotional neglect. Maybe her fate would be no different from her mother's. Of course escape is possible, but the conditions are not conducive to her becoming educated, or happy. In the event that she were to "return" to Somalia—a word that is a falsehood, although all Somalis use it, for Su'ad was born in the UK, not Somalia, and she holds British citizenship— she would not last long. In Somalia my grandmother's clan mentality is omnipresent, and Su'ad doesn't meet even the lowest of my grandmother's standards: she is *wa'al*.

Magool told me another story about a cousin of ours, Anab. Anab had arrived in America a little before I did, in 2006. She was younger than I, and although I had never met her, I knew *of* her. All of us did. She was said to have stabbed her husband, killing him, somewhere in Kenya or Tanzania, where she was living as a refugee. What actually happened—or who was at fault—was not clear to me. But what was clear was that Anab's husband's family considered her a murderer.

Another cousin, Hassan, had also established himself in the United States. He was pious and respectful and good. Hassan was working as a cab driver. Almost every cent that he made went back to the family. His father was by then almost seventy, but he continued to marry young wives and had well over forty children.

Hassan supported many of those children and their mothers. (Many of them were adults, but Somalia has few jobs and high unemployment; never having learned any skills, most of his siblings had little or no income and no visas.) Hassan had also applied for resettlement visas for several of them to enter the United States as refugees. I felt pity for him. Like Farah Gouré, the clan elder in Nairobi who for years helped my mother, and countless other Somali refugees, he was denying himself the fruits of his own labor, bleeding himself dry in order to meet the endless needs of others.

When Anab killed her husband, Hassan's family begged him to contribute to the payment of blood money to the husband's family. The clan, for reasons of honor, must collectively pay for the acts of its member. Next they implored Hassan to take her to America, to prevent a revenge killing by her husband's family and the blood feud that could follow.

From my Western viewpoint I struggled to understand what I was hearing, but from my old tribal mind-set it made all the sense in the world. According to Shari'a, which is incorporated into Somali clan law, murder is settled in one of three ways. A chain of revenge killings is set in motion that can last for generations and can even lead to civil war. Or the family of the perpetrator has to compensate the family of the victim with a payment in money, livestock, or one or more brides, free of charge. Or an agreement is reached by the elders to kill the murderer and thereby end any possibility of a blood feud.

When she finally arrived in America, Anab was twenty years old and already had a child. She soon met and married, under Shari'a law, a Somali living in America named Shu'ayb. (Apparently they never bothered to marry under American law, so this Shari'a wedding was not actually legally valid.) But now I learned that, just two years after she arrived in the United States, Anab was under indictment for attempted murder; the authorities believed she had tried to kill Shu'ayb when she discovered him on the phone with another woman. She realized that he was speaking to a woman with whom he was very intimate, perhaps even married. With her baby asleep in the room, Anab eavesdropped on the conversation. Then, overcome with rage, she drew a knife and began stabbing him.

The clan raised enough money to bail her out of jail. Anab's husband survived the attack. Her trial was pending, and her daughter was in the custody of social services.

For hours I thought about these stories. Hassan was still working for the bloodline, dutifully obeying the constant demands to send the family money and to rescue them from the challenge of perpetual hunger, disease, and the general uncertainty of life outside the West. He saw this as compassion and goodness: this rule of behavior was visceral, instilled in him down to his marrow. In a tribal context, it was the right thing to do. But look at the consequences.

When someone applies to live in the United States, he has to produce a clean police record from every country where he's lived. But the American resettlement officials probably hadn't realized that in Kenya and Tanzania you can *buy* a clean police record from the police, and in a place like Somalia there's no one to even buy it from. The American resettlement officials also might not have realized that the more close-knit an ethnic community is, the more loyal its members are to the strictures of their clan and religion, and the less likely it is for those members to succeed in America, for the simple reason that they put kinship and Shari'a law above a secular law that they feel is alien to their way of life.

A few days later, in a long, late-night conversation, Magool told me about another relative of ours, Hiran, who was in a mental institution. She had gone mad. Magool told me that Hiran had learned in 2003 that she was HIV-positive. But then she met a boy who was good to her, who truly, Magool said, loved her. Yet Hiran never told him she had the virus or took precautions. Now she could no longer hide her diagnosis, for she had full-blown AIDS.

The horror of these stories of Magool's took me back to my years as a translator in Holland, and the countless girls for whom I had acted as interpreter after they got into trouble because of their ignorance of the Western ways of sex and affairs of the heart. One desperate girl refused to accept a positive test for pregnancy and maintained against all evidence that she was a virgin. She hysterically demanded that the doctor do a second and a third test. Test after test, over the span of three weeks, showed that she was pregnant, and her period never came. When she finally faced the reality that she was indeed pregnant, that she had indeed had intercourse, the doctor offered her an abortion. At the sound of the word, which in Somali is less technical, translating as "pulling out" or "flushing out" the baby, she sobbed. She called herself a sinner and a fornicator and cried that she deserved to be flogged and stoned, for she would no longer have a place in heaven. She told the doctor she could not compound her sins by adding to them what she felt was the murder of an innocent child. She finally decided to have the baby, knowing that she would be taunted as a whore by her relatives and that the child would forever be branded as *wa'al*.

Such is the tragedy of girls and women who by the strictures of their upbringing and culture cannot own up to their body's desires, even to themselves. But this attitude is not limited to women. Many times I would translate over the phone—never, in such cases, in person—for a Somali man who had agreed to take a blood test to discover whether he was HIV-positive. I would hear the Dutch doctor say those three horrible words, "You are seropositive," and the wheels in my head would churn to find a way to describe such a thing in Somali.

The first time, I admitted my ignorance. I told the doctor, "We don't have a word for *seropositive* in Somali. How can I best describe it?"

He said, "In the blood test, it shows that there is a virus in your immune system."

I struggled to find the Somali word for *immune system*, or even *virus*, and finally told the man, "In your blood test, invisible living things were found that slowly will destroy the army of defenders in your blood." I went on to describe that the blood is made up of white blood cells—though we don't have the word *cells*—and red blood cells. "The white blood cells are an army that keep away enemies that come into your body and make you sick. But some things, like the one that was detected in your blood, are too strong for your soldiers without the help of medicine."

My explanation was taking some time, and the Dutch doctor interrupted me. "Is all that necessary?"

I explained to him, "There's no Somali word for *seropositive, white blood cells, red blood cells, viruses, bacteria,* or *AIDS*."

The Somali man's voice, sounding very alarmed, cried out, "AIDS?" He pronounced it *aydis*. "Aydis?! I don't have that! I'm a Muslim! And I'm a Somali! We don't get Aydis!" Confused, embarrassed, but relieved that my client understood me, I clung to the word *Aydis* and told him, "Yes, they found, in your blood, the thing that will make you get Aydis later, but you don't have it now. Not yet."

The doctor interrupted me again. "He does not have AIDS now. He's only seropositive. We can give him medication to prevent the HIV virus from turning into AIDS."

The Somali man yelled through this, "Aydis! Tell him I don't have Aydis! Muslims do not have Aydis!"

Subsequently I endured several similar conversations. Now, I imagined my cousin Hiran in 2003 going through the same ordeal and hearing, no matter what words of explanation were actually said to her, only *You are going to die, and what you are going to die of is an outcome of sin, of fornication, of denying the laws of Allah.* So many patients, after finally accepting that they did, in reality, have Aydis or something that would give them Aydis one day, perceived it as Allah's punishment, an internal flogging or stoning. Often they refused treatment, for that would compound their initial sin by denying Allah's judgment. Others remained in denial and continued having sex with others, even their innocent spouses, passing on the virus.

I fully understood my cousin's context. Islam and tribal culture had mystified and denied her understanding of something as natural as her own sexuality. Now that she was living in the diaspora, this religious control mechanism could lead only to denial and hypocrisy, self-undoing and destruction.

I wondered what Hiran's boyfriend thought of the personal cost to him of his trust in her. I haven't spoken to him; I don't know him.

But I imagine he might have thought when he met her, *She's a Muslim girl, she wears a headscarf, she condemns any kind of sexual activity before marriage, so she must be a virgin.*

When proponents of cosmopolitan, multicultural ideals wax lofty about tolerance and welcoming and warmth, they overlook these consequences, which people like my cousin's Irish boyfriend end up suffering. It is these people who become disillusioned with welcoming people like us into Western society.

How does one judge Hiran's actions, or lack of them? She knew she had tested positive for HIV. She knew that she had acquired it through sexual intercourse and that she could pass it on. She didn't tell her boyfriend because it was too hard for her to admit it, even to herself. She didn't insist that he wear a condom because she denied her condition even to herself. She made it unreal.

Two people from different cultures met. One was from a society that stresses individual responsibility (in this case, sexual responsibility), and the other was reared to think in group terms. She was brought up in fear of her own sexuality, steeped in self-loathing for having sex outside of wedlock, taught to distrust the infidel. He felt trust; she betrayed it.

When Hiran was finally diagnosed with full-blown AIDS she could no longer cope and went into temporary psychosis. Only then did her boyfriend discover her illness, and he immediately had himself tested. He discovered that he too was infected. According to Magool, after he got over the initial shock and devastation, he continued to visit Hiran in the hospital. When she was well enough to talk, according to Magool (who was present), he asked Hiran why she had never told him. Hiran said, "You gave it to me. I got it from you." Only then did he stop visiting her.

At the heart of the clash of values between the tribal culture of Islam and Western modernity are three universal human passions: sex, money, and violence. In the Western perspective, the debate now raging about how to assimilate minorities (read, Muslims) into Europe and how best to wage the "war on terror" that began in America in response to the 9/11 attacks boils down to fundamentally different views on sex, money, and violence—or, transposed into loftier vocabulary, demography, buying power, and military capability.

Having studied the rhetoric of radical Islam, and having tried as a young woman to live according to its principles, I know that the same three themes are the yardsticks by which Islamists measure what they consider the decadence and moral turpitude of the West.

My cousins, like so many individuals in a globalized world—including myself—are caught between the two worlds. They were never prepared for life in the West. European and North American societies have been fundamentally reshaped by the values of the eighteenth-century Enlightenment, which shifted the balance of power from the collective to the individual. During these hundreds of years, thinkers and activists developed and refined ways of allowing as much individual liberty as possible within the realms of these three urges without sacrificing the common good. (Who determines the "common good" shall forever remain a subject of debate, in open societies as in all others.)

These three passions lie at the center of Muslims' journey from tribal life to Western societies that are based on the values of the Enlightenment. Immigrants from traditional societies that have been dominated for centuries by the bloodlines and values of clan and tribe make the physical transition to the West in a matter of hours. Often they have been driven to look for a better life when home has become a nasty, unwelcoming place. Yet both the immigrants from the tribe and bloodline and the activists of prosperity share a common delusion: they believe that it is possible to make this transition without paying the price of choosing between values. One side wants change in their circumstances without letting go of tradition; the other, overcome with guilt and pity, wants to help newcomers with the material change but cannot bring themselves to demand that they excise traditional, outdated values from their outlook.

Ladan, Hiran, Hassan, and Anab, like me, succeeded in coming to the West with personal high hopes of a better life, and at least in the case of Hassan, with the additional hope of success for his father, his aunt, our uncles, my mother, and a host of siblings and cousins. We were resilient and resourceful; we were survivors, even (in the case of Anab) a warrior. But their lack of clarity about where they stood on the core issues of sex, money, and violence—their failure to recognize that where they live geographically must change where they stand ideologically—has led them to human tragedies of disease, debt, and death. I too was ill prepared for the West. The only difference between my relatives and me is that I opened my mind.

Ladan and Hiran grew up in families from a merchant clan. Their families were among the wealthiest in Somalia, with international business interests. Because of their wealth and commercial ties to foreign countries, these families could purchase the gadgets of modernity. These girls were used to having a car, televisions, videos, and other modern possessions.

The circle of people with whom they interacted in Somalia followed Western fashions and proclaimed (almost too loudly to be true) their Western attitudes. Ladan in particular spent much of her teenage life with female role models who knew more about Valentino, Armani, Prada, Gucci, and Chanel than chapters in the Quran or the sayings of the Prophet. They conducted a grim competition about who looked sexier, because Western fashion is about displaying the female body.

Ladan and Hiran wore makeup, styled their hair, and even mixed with boys. Yet their modernity was only skin-deep. Their fathers were both very successful and frugal, yet they allowed their daughters the trappings of Western culture. Even so, they didn't educate them about how to make money, let alone save or invest it. And their apparent ease with the visible markers of a Western lifestyle did not translate into a stable sense of identity or a coherent, resilient approach to the vicissitudes of life.

Many Westerners entertain a general belief that non-Westerners who have grown up in large cities with wealth and cultural ties to Western countries are better prepared for life in modern societies. But Ladan and Hiran did not grow up with a complete set of moral values, either Islamic or Western. They looked modern; they played the part and dreamed the part, but they were not anchored in Western sexual mores. They indulged their desires as if they were indeed Western young people, but they did not escape the culture of shame. They buried their shame under elaborate layers of secrecy and hypocrisy; they hid, even from themselves, the bare, bold fact that they were having sex.

* * *

As I heard about the troubles of my family, I was once again filled with a sense of guilt and regret. But this was different from the earlier guilt I had felt at escaping my arranged marriage and from my regret at betraying my father and compromising his honor; it was different from the guilt I had felt at putting my mother in a position where she was blamed for what I had done. I no longer had that old, constant remorse, that constant guilt about what I could have done for my family in those years of silence and anger, after I had fled from my clan to a society that was free, informed, and affluent, to a new world in which I had learned to survive.

Now my guilt stemmed from a new feeling: that I should have shared some of those tools of survival with the closest members of my family. Instead of cutting them off, I should have called them more often. If I had kept up with Hiran and Ladan, perhaps I could have helped them to shed their religious and clan convictions—to learn about contraceptives, for example, and face up to their sexuality, instead of pretending (even to themselves) that they weren't really having sex and thus taking no precautions.

My actions were selfish, but they were not malicious. They were selfish because I had chosen to improve *my* life, pursue happiness in *my* way. They were treacherous because, in achieving my personal goals, I was aware that I was disregarding long-held traditions of my family and religious edicts.

One evening, about three months after my father's death and after conversations with my mother and Magool, I sat down to dinner with an American couple who had become very close friends of mine. While I ruminated over the ruins of my family, we talked about the books of Edward Banfield, who maintained that the tightly inward-looking focus of traditional societies impedes their members from progressing in the modern world, for it prevents them from making bonds outside their clan.

Afterward I asked myself, *What is it about our Somali culture that holds us back?* Perhaps part of it is that we do not have much to call culture anymore. There are no Somali historians, few authors, few if any artists of any kind. The old ways are broken, and the new ways involve only violence and disorder. As a tribe we are fragmented; as clans, scattered; as families, dysfunctional.

Slowly I sought reconciliation with my family, and yet with every renewed tie I felt more alienation and more sadness at how far and fast our family had regressed. Haweya, gone. Mahad, a shadow of himself. Hiran, broken. My half sister, Sahra, denying modernity, choosing to entomb herself in her veil. Ladan, unaware of the volumes of books, videos, and DVDs on parenting, now preparing to bring another child into the world, oblivious of the risks to which her addiction and poverty expose her daughter. My conscientious cousin Hassan, spending his money to prop up people invested in outdated values.

I wanted to tell Hassan, *Save your money, buy a home, get an education—above all, rethink the values of our grandmother, and teach your children new ethics. Help them develop the tools to be successful and get ahead in America. Our grandmother was disciplined and resolute, but her lessons about traditions and bloodlines cannot carry us through this new landscape. If we try to hold on to them we will break apart, for the old ways have failed. Even Somalis can learn to adopt the values of a liberal democracy.*

One evening, staring at my grandmother's photograph above the fireplace in my apartment, I began thinking about her first voyage away from the lands of her ancestors. She must have been only about forty when she crossed the Red Sea in a dinghy, traveling from the port of Berbera, in Somalia, to Aden. Her husband's third young wife had just had her second son. Shame and jealousy burned within her and propelled her out of the desert with her youngest daughter, who was still not married.

I imagined her, afraid perhaps, but excited by the motion of the sea and the challenge of the unknown. Perhaps, secretly, she desired to escape the monotony of the nomadic life, a life with a very short span, vulnerable to natural disasters and war.

My grandmother used to talk to the dead. She talked with our forefathers, calling them by name. Many a time she warned us not to cross them, not to bring down their fury. As I stared at her photograph, I realized that I no longer feared my forefathers, and I marveled at that. I looked at her dark, piercing eyes, so full of judgment and accusation, and in my mind I spoke to my grandmother. And then, because my literacy has robbed me of my grandmother's flawless memory, I did as I always do when something is important: I pulled out a notebook.

It began as fragments, part English, part Somali. It was not a conscious composition, like an article or a manuscript. I had no clear idea that what I was writing was a formal farewell, a statement of adieu to every family tie I had ever known and to all the bequests my clan, tribe, religion, and culture had ever bestowed on me. But gradually it dawned on me that, just as she would have done, I was talking to my forebears. I was writing my grandmother a letter.

CHAPTER 7

Letter to My Grandmother

Dear Grandmother,

I do not wail for your passing. You were ready to go. Ma said you kept asking your forefathers to take you. Your legs refused to carry you. Your joints jammed. When straight, they hurt you to bend them; when bent and curled for a few minutes, they refused to straighten. They creaked with effort. Your side ached from sitting and from lying down. Your skin creased into folds hard to clean; the sweat collected in them and you itched. Your long, thin, and lovely fingers curled inward into stiff and crooked branches. You scratched the itch in your side with them, but the nails cut you instead. Your ears refused to serve you any longer; your eyes wouldn't see anymore. Your daughters and granddaughters comforted you as best they could, but they could not ease the pain of old age.

I do not wail for your passing, but I am filled with a sense of guilt: I wish I too had been there for you. You held me in my childhood when I was in pain; you whispered words of consolation in my ears as I was shaken by the fevers that attack a body so young it doesn't know how to defend itself. You called in the help of your forefathers on my behalf; you chided me not to give in; you took me to the witch doctor, who took your money and your sheep and burned wounds in my chest with a long blacksmith's nail he held with tongs. That hurt me more than the fever, Grandmother, and I still have the scars. They are a symbol of your love for me. It was not the witch doctor but you who spurred me to fight the demons in my blood and recover.

I am sorry, Grandmother, that I was not there in your old age as you were there in my childhood. I would have summoned the spirits of my new world. Here, they have salves to cleanse and soothe the itch in folded skin; they have hearing aids; they have walking sticks on wheels to help you roll smoothly along the road. They have all these props and more, and painkillers. I am sorry, Grandmother, for abandoning you when I could have been a source of comfort in your old age.

I have lived with the infidels for almost two decades. I have come to learn, appreciate, and adopt their way of life. I know that this would make you sad. Before he died Father tried to convince me to change my mind, and Ma does the same every time I speak to her on the phone. I think, at first, you would do the same as my parents, and tell me to respect the traditions of our fathers and forefathers. But I have this odd feeling that you, Grandma, would come to see my point of view.

Still, I do not wail for your passing.

Gone with you are the rigid rules of custom. "Repeat after me: I am Ayaan, the daughter of Hirsi, who is the son of Magan, who is the son of Guleid . . ." Gone with you is that bloodline, for better or for worse, and gone is the idiot tradition that meant you cherished mares and she-camels more than your daughters and granddaughters.

When a boy was born into the family you rejoiced. Your eyes twinkled, you smiled, and with a burst of energy you would weave impossible numbers of grass mats to give away as gifts. As you wove you would tell us your warrior legends—about courage, resistance, conquest, and *sharaf, sharaf, sharaf*. Honor, honor, honor.

When we heard news of the birth of a girl in the family you clicked and pouted and sometimes sulked for days. Squatting under the talal tree in Mogadishu, on the huge straw mat, you wove, your fingers orange with henna, working away with your *muda* needle. You would chase us away and speak of ominous events. Then, when you had been quiet for days, you would tell us endless tragedies of the misfortunes that befall a family of too many girls—gossip, betrayal, bastard children, and *a'yb, a'yb, a'yb*. Shame, shame, shame.

You squinted and clenched your teeth as you wove the grasses tightly into mats and bowls, cursing if ever the pattern was even remotely wrong. Grandma, you were so diligent and you preached the same diligence to us. "Here, girl, sweep this dust. Shake the mats. Go milk the goats. Light the fire. Fetch more water. Clean the meat, chop and cook it. Pick the rice." I hear your endless orders still, today. You taught us to memorize our father's bloodline instead of the ABCs. You will be sad, very sad, to learn that Abeh is dead and there is only one son, my brother Mahad, to carry on the bloodline. And although Mahad is over forty he has only one child, Jacob, who was born two weeks before Haweya died, almost eleven years ago.

Jacob cannot be taught his culture by his elders, because the lessons they will try to teach him are no longer valid in the time and place in which he lives. Those lessons will seem even more fragmented and nonsensical to him than they did, long ago, to me.

I am far away from the shade of the talal tree now. Like hordes and hordes of our relatives and fellow Muslims, I have settled, forever, in the land of the infidels.

I find it hard—as I always did—to explain to you what countries are. I remember putting my school atlas on your lap in Nairobi when we came to live in Kariokor. You were deriding Haweya and me about getting too close to our Kenyan schoolmates; you called them slaves. I told you that we need to respect people in whose country we live. You were puzzled by this word *country*, just like you were puzzled by the idea of a country called Somalia. You asked how the proud sons of the great clans, Isaq and Darod, could accept some invisible line that they were not allowed to cross. You pushed the atlas off your lap and said that, through tricks and magic illusions like these pictures, the infidel convinced people who belonged apart to accept silly fences and imaginary borders. You insisted that we remain loyal first and foremost to God and the bloodline.

Grandma, countries do exist. But your instinct about the disunity of the proud sons of Darod and Isaq was right. There is no Somalia. We are famous now for lawlessness and vicious violence; we are known as bandits of the sea and for our religious zeal, our will to kill and die for nothing.

Everywhere today Muslims live in trying circumstances. Most Muslim countries are ruled by violence and threat; they fail to produce goods and minds of quality. There is no union in such countries, no sense of making a better future.

But in the *Qurbe*, the lands of the white infidels, life is different. Here, flags represent real union. You taught me to admire strength, to learn and to keep an eye open for strategies of survival that work. Grandmother, the infidels' strategies for survival work better than ours.

Remember how the milk ladies in Mogadishu would crouch for hours, tugging and pulling and squeezing between the legs of those grouchy cows to get as much milk as they could? How I wish you were with me the day I visited the farm in Holland where Ellen, my first Dutch friend, grew up. Her family had fewer cows than the Hawiye milk maids, but they were much fatter and more patient. When it came time for them to be milked, Ellen's brother unhooked thin tubes, like the ones we used when we ran water from the storage barrel to our bucket. He attached them to the udders of the fat cows while they grazed on hay. Then he turned on an electrical switch, like the one we used to turn on the lights in Saudi Arabia. And to my amazement and wonder the tubes sucked and transferred the sweet milk from their swollen udders to the empty pails. Within the hour Ellen's brother had more milk than all the women in the markets of Hodan and Hawlwadag.

The wonders of the infidel are not limited to the milking of cows. I see firsthand their way of life and think that if you had had the chance, like me, you would have been glad to witness it and grateful to learn a few of their tricks to keep you alive.

The secret of a Dutchman's success is his ability to adapt, to invent. The Dutchman's approach to solving problems encourages him to bend nature to his wish rather than the other way around. In our value system, Grandma, like the thorn trees, like the baobabs, like dawn and dusk, we are all set firmly as who or what we are. We bow to a God who says we must not change a thing; it is he who has chosen it. When our people wandered through the desert from oasis to oasis, we did not create permanent wet spaces, we didn't bend rivers and lakes to our will or dig deep into the earth for wells.

Grandmother, do you remember when you traveled from Sool, in the Dhulbahante lands, across the sea, to Yemen? You must have walked several days to the road, wondering what you would find there. Perhaps you paid a man with a cart or a truck to take you across the desert to the port of Berbera. Then you crossed the sea on a small boat. You voyaged in a time machine. You sat in a magic boat that carried you to a different era. You did not realize it, but you had sailed, all at once, hundreds of years into the future.

You were not alone in this adventure. Thousands of others also moved from their huts built in the shade of thorn trees, from their springs, wells, and oases and the routines of millennia, from their kith and kin, from their gods, their spirits, their narrative of what life is, what to look forward to, and what pitfalls to avoid. Thousands from all corners of the world made the same sudden leap into the future.

But even if you had done nothing and stayed in your hut made of thorns, even if you had lived all your life dismantling the hut, loading it on the back of patient camels, traveling in a caravan to the next green pasture with your husband and children, and their children, and the wives and children of your husband's kith and kin—even so, modern life would have come to you. In the shape of bullets and bricks, decrees, men in uniform—it reaches into every part of the world.

Grandmother, I have compared the infidels' morals to those that you taught us, and I must report that they have, in practice, a better outcome for humans than the morals of your forefathers.

You taught us the virtues of suspicion and distrust, and Islam taught us to survive by *taqqiyah,* pretending to be something you are not. You were fierce to me when Mahad threw me into a latrine pit full of excrement, because in your eyes, trust, even of my brother, was equal to stupidity. "Be wary" was your motto. But wariness leads to weariness. It is exhausting never to let down your guard in case someone takes advantage of you. It means you cannot truly collaborate with anyone, and you cannot risk public error for fear of shame.

The infidel insists on honesty and trust. Everywhere you turn here, you must trust someone: to fly the airplane you travel in, to teach your child, to take care of you when you are sick and feed you food that is edible. And everywhere your trust is borne out.

The infidel does not see life as a test, a passage to the hereafter, but as an end and a joy in itself. All his resources of money, mind, and organization go into making life here, on Earth, comfortable and healthy. He is obsessed with cleanliness, a good diet, and the right amount of rest. He is loyal to his wife and children; he may take care of his parents but has no use for a memory filled with an endless chain of ancestors. All the seeds of his toil are spent on his own offspring, not those of his brothers or uncles. He shows special love, generosity, and compassion to people he chooses to befriend, on the basis of common interests rather than the dictates of blood relations.

Because the infidel trusts and studies new ideas, there is abundance in the infidel lands. In these circumstances of peace, knowledge, and predictability, the birth of a girl is just fine. There is no need to pout and sulk and every reason to celebrate and rejoice. The little girl sits right next to the little boy in school; she gets to play as much as he does; she gets to eat as much as he does; she gets the same care in illness as he does; and when she matures she gets the same opportunity to seek and find a mate as he does.

Grandma, I know this will shock and offend you when you first hear it, but when you calm down and think about it with a cool head, you will understand that there is no need to groom one child to obey and be a slave to the other child when they reach adulthood. And there is no need to cut and sew a girl's genitals to preserve her for a man who will purchase the right to her body.

The infidel praises frugality, just as you did, but here the display of wealth is everywhere considered important, so much so that they have classes of people divided according to their wealth or lack of it. They are also divided along ideas and ideology. These divisions—for man shall always live to dispute—are more practical than the false promise of brotherhood in the name of a shared great-great-grandfather. Organized around real and practical common interests, the association is more genuine and forthright than the pretense of unity between men just because they can recite their lineage to a common ancestor.

Do you remember Farah Gouré, the clansman who took care of us in Nairobi? He worked, earned, invested, and saw his wealth grow, but in the name of your morals he had to share, to give away his wealth to the family of the man who never bothered to leave his bed, the man who chose not to work, the man who abandoned his wife and children. They all fed off Farah Gouré until he was squeezed dry. This is now happening to your favorite grandson, Hassan, who lives in America, the country where Abeh went to university, before he met Ma.

Abeh is dead now, and so are you, and I do not wail for you, or for the passing of your world.

You recited old poems and tried to make me memorize them. I did not. I failed you and the next generation. I did not learn them by heart; I did not write them down. Now you are gone, and all those poems of adversity and triumph, of longing and love, of fear and valor, pride and humiliation, generosity and pettiness—they are gone with you. The parables of intrigue and old wisdom were buried with you when you were laid in a hole in the sand.

I wail for that loss of memory, but in this new world those poems no longer have the power to sustain us. The Somali clans are now adrift on a violent sea of uncertainty whose waves bring sudden, sweeping changes, and we have no props, or tools, or boats for support. The bloodline is tired and impotent; adhering to it leads only to violence. It is no strategy for unity and progress.

Your children and grandchildren are left without foundations or guidance. Take Ladan. You were always full of contempt for her because of what you saw as her waywardness, her attraction to the music and entertainment of the infidel. She is in Britain now, and the people who once felt sorry for her and gave her food, shelter, and alms are now also full of contempt for her. She cannot meet your standards, nor can she meet those of the infidel. She feels a part of the clan, but it means nothing to her. She is lost.

Salvation lies in the ways of the infidel, Grandmother. He has printed and bound books full of memory. He peeks through lenses that allow him to see an invisible world of creatures that live in us and with us, and he has sought and found remedies that attack them and defend our bodies. Grandma, fevers and diseases are not caused by *jinn* and forefathers rising from the dead to torment us, or by an angry God, but by invisible creatures with names like *parasites* and *bacteria* and *viruses*. The infidel's medicine works better than ours, because it is based on facts, inquiry, and real knowledge.

The sooner we adopt the infidel attitude toward work, money, procreation, and leisure, the easier and better life will be. I know your thoughts on the easy life: too much ease leads to a loss of discipline and moral muscle. You passionately condemned even the washing machine. If machines washed our clothes and dishes, you seethed, young girls and women would find themselves with too much time on their hands. We would be tempted into all sorts of mischief and risk becoming whores.

In a way you were right about washing machines, and in a way you were wrong. The best medicine against decadence is to focus on goals. You might add prayer too, but I don't know if that helps anything at all. Since I came to the lands of the infidel, where machines wash our clothes and dishes, where we order food from stores online and where we save hours and hours of the day, I have not been idle. I have been more useful, and I have had pleasure. And pleasure is good.

Grandmother, I no longer believe in the old ways. The world began changing in your lifetime, and by now the old ways are not useful to me any more. I love you, and I love some of my memories of Somalia, though not all. But I will not serve the bloodline or Allah any longer. And because the old ways hamper the lives of so many of our people, I will even strive to persuade my fellow nomads to take on the ways of the infidel.

PART II

———•———

NOMAD AGAIN

CHAPTER 8

Nomad Again

After my father died, memories flooded into me unbidden. Some of them were painful, others sweet, but strangely, most of them were of Holland, the country I had recently left.

Holland was the safest place I had ever lived, and the place where I was happiest. I remember with particular nostalgia the summer of 2001. I had just graduated from the University of Leiden with a master's degree. I had made enough money, working as a Somali translator for the Dutch social services, to buy a place of my own with my best friend. I had learned the language of the society I immigrated to, and I had just found a meaningful job at a think tank for an important Dutch political party. I had friends with whom I could share the gifts and trials of life.

In those days, when I reflected on what I had achieved and where I was going, I felt a sense of accomplishment. Yes, I was disobeying many of the laws of Allah, and I had taken a huge risk in exiting the world of my clan. Yes, I had plainly hurt my parents and put myself at the mercy of a wrathful God. Yes, I had lost my sister and felt deep pain. But I also felt that I was succeeding at something important, something that my family had always warned me I would fail at.

In every story I was ever told, the girl who left her family—or, even worse, her clan—to pursue her own goals found that her story ended swiftly in horrible depravity and bitter regret. I had not just left my family and clan; I was on my own *in an infidel country*. But I felt I could still hold my head high. I had not fallen into the pitfalls of depravity; I had hoisted myself onto the road of progress. And I felt that I was still basically a faithful Muslim, just a slightly lapsed one. I didn't pray, I drank alcohol, and I had sex out of wedlock, but I felt (uneasily) that in essence I still obeyed Allah's main rules and would one day in the distant future return to his narrow path.

I had been reconciled with my father. He had even acknowledged that he should not have forced me to marry against my will, and he worked for months to get me a divorce. I felt it was proof that not only had he forgiven me, but he had accepted my chosen path in life. I was in constant touch with my mom and sent her a monthly allowance. Mahad had been taken ill, which saddened me, but when he felt well he and I could speak on the phone. Once in a while I exchanged emails and phone calls with my cousins: Hassan, Magool, Ladan, Hiran, and others. The family circle did not by any means embrace me, but as time went by I sensed that my difference was becoming accepted. My professional success in Holland brought me respect, and I felt that I again belonged to my family, but on my own terms.

My life back then was not yet politicized. I had not yet made the public statements about Islam that would bring me notoriety, fame, a seat in the Dutch Parliament, a mission to improve the lives of millions of women I have never met, as well as drama, death threats, and bodyguards. My best friend, Ellen, and I used to take bike rides with friends—a crowd of young women riding our bicycles six or seven miles to the beach, flying down the roads with a picnic as our goal. We splashed in the freezing cold North Sea waves and walked across the sand dunes to get bags of spicy *patat-oorlog,* "warlike French fries," in swimsuits that were still covered in sand. I felt full of joy, freer than I had ever been in my life. I looked forward to a future that promised no upheaval, but a safe, steady, and predictable existence surrounded by loving friends, a slightly blurry but undoubtedly wonderful mate, and children, perhaps even an inquisitive little girl who looked like me.

But my life in Holland ended abruptly in May 2006, in an atmosphere of high drama and low farce. Although I was then a relatively prominent member of the legislature, the Dutch Minister for Immigration and Integration, Rita Verdonk, stripped me of my citizenship—only to be forced to restore it a few weeks later, after a debate in Parliament that led to the collapse of the government and new nationwide elections.

When I first arrived in Holland, I was told by refugee advocates that in order to obtain permission to stay, it was not enough to say that I was running away from a marriage that was forced on me. If I said that, I would be sent back to Africa. To receive permission to stay in the Netherlands I had to state that I was being persecuted in Somalia for my political opinions or clan. So, although it was not true, that was what I claimed, and I duly received refugee status.

Years later, when I was asked to join the Liberal VVD, a political party founded on the principles of individual freedom, limited government, a free market, and national security, and to run for Parliament, my party leader asked me if I had any skeletons in the closet. "Yes, I do," I said. "When I came to the Netherlands I changed my name, I changed my year of birth, and I pretty much lied my way in." I told him the whole story.

My party leader talked to some of the party's legal advisers and lawyers, but everyone treated the whole affair as something insignificant, a small lie told years before. They emphasized that I had managed to assimilate to Holland; this, they clearly felt, was far more important than the lie I had once told. They wanted to tout me as an example: if immigrants seriously chose to adopt Dutch values, learn the language, study and work, then they too could succeed as I had. Besides being a role model, I was also seen as an expert on the social and cultural obstacles to integration, and how to surmount them.

Rita Verdonk was my colleague in the Liberal Party; indeed, she and I had been recruited into the party's proposed parliamentary list at almost the same time. She had run a prison and had been director of a civil service unit, the Department of State Security of the Ministry of Interior Affairs. I had written articles about Islam. It was a time of turmoil in Dutch politics. Pim Fortuyn, a powerfully charismatic speaker and an openly gay man, had recently surged to political prominence, only to be assassinated by a deranged animal rights activist when he was on the brink of taking power. In appointing Rita and me, the Liberal Party was clearly seeking people who might attract some of Fortuyn's voters.

I was to be the face of the Muslim woman who had sought and found freedom in Holland. Unlike white commentators, who were hamstrung by the fear that they would be labeled racists, I could voice my criticisms of the feudal, religious, and repressive mechanisms that were holding back women from Muslim communities. Rita Verdonk, meanwhile, would be the face and voice of those Dutch men and women who had voted for Pim Fortuyn, who felt that they were disenfranchised in their own country, who felt invaded, their society pushed into mayhem.

A fifty-plus woman who looked her age, with dark, short hair styled around her face, Rita was plump in a muscular way that made her look strong yet warm and even motherly. She was a perfect image of Dutch rectitude, exuding hard work and competence; she had that direct, slightly disapproving clear gaze that is particular to a certain kind of Dutch person. This had intrinsic appeal to Fortuyn's voters. Moreover, Fortuyn had been an outrageously gay academic who spoke with the haughty vowels of the upper class; Rita more closely mirrored his voters' mannerisms and values, in addition to sharing many of their views. The plan was clearly that together, behind closed doors, she and I would find consensus, issue by issue. Many in the establishment saw us as rebels; others, as puppets. But the goal was that we would make separate, rebellious parties such as Fortuyn's unnecessary, for we would gather his now docile voters within the steady embrace of the impeccably well-behaved Liberal Party and all would end well, the Dutch way: in consensus.

Who were these voters of Fortuyn's? Policemen, teachers, civil servants, owners of small family businesses—the baker, the butcher, the florist—who felt tyrannized by regulations and taxes and saw immigrants from Morocco and Turkey both as competitors (with small shops that could sell cheaper goods because they hired cheap, illegal workers) and as bad employees (unpunctual and disrespectful slackers who could not speak proper Dutch). They perceived immigrants as *verloedering*, debasing, corrupting. They did not scrupulously separate their recyclable from their non-recyclable trash. Their children did not ride their bicycles only in designated lanes. They had no respect for public or private property. They vandalized shops, committed crimes, molested and harassed women, and turned once pristine neighborhoods into areas both unsafe and unclean. If picked up by police, they would be set free by the judge on grounds of being minors. They were dropouts from school. Their families lied their way into generous welfare payments and out of proper payment of taxes; they jumped the queues for public housing. None of these generalizations was exactly or universally true, but they were true enough for this perception to be widely held.

There was a real tension between this "Rita class" of voters and the elite ruling class. Fortuyn's voters no longer trusted their rulers, for they had opened the borders of Holland to foreigners. Even though the middle and upper classes could still afford to move to airy, expensive neighborhoods and send their children to safe schools, and could lobby for informal favors to keep from being fully exposed to disruption from immigrants, the Rita class felt that they and their neighborhoods were bearing the brunt. But when they voiced their concerns, they were chastised for being provincial and intolerant.

Having run a prison, "Iron Rita" was plainspoken to the point of bluntness and scrupulously respectful of the law. I rather liked her. She became the most popular politician among the voters of my party. As minister for immigration and integration, she was a powerful member of the cabinet. I was merely a member of Parliament, but I had been appointed our party's spokesperson for integration and emancipation. (My title did not specify integration into what or emancipation from what.)

It was common knowledge that my views on immigration were different from Rita's. For instance, I supported an immigration amnesty for the twenty-six thousand asylum seekers who, after more than five years of living and working in Holland, had been turned down for refugee status, and who thus had no further right to live in the country. But on other issues we agreed. We both supported immigration quotas that would favor the entry of people from Poland and other Eastern European countries over those from Morocco and Turkey. Our point was that Holland should attract immigrants who work; we needed nurses, caretakers of the elderly, fruit, vegetable, and flower pickers, workers in restaurants and hotels, electricians, painters, and construction workers. The immigrants from North Africa and Turkey were being admitted on the grounds of family formation and reunion. They went straight into welfare or applied for unemployment benefits after hardly a year in the workforce. Most of them were unemployable or unqualified or had a work ethic that employers found unsuitable.

Like me, Rita also wanted to confront Islam's treatment of women head-on. I applauded her in 2004 when she walked into a mosque and extended her hand to an imam, knowing that he would reject it. It was an image that produced a great deal of anger and confusion in Holland, but the gesture she provoked—a blatant expression of contempt for a government minister—encapsulated not only what some imams in Holland were saying about women, but their scorn for Dutch values, society, and law. Like Rita, I thought that people needed to see this; once they saw it, they could no longer pretend it wasn't there.

So Rita and I had a warm working relationship. We had occasional chats on the phone; we exchanged information before a debate; we shared meals; and sometimes we met for drinks.

When our party leader, Gerrit Zalm, stepped down in 2006, Rita decided to campaign for the post. She was running against Mark Rutte, a boyishly attractive, much younger man who was considered a rising star in the party. Just before Parliament broke up for spring break, I was with her in her office, talking about policy. The conversation veered to politics, a very different thing, and she asked me to support her publicly, a request that made me uncomfortable. Gerrit Zalm and Jozias van Aartsen, another leading Liberal, had asked all the members of our party to refrain from openly endorsing either of the candidates in order to avoid making public the splits that had begun spreading through the ranks. Consensus is a sacred article of faith in Holland, and although the media love any sign of dissension and will seize on it and amplify it with glee, any kind of public disagreement within a political party is frowned upon by party leaders, who consider it unprofessional and damaging to the party's goals.

I told Rita, "I am not doing any public endorsements. You know what Gerrit and Jozias will say."

Rita's smile seemed forced. "Come on, Ayaan, don't give me that! Since when have you respected what Gerrit and Jozias have to say?"

Shifting my weight, I reached for my drink. "You know, there's enough tension between me and Jozias. Gerrit has been very patient with me. I'm not looking for trouble."

Rita countered, "Ayaan, you know it's not about me. It's about the people. They're angry. When I go around the country, they take me into their homes, they tell me about their problems. It's not just the welfare state and globalization, all these lofty themes. It's about trash on the street. It's about your daughter being raped. It's about seeing your earnings disappear. They're suffering. These are the men and women who voted for Pim Fortuyn, and now that he's dead they're politically homeless. Jozias and Gerrit won't say so in public, but they're endorsing Rutte. Do you think Rutte is capable of getting that vote for our party?"

I wanted to tell her what I really thought, which was that she and Rutte were *both* unqualified for the job. They were both beginners in politics (as I was), and neither seemed to have any real clue about how they wanted to change the country; they seemed driven by personal ambition and nothing more. The man I favored as candidate, Henk Kamp, had decades of political experience and had run two ministries. He was a far more skillful political operator than Rita, and yet there was humility about him, and a quiet intelligence. I felt that it was very unfortunate that he refused to run. But I did not want to offend Rita by saying so. I began rambling through a rather uncomfortable soliloquy about the nature of Dutch politics when Rita interrupted me, her gaze now steady. "I've lived here all my life. I know this country better than you do."

I nodded and managed to conceal the instant pain of exclusion this remark triggered. Rita was not the only one who said this sort of thing. People who disagreed with me often invoked their native Dutchness, their instinctively greater understanding of all Dutch problems. It's an easy way out: you are the outsider, I am the insider, therefore I win.

Her attitude shifted from charming seduction to indignant impatience that I would not give in and give her my support. This job needed to be done—she repeated the phrase more than once—and I was preventing her from doing it.

She grew more abrasive. She confided to me her tension with our colleague Piet Donner, the minister of justice, and the left-wing mayor of Amsterdam, Job Cohen, representatives of what she saw as a small clique, mainly men, who had attended the same universities, belonged to the same fraternities, spoke with the same accent, and who ultimately, though they might identify with different political ideologies, served only the interests of their common class. Rita often attributed any hostility to her as the snooty, entitled disdain of the upper classes for a woman who did not hesitate to put her hands in the muck of real life, so I had heard this line before. It had some truth to it.

Pim Fortuyn had called the political leadership class of Holland the *regenten,* the regents, who control real power behind the scenes. The *regenten* form an elite triangle: the upper class and royalty (although Dutch people are fond of calling Holland a classless society, that is far from reality), leaders of the unions, and directors of corporations. These three groups have divergent interests, but their prominent leaders gather in five-star hotels, elite clubs, and government institutions, and once in a while the queen opens her palace to them. These men and women—mostly men—are immersed in the culture of Holland's celebrated consensus politics. Whenever there is divergence among them, their positions are staked out at a safe distance, in the media; journalists will report excitedly that there is an impasse. Then, after this ritual saber rattling by proxy, the parties at dispute will withdraw into whatever chamber is available and emerge days later waving an agreement: the breach is healed. Powerful members in all corners of this triangle are trained in academia and the media; it is not at all unusual to see the head of a faculty become a minister, the editor in chief of a newspaper become the head of a faculty and then be appointed mayor.

Pim Fortuyn was a member of the *regenten* class, a professor in Rotterdam who made a career out of writing books and articles. Rita did not belong to the political class and they disdained her for it. I did not belong either, but I had a degree of friendly support from high-ranking party members and our party's sage, Frits Bolkestein. This probably made Rita suspicious.

It was time for me to leave. "Rita," I said, "let me think about it." My discomfort was acute, for we both knew that, in Dutch politics, this was a clear message, meaning *I've already made up my mind, and I'm not going to endorse you.*

It crossed my mind that I might lose her political support, but that didn't matter very much. I had already decided to leave politics; in fact I had even confided to Rita that I didn't plan to run again for Parliament in the next general election.

When I left the room we kissed each other three times on the cheek, as is usual in Holland, and wished each other a happy spring break.

I am certain that Rita knew, and had known for a long time, that I had lied on my application for refugee status when I was twenty-two. Even if she hadn't read the many interviews and statements I'd given in various local, national, and international newspapers and magazines, in which I had freely admitted the fact, we had spoken of it several times. The last time was just a few days after that uncomfortable conversation in her office. I had phoned to ask her to reverse her decision to deport an eighteen-year-old girl from Kosovo, Taida Pasic, who was due to take her final high school exams.

"She lied," Rita told me. "My hands are tied."

"But Rita, you don't understand," I pleaded. "Almost all asylum seekers lie. That's how the system is. I lied too."

Rita was adamant. She said—and I suppose it should have been a warning to me—"If I had been the minister when you applied for asylum, then I would have deported you as well."

A couple of weeks later, during the parliamentary spring break, the television program *Zembla* aired a documentary that prominently featured the fact that I had lied on my refugee application. Just a fortnight away from the election for our party leadership, Rita let it be known that she was now investigating my immigration file and that my status in Holland—not only as a member of Parliament but as a citizen—was in doubt. A few days later she announced that she was stripping me of my Dutch citizenship. To be precise, she claimed I had never had Dutch citizenship in the first place because I had applied for it under false pretences.

Iron Rita's decision to render me stateless was perceived by many of my colleagues in Parliament (even many who rarely agreed with my policy decisions) as arbitrary, vengeful, and even downright strange. There was certainly something of the action of a banana republic about it. After weeks of very un-Dutch furor in Parliament, the press, and the wider public, the prime minister, along with the cabinet ministers and an overwhelming majority of the members of Parliament, forced Rita to reinstate my citizenship. She finally did so, but only on the condition that I sign a letter stating that I had lied to her about lying about my asylum application. Signing that letter made me lie for a second time, but I had to sign; otherwise, Rita could not save face.

But consensus could not so easily be restored. The D66 party, a small pseudo-libertarian party that was also a member of the governing coalition, deemed this procedure outrageous and demanded that Rita resign or D66 would leave the coalition and the government would fall. She would not resign. She was forced into this situation by a trait of character that was also, at other times, her strength: her inflexibility, which was also an inability to adapt to circumstances or admit a mistake.

The government fell. New nationwide elections were scheduled. Rita lost the race for party leader. A few months later the VVD lost ground in the new elections; it could no longer claim any seats in the cabinet. In September 2007, after she had criticized the party's "invisible position" on immigration, she was expelled from the Liberal Party by her old rival, Mark Rutte, who was now the party leader, and from that charmed, smooth-sided triangle that is the Dutch political establishment. She founded her own party, which she named "Proud of the Netherlands." Its public support has slowly dwindled. Rita has become a political outcast.

I learned an important lesson in this about the nature of Dutch politics. Rita, I realized, had violated the most sacred taboo of the political elite, the *regenten,* not so much by what she said as by the way she said it. A consensus society like Holland's requires a great deal of conformity: the tone, flavor, timing, and context that you choose to articulate your message will make or break you. When individuals from groups that historically have had no power are invited into the ranks of the *regentem,* they are taught to express their wishes and grievances in the same way that the *regenten* do. In Holland you must negotiate and compromise; your freedom of speech is limited by the boundaries of what is viewed by the *regenten* as acceptable. This was always going to be hard for someone from Rita's class and temperament, for she could not bear to compromise, and she did not even recognize those subtle perimeters of conformity. Her criticism of immigrants, regardless of the rights and wrongs of the issue, seemed unacceptably rude, parochial, or simply racist.

*   *   *

Another lesson I learned was that it was time, once again, to pack my bags and move on. So I left Holland soon after the crisis about my citizenship erupted. As if to compound the insult of losing my citizenship, my neighbors in the condominium in which I lived had recently managed to win a court case to have me evicted because, they said, my security detail was invasive and the death threats against me were a danger to them too. Now I was not just stateless; I was also homeless. Instead of being perceived as contributing to solving the problems posed by massive waves of foreign immigrants into Dutch society—which I had sought to do—I was now seen as part of the problem.

In fact I had been exploring the possibility of leaving Holland for my own self-preservation even before Rita struck. In Holland I had become too recognizable for my own sanity. Earlier that year I had made up my mind to try to move to the United States, where I thought I would have more freedom, and I had asked a friend of mine, a former U.S. diplomat who is now a university professor, to help me find a job. I had already scheduled a visit to the United States during the parliamentary spring break in order to promote a book of essays I had just published, *The Caged Virgin,* and my friend had proposed to introduce me to people at think tanks of various persuasions on the East Coast, including the Brookings Institution and RAND, and Johns Hopkins, Georgetown, and George Washington universities.

Everyone I met there was effusively polite, but I felt their support for me and my ideas was tentative. The man who interviewed me at the Brookings Institution seemed overly concerned with the possibility that I might offend Arab Muslims and therefore frustrate a series of programs they had just initiated in Doha, Qatar. Then my friend took me to visit the American Enterprise Institute.

The role of American think tanks like the AEI is widely misunderstood. Like their counterparts at liberal and libertarian institutions, such as Brookings and the CATO Institute, AEI scholars do not write policy, they publish their views on policy. These views are often quite diverse. But over the years I had met many people in the media who see the AEI as an arch-conservative club, and I do not consider myself a conservative. (My reasons for not being one are the same as those convincingly put forward by Friederich Hayek in *The Constitution of Liberty*: most essentially, I do not wish to *conserve* the status quo but to alter it, radically.) So I went to see the AEI with some qualms.

To my surprise, they instantly offered me full support. There was no discussion about what I could and could not say. I was pressed on the need to have empirical data and consistent arguments and to think through the benefits and disadvantages of my proposals. I asked whether my pro-choice views on abortion and gay rights would present a problem, and Christopher DeMuth, the president of the AEI, answered that I was free to have whatever opinions I wanted. There were no restrictions on what I could think, say, or write.

Here was another political lesson, one of the first I was to learn in the United States. American liberals appear to be more uncomfortable with my condemning the ill treatment of women under Islam than most conservatives are. Rather than standing up for Western freedoms and against the totalitarian Islamic belief system, many liberals prefer to shuffle their feet and look down at their shoes when faced with questions about cultural differences. I began to understand that *liberal* means different things, depending on which side of the Atlantic you are on. What Europeans would call Leftists are confusingly termed "liberal," with a small *l*, in America, while in Europe liberals are what Americans now call Classical Liberals: they stand for the free market, respect for property rights, the rule of law, limited government, and personal responsibility. European Conservatives support all of these things too. But American Conservatives are more likely to add a list of social and cultural values associated with their Christian faith. Even though their predecessors had once agitated for the rights of workers, the rights of women, and the rights of blacks, American liberals today are hesitant to speak out against the denial of rights that is perpetrated in the name of Islam. So Brookings said no to me and the AEI said yes.

Following our first meeting in 2006, Chris DeMuth formally invited me to become a resident scholar at the AEI in September. When Rita suddenly took away my Dutch passport, this offer had not yet been formalized; he hadn't had the opportunity to consult the AEI's board of trustees. But clearly I could no longer be a member of the Dutch Parliament, for I was no longer Dutch. On the morning of the press conference at which I had decided to announce that I was resigning my seat in Parliament, I received a call from the daily *Volks-krant*: Was it true I was going to take a job at, of all places, the AEI?

I couldn't answer. I had no idea whether the AEI would now take its job offer off the table. I called Chris to tell him I was being badgered by reporters and had to answer them; he told me he would have to consult with his trustees before I could formally announce my new job. My heart sank because I thought that the trustees would be bound to say *Why import scandal?* But only thirty minutes later Chris called back and said I would be welcome at the AEI on September 1.

When the Dutch newspapers wrote that I was headed there, many people warned me that I was making the biggest mistake of my life. They had Googled the AEI, they told me, and it was an evil place, a nest of neoconservatives who had conspired to create the Bush presidency and invented the Iraq war. Why on earth would I choose to consort with this nefarious mob? Well, having just lost my home, my livelihood, and almost my citizenship, I replied that I would take my chances and once again trust in the kindness of strangers.

I was a public figure. Before I left Holland I was given three farewell parties, for at least 150 people claimed to consider themselves my best friends. Some of the speeches my friends made almost compensated for the pain I was feeling. They helped me remember that there were still at least some people in Holland who not only agreed with me but saw past my nonconformist tone and style. I was deeply touched and understood once more why I love this country that I was leaving.

I was born into a political family, and I've always understood that, in politics, things are not always as they seem. Compared to my experiences in Somalia, Ethiopia, Saudi Arabia, and Kenya, my collision with power was very benign in Holland. I was neither tortured nor thrown into jail. In fact one of the farewell parties was in the parliamentary building and attended by some of my most passionate critics. In the Dutch way, I received a small gift and three big smacking kisses on the cheek from every single one of them. It was a very consensual leave-taking.

I was a nomad once more.

CHAPTER 9

America

A few days later I woke up in a Washington hotel and got dressed for my first day of work at the American Enterprise Institute. But I discovered that the office was closed: it was Labor Day. The first pang of my homesickness for Holland came with the realization that Labor Day was not on the first of May, as it is everywhere in Europe, but on the first Monday of September. I had a lot to learn.

This wasn't just a new job, it was a new country: new culture, new holidays, new history. Even my old friend from Kenya, the English language, seemed very different on the streets of the District of Columbia. Would I ever take root here?

I went back to my hotel and thought about it. The first and most striking feature of America is its ethnic diversity; that was the first thing I noticed at the airport when I made my first visit to New York. Everywhere I went I saw Africans, Asians, Hispanics, and more ethnic blends than I could even dream of identifying. I noticed too how positive they were about America. Immigrants spoke easily about how *glad* they were to have come to this country, that they had no intention of going back home because America offered their children opportunities that were unthinkable where they came from. This was so different from the constant complaining about Holland that I was used to hearing from immigrants who sent their money home and who remained cultural and emotional foreigners for generations.

Unlike many immigrants to Holland, when I immigrated to the United States I already spoke the language of my new country and I already knew a few people. I had a visa in my passport that was reserved for people possessing "extraordinary talents" that were "indispensable" for the United States of America, a visa for "exceptional aliens." I enjoyed the phrase, but I wondered: What extraordinary talents did I really have? This visa meant that I was being given a very smooth, privileged admission into a nation where many people in the world would give a lot to go. Other immigrants endure a much more arduous and lengthy application process.

I told myself to be worthy of that visa. It had been given to me because I was a Muslim woman who had found her way to freedom and independence, who was actively propagating the ideals of democracy.

I quickly felt that I belonged at the AEI. The week I arrived in Washington I was introduced to a man I had long hoped to meet, Charles Murray, who in 1994 cowrote *The Bell Curve*. When his book was published I was still a student at the University of Leiden, where it seemed everyone was talking about this horribly racist book that argued that black people were genetically of lower intelligence than white people. I read it, of course, and I found it to be the opposite of racist, a compassionately written book about the urban challenges that confront black people more than white. All black people should read it.

When I was introduced to Murray, I couldn't help thinking that even his head was shaped like a precise bell curve. While we exchanged greetings, I mentioned that I recognized his name from reading his book, at which point he gritted his teeth, no doubt bracing himself for another attack from an offended black person. When I said how great I thought his book was, his smile was so broad and so surprised. We became instant friends.

Despite my initial suspicions and my Dutch friends' prejudice against the AEI, my fellow scholars were well-read and knowledgeable, as well as friendly. Far from being dogmatic warmongers, they showed themselves entirely capable of criticizing the Bush administration. Chris DeMuth proved to be a man of exceptional intellectual depth and breadth, who asked sharp questions about matters ranging from the Iranian nuclear program to the moral crisis of feminism.

In the main, the AEI's focus is on economics, and the major principles on which the scholars seemed in rough agreement are individual responsibility and limited government. Working at the AEI wasn't like working for the think tank of a political party in Europe, where people are obsessed with preparing elections and avoiding controversy. I was able to write, to read, to think, and to attend discussions chaired by the other scholars on subjects that ranged from national security to religion, genetics, Medicare, global warming, and development aid to other countries.

It added to my pleasure in my new life that Washington, D.C., is such a miraculously easy city to navigate, laid out in straight lines, with streets whose names run through the letters of the alphabet and the numbers up to twenty-six. I felt I could never get lost.

When my memoir, *Infidel,* was published in the United States in February 2007 I began promoting the book around the country. This was very instructive. To my amazement, it could take five or six hours simply to fly from one city to another; there were four different time zones (five, including Hawaii) and numerous different weather zones. Of course, I had known these facts since my school days, but it was now that I finally grasped the sheer staggering physical scale of the United States.

In Holland, after you drive for two hours you're already in another country. The land there is flat and all the fields are manicured squares; every acre of Holland has been touched and engineered by man. In contrast, entire European nations could fit inside a big state like Texas or California. The rugged landscape of America, with valleys, mountains, creeks, ravines, and canyons, is almost as untamed and challenging as Somalia's. Flying across the country, peering out of the small windows of airplanes, I began to see why people in the rural United States believe they have a right to carry guns.

I always feel a sense of wonder when facing the geography of America. I traveled for over an hour from Santa Fe to Albuquerque without seeing a single human being. The land was a moonscape of strange rock formations and craters studded with cactuses, and though it was warm in the car, snow-topped mountains rose in the distance.

There's nothing wild about Holland. There the protected species are muskrats and certain obscure insects; anything larger was eliminated centuries ago. In the United States, simply hiking up a hill I have seen trees so tall they seem primeval, and among them coyotes and elk.

* * *

I admired the vast new landscape of America and liked my job in Washington, but I felt most at home in New York City, which I often visit in order to stay with friends. One beautiful weekend late in June 2007 I took a walk in Central Park. Summer was about to begin—I could tell from the thunderstorms and torrential rain we'd been having—but that morning was glorious: bright and sunny, with hardly any wind. It was the sort of day for running around in the park in a bikini.

I walked past the bronze statue of the Angel of the Waters and her four cherubs and on toward the lake. A couple of roller skaters dashed past me; a woman with two children in a twin buggy jogged up. All around me Europeans were talking in familiar languages: Italian, French, and Scandinavian. The dollar was low and the weather was great.

I was tapped on the shoulder and almost jumped. A nice young Dutch couple, in jeans and leather jackets, were smiling broadly, cameras in hand. It was a reminder of my last, lost home. It was also a reminder of my continued insecurity. My bodyguards moved closer. I gestured that I was okay.

"*Mevrouw* Hirsi Ali," said the man, in Dutch, "may we take a picture with you?" *Mevrouw* in Dutch can mean "Miss." or "Mrs."

"Of course," I said, smiling back, and one of the bodyguards offered to take the picture with their camera. As we posed the woman asked me, "Will this ever come to an end?" She meant my needing bodyguards.

"I don't know. I don't know when it will end."

"Do you still receive death threats?"

"It is hard to say. I get threats via e-mail. But people who mean real harm will not bother to send me an e-vite."

During my book tour for *Infidel* I was scheduled to give a talk at the Philadelphia Public Library. A week before, I was informed by my security detail that threats against me had been intercepted on a Muslim website. They were explicit about the venue and the details of my talk and outspoken about their plans to prevent me from carrying out my engagement. I was sitting in a restaurant in Los Angeles when I was given this news and was advised to cancel the appearance. Without hesitating I exclaimed, "You cannot be serious. This is a free, democratic country. I will give this speech, and it is because I have protection that I am able to do so. This is exactly why I have protection!" Once I had calmed down, I called Chris DeMuth at the AEI to ask his advice. I didn't want to risk other people's lives. Without hesitation he said, "You go and do what you should."

The speech went ahead as planned, thanks to the concerted efforts of a number of security organizations, including the local police.

People often ask me what it's like to live with bodyguards. The short answer is that it's better than being dead. It's also better than wearing a headscarf or a veil, which to me represents the mental and physical restrictions that so many Muslim women have to suffer. Still, the irony of my situation has not escaped me: I am supposed to be a great icon of women's freedom, but because of death threats against me I have to live in a way that is, in a sense, unfree. It's not much fun to be followed around all the time by members of a team of physically intimidating armed men. It's a little like wearing an astronaut suit, a protective casing that prevents your contact with the elements. It slows you down and makes every movement very conscious and stiff. I don't like to be watched all day and night.

Yet bodyguards keep me safe. They make me feel less fearful. When you live with death threats all the time, you do feel fear, and you do have horrible nightmares. When a car is parked outside for too long, I ask myself whether I am being watched. If the man at the newsstand stares at me, I wonder if he knows who I am. If a delivery boy rings the bell, I hesitate: Is he really who he appears to be? Should I answer the door?

I try to stay vigilant. I don't keep a routine. But I have decided not to stop writing, not to stop drawing attention to the plight of Muslim women and the threat that extremists pose to free thought, free speech, and democratic governments. If I were to stop, I don't think it would help my situation, because once an enemy, always an enemy. There will always be someone happy to take me with him to the hereafter.

In a way these threats motivate me. They have given my voice *more* legitimacy.

That afternoon in Central Park I lingered for a moment in the sunlight, talking to the Dutch couple. They told me how upset they were at how I had been treated in Holland and how much they would like to give me support. It was a lovely encounter, completely surprising, as it often is when I encounter Dutch people; some are hostile to me, but most are very loving, extremely warm. This chance meeting gave me a pang of homesickness for Holland. Hearing Dutch in Manhattan produced the familiar, affectionate, almost unconditional feeling of being *connected* that a people share when they are from the same place. It is the feeling that a nomad is always grasping for: that elusive sense of family.

By Christmas of 2009, three years after my immigration to the United States, I was more than ever living the life of a nomad. I did not spend much time in Washington. My job was a cross between academic work and activism. In research I discovered that debates on Islam, multiculturalism, and women had been exhausted in the late 1980s and 1990s, long before September 11, 2001. As far as I could see, there was nothing original I could add to the existing volume of scholarly work. My academic job as I defined it was to follow closely new attacks in the name of Islam. The activist part of my job took me all over America as a speaker. This meant I spent much of my time traveling from one city to another on the lecture circuit and to conferences.

Globalization and the threat of terrorism are best experienced at airports. Most of the American airports that I have used are better than those in Africa and far worse than those in Europe, except for London's Heathrow. The Dallas, Denver, and Los Angeles airports are excellent, while Chicago's O'Hare is as confusing as Paris's Charles de Gaulle but not quite the nightmare that Dulles and JFK are. The further inland you go, to places like Aspen, Beaver Creek, and Sun Valley, the smaller and more efficient the airports become. These little airports are almost a relief to travel through.

My first taste of an American airport was in 2002. I landed at Kennedy Airport, en route to Los Angeles. For a minute I thought that there was some mistake, that I had taken the wrong flight to somewhere in Africa. Crowds of people huddled in large groups, some in transit, others just arrived. At Immigration there were stanchions with lanes marked by ribbons that wound around for hundreds of yards to keep us moving along in an orderly way. The civil servant who checked my passport spoke poor English and seemed to be angry, probably because he was trapped in such a tiny cubicle. The lines seemed to last forever; the luggage carousels spilled over with bags, and some men were throwing the bags back onto the few empty spaces that were left. People in uniform were yelling at passengers, and a cacophony of voices came from loudspeakers admonishing us, as did the television screens at every gate, "Do not leave your bags unattended. The terror alert is on orange."

I soon grew accustomed to such scenes at major hub airports. If anything, the Departure areas were even worse: endless lines of people slowed down by the new safety rules; laptops removed from their bags; shoes and belts and even jackets tediously put in gray plastic trays. Flights operated by almost bankrupt airlines nearly always departed much later than scheduled. The erratic American weather—thunderstorms, hurricanes, wind gusts, and snowstorms—periodically threw everything into chaos.

I had come to America looking for a new home, but I soon found that I was living out of a suitcase, moving from airport to airport and from hotel to hotel. I began to consider the obstacles of modern travel to be similar to those of the caravans Grandma used to talk about. In her time the risks came from marauding warlords and their militias, from severe drought or floods, from beasts of burden that were overused and underfed. In modern America the equivalents were terrorist alerts and snowstorms.

After months of such nomadism, my American friends took pity on me. It was time, they said, to discover that life in the United States was not all about work. One friend asked if I had ever been to Las Vegas. My immediate thought was gambling. That was the only sin I had not yet committed that is expressly forbidden by Islam. "Not Las Vegas,"

I stammered. "It's a place of crime, gambling, and fierce neon lights. I don't think I want to go there."

"Oh, come on," replied my friend Sharon. "You don't know what you're missing. It is such a part of America, you must see it."

So one weekend she drove me from Los Angeles to Las Vegas. L.A.'s sprawl can seem infinite, but as we sped along the highway the buildings eventually became fewer and fewer and the landscape became steadily less green until there was only desert, barren land with mountains, hard rock, soft mounds of sand whitish in color but brown and gray too. We passed by places with bizarre names like Zzsyk. My interest was caught by a sign proclaiming "Ghost Town Road."

"Spooky," I said pointing to the sign.

"Maybe we should stop in one of those places on the way back," my friend replied.

After several hours of desert landscape we finally reached Las Vegas. I was dazzled. Turning right at Mandalay Bay was like entering a magic island with surreal replicas of New York, Paris, and Rome. At the Wynn Hotel, where we stayed, there were not only bedrooms and restaurants but also full-scale shopping malls; high-end European stores with the latest in fashion; jewelry stores displaying gold, platinum, and diamonds and other precious stones; and at the center of all this splendor, rows and rows of gambling machines and gambling tables. And of course, strip clubs for men and spas for women.

Sharon urged me to try one of the machines. I lost eight dollars and won a dollar twenty-five at one machine; at another I won ten dollars and lost twenty; and at a table we played a game called blackjack. Sharon and I put in a hundred dollars. We lost sixty. It was weird. We had to buy chips of five and ten dollars each; the game started with fifteen. A dealer gave you two cards while he held two. You could play a hand or ask for an extra card. If all three cards added up to twenty-one, you won—that is, you won more chips.

I must have looked as if I had walked in straight from the bush. To play, you had to make tiny gestures, like moving your forefinger back and forth or waving your palm slowly to and fro as if you were stroking the table without touching it. The dealer would nod and my friend would nod back in a strange way. Blackjack is supposed to be the simplest of the card games, but I felt that it would take me a long time to grasp all the secret signs, and even longer to analyze the probability of what the next card would be. By then I would have run out of cash. So we stopped playing.

To round off the night we went to the Palace Hotel to see the musical *Jersey Boys*, which tells the story of a band of poor kids growing up in New Jersey. I was soon captivated by this classical American account of the price of fame. At first it seems like a good idea to form a band, though their path to success is strewn with obstacles. When at last success comes, not only has the band split up, but the protagonist's marriage breaks down, his girlfriend leaves him, and he loses his daughter to drugs; sadly he sings about being abandoned by everyone. The show ends with solos from all four men as they look back on their lives.

On the way back to L.A. we stopped for gas very close to where Ghost Town Road went, winding up a hill of colored rocks. "Would you like to take a look at the town?" Sharon asked, remembering my earlier curiosity.

Why not? I was up for more adventure. We drove to the ghost town of Calico.

At the entrance to what was once the town is a cubicle with a thatched roof manned by a guard who collects a small fee from the tourists. The ghost town is essentially an open-air museum. A century and a half ago Calico was known for silver mining and attracted crowds of prospectors who wanted to get rich quick. It had had a couple of provisions stores, a couple of shops that sold garments and household goods, and a saloon with a brothel attached to it. A simple family home had been restored to give you a glimpse of how people had lived in the Wild West.

A nineteenth-century stove caught my attention because it was far superior to the charcoal braziers we'd used in our homes in Mogadishu and Nairobi and which are still in use in many African homes today. Even the rustic furniture in this old and abandoned home was better-designed and sturdier than ours. The townspeople of Calico had walked about two miles to fetch their water, as many Africans have to do; they washed their garments (uncannily similar to many still worn in Africa) by hand. Their woven floor mats, bowls, and placemats transported me back to Mogadishu, Addis Ababa, and Nairobi. Grandma used to spend hours weaving such mats.

The ghost town vividly illustrated the difference between my grandmother's traditions, which insist on keeping things as they are, and American traditions, which continuously innovate. The American mind seeks new, better, and more efficient means of cooking, washing, and finding fuel, the most basic and most universal activities of human life. In my grandmother's tradition people get stuck, almost imprisoned, by the cycle of finding food, preparing it, and eating it. I can't think of anything useful a Somali man or woman ever invented to make that cycle easier.

Even this long-abandoned ghost town in the no-man's-land between Nevada and California contained relatively more luxury than my mother's house did. Moving from that town back to L.A., I saw how incredibly fast the early settlers in America had moved forward, how swift their progress had been.

A couple of months before my Vegas trip I was back on the East Coast, at the Metropolitan Museum of Art in New York City. The director of the Rijksmuseum in Amsterdam, Wim Pijbes, and the Corporation of Tulip Breeders had proposed to hold a small ceremony in my honor. I was to be given a hundred Black Tulip bulbs as a symbol of (so Pijbes explained) diversity in the Netherlands. I invited some of my closest American friends, and Pijbes invited a few Dutch visitors. I mentioned that Chris DeMuth had a weakness for the artist Vermeer. Coincidentally the Met had just mounted as complete an exhibition of Vermeers as they could find.

Chris was late, but I went down to see the paintings, led by Pijbes. We paused for some time in front of Vermeer's *The Milkmaid*. Pijbes went into an in-depth explanation about the genius contained in that small painting: the precision, lights, colors, shadows, and the choice of a milkmaid as a subject. But as I stared at it what struck me was the room; it was poor, dark, and small. Many rooms in the neighborhoods of my youth were just as small.

After the short tour of the exhibition I got into a conversation with another of the Dutch visitors. I was disappointed to hear her recite the usual prejudices about Americans being *plat*. This is a very difficult word to translate; it means something like "plebeian," unrefined and with little or no history of art or proper culture. In this view everything in American culture is pop, if not pap, and produced for the masses. Certainly much nonsense passes for culture in the United States, including an obsession with celebrities of all kinds. But that is scarcely representative of the vast wealth of extraordinary art, literature, and music produced by Americans in the almost two and a half centuries of the country's existence.

As a stranger to America I often find myself excluded from conversations because so many references are made to musicals and movies I have never heard of. Once in Boston while chatting with friends, I let slip that I did not understand some of the cultural references in the conversation we were having about prejudice. "Did you ever see *South Pacific*?" one friend asked. For some reason it sounded familiar, but I had not. (It is typical that a lot of American references sound familiar but really are not.) She and her husband promptly invited me to join them in New York to see it.

A love story in wartime told on stage with songs and acting that left you more cheerful than if you had been to a comedy, *South Pacific* enchanted me. It was a relief too, after European opera. Opera's love stories almost always end unhappily, even though the lovers are accompanied to their doom by the most splendid music. By contrast, couples in American musicals can sing and dance their way around massive issues like war and racism, only to end the love story on a happy note. At the end of the show I found myself humming the tune "You've Got To Be Carefully Taught."

> *You've got to be taught*
> *To hate and fear,*
> *You've got to be taught*
> *From year to year,*
> *It's got to be drummed*
> *In your dear little ear,*
> *You've got to be carefully taught.*
>
> *You've got to be taught to be afraid*
> *Of people whose eyes are oddly made,*
> *And people whose skin is a different shade,*
> *You've got to be carefully taught.*

You've got to be taught before it's too late,
Before you are six or seven or eight,
To hate all the people your relatives hate,
You've got to be carefully taught!

This show and the conversations that followed gave me a window into America's seemingly endless struggle with the issue of race. More than any number of sermons from politicians or pundits, such songs designed for mass consumption served to weaken racial prejudice by ridiculing it .

Another couple took me to Leonard Bernstein's ninetieth-birthday-gala concert in New York. I was a little embarrassed to admit that I did not know who Bernstein was. No problem, they said in unison. Tonight will be a good introduction. One of the performances that intrigued me was by a couple of poorly dressed teenagers who imitate an encounter with their neighborhood policeman and then sing about it:

Dear kindly Sergeant Krupke,
You gotta understand,
It's just our bringin' up-ke
That gets us out of hand.
Our mothers all are junkies,
Our fathers all are drunks,
Golly Moses, natcherly we're punks!

After the show I asked my friends about that song with the teenagers. They were astonished. "Haven't you seen *West Side Story*?" Just a few days later I was watching it on DVD and savoring the swings that the lyricist took at the soft psychology that talked teenage delinquents into believing that they were "victims of society." I also heard for the first time the unforgettable immigrants' song, "America." It is a conversation in song between men and women immigrants from Puerto Rico. Below are a few of the lines that I think are timeless; they also illustrate the different perspectives that people from the same place, indeed the same family, have on America. For the women it is a land of freedom and unlimited opportunity, for the homesick men a place of poverty and bigotry if you are not white.

I like to be in America . . .
Everything free in America. . . .
Buying on credit is so nice.
     One look at us and they charge twice.
I have my own washing machine.
     What will you have, though, to keep clean? . . .
Industry boom in America.
     Twelve in a room in America.
Lots of new housing with more space.
     Lots of doors slamming in our face. . . .
Life is all right in America.
     If you're all white in America.
Here you are free and you have pride.
     Long as you stay on your own side.
Free to be anything you choose.
     Free to wait tables and shine shoes.
     Everywhere grime in America,
     Organized crime in America,
     Terrible time in America. . . .
     I think I'll go back to San Juan.
I know a boat you can get on.
     Everyone there will give big cheer!
Everyone there will have moved here!

That dialogue still rings true today. For most immigrants, coming to America means exchanging a home plagued by joblessness, violence, and apathy for a new land where the alluring opportunities come packaged with residential grime, gangs, and organized crime.

By contrast, I have been exceedingly fortunate in having many of my American dreams realized almost on arrival. I have not only been to Las Vegas in the past year; I have been on a cruise to Alaska, where I saw high mountains, glaciers, bears both black and brown, and whales that sneezed meters of water straight into the air and then dove to show off their tail fins. At Thanksgiving another friend suggested, as if offering me a cup of tea, a ride on a four-wheeler on a Texas ranch. I ended up getting a riding lesson on a cowboy's horse too. I have attended conferences at which the assortment of postprandial activities ranged from playing golf to tennis clinics to white-water rafting.

I am lucky to have come here in the way I did. I am lucky to have the friends I have. But that does not mean that I underestimate what it means to come to America as an illegal immigrant, sneaking across the Mexican border, or to be born in the inner cities of Chicago, L.A., or New York. On my visits to the Bronx I have seen that there are indeed pockets of America where people barely have enough food to eat, where girls get pregnant at thirteen, where teenage boys acquire guns all too easily and shoot one another, where school entrances need to be bullet-proof and students need to pass through metal detectors. In some ghettos the life expectancy of a black boy is estimated to be only eighteen.

These are serious social and political problems, no doubt. In some cases they are clearly more serious than equivalent problems in European inner cities. But they are not problems that affect mainstream America the way such problems in Africa affect that continent.

What is it that makes America different from Europe and Africa? Clearly it is not just the homicide rate in poor black neighborhoods. To answer that question I need to take you with me to a wedding. In the Stanford Memorial Church in Palo Alto, California, a week before my fortieth birthday, I watched my friends Margaret and John get married.

At thirty-one, Margaret looked exquisite. John had the look of a man about to embark on a serious mission. I had never been to an all-American wedding before. In movies, it seemed to me, brides were always blonde and grooms always had dark hair. Margaret is blonde, John has dark hair, but beyond this nothing about their wedding was like the movies I watched. Weddings in movies are usually comedies: the priest messes up the vows (*Four Weddings and a Funeral*); the bride runs away (*Runaway Bride*); the parents get themselves in a fix (*Meet the Parents*). This, by contrast, was no comedy. The ceremony was impeccable. The food was plentiful and good, the wine excellent, the church breathtaking, the bride in her grandmother's wedding dress had tears in her eyes, and the groom was visibly moved. Solemnly they took their vows. I quietly wondered if any human could keep such promises: "To have and to hold, from this day forward, for better, for worse, for richer, for poorer, in sickness and in health, to love and to cherish, till death us do part."

I was so stunned by the intensity of the service that I asked the female guest next to me, "This is pretty serious, isn't it, for so young a couple?"

"Yes," she replied. "Marriage has little to do with age and everything to do with family, and here in America family is serious."

That day I learned that the core unit of American society is indeed the family. In theory, of course, the core unit in any truly free society is the individual, who is the starting point in a democratic constitution and in law. Individual responsibility is required and urged at all times. But pretty soon you realize that, to be happy and fulfilled, the individual must be embedded in a family. Americans are constantly asking after one another's families. The American family is not as extended as in the clan culture I grew up in and not as tightly nuclear as the Dutch model. Nor is there any of the experimentation I encountered in the Netherlands.* In America I have met married couples, single people seeking to marry, engaged pairs on the point of marriage, and divorced ones who constantly talk about how to start the whole process afresh. Cohabitation, except in some circles, is not seen as a long-term option, and often couples who live together tend to be engaged. Only in New York does it seem acceptable to remain single on a long-term basis.

The other thing I learned at Stanford is that families are the building blocks of American society, for it is out of families that the communities grow that form the American nation. Margaret and John's wedding exemplified for me so many of the characteristics of the United States I had come to appreciate.

America is a country with its own foundation myth, that of a new and virtuous republic, built in a virgin land by brave and hardy pioneers. This founding myth is told and retold in countless ways and through all available media, but for me the American wedding is the most powerful version. It is all there: the optimistic faith in the suc-

---

*In Holland after the 1960s all sorts of new family models became fashionable: the *Bewust Ongehuwde Moeder* (the deliberately unmarried mother); the *Bewust Ongehuwde Vader* (the deliberately unmarried father); the Living-Apart-Together; the gay families, consisting of two lesbians and children of which one partner is the mother or gay men with adopted children; and the experimental communal families that vary in size and longevity but oppose the traditional family model of father-mother-children.

cess of a new partnership; the lofty, Christian ideals and vows; and the patriotism that finds its way into every American family ritual. Most striking of all is the way so many American weddings epitomize the ideal of the unity of diverse peoples.

Margaret grew up in Colorado and is the great-granddaughter of Herbert Hoover, the president of the United States from 1929 to 1933; her husband's forebears came from Greece. The guests were even more diverse: the bridesmaids alone were of six different shades of color. In terms of class and religion, the guests ranged from local farmers to Stanford professors. There was not the faintest trace of snobbery. In the various speeches, this cocktail of races, religions, and classes was mentioned repeatedly with unconcealed pride. *Look,* they seemed to be saying to me, *this is who we are: a family that welcomes all peoples who share our family values.* That for me is America: a large family where anyone can belong, so long as you accept those values.

The big question, of course, is: What exactly are those values, and what if you do not accept them, or even take them seriously?

I admit I came to America full of African as well as European prejudices. One of those prejudices was that Americans were hypocrites when they lauded family values, particularly monogamy. In my first three years in America scarcely a month passed without some major public figure being exposed for cheating on his wife. The divorce rate seemed to bear out my suspicion that high-flown talk of family values in America was just that: talk.

But the United States is not utopia, and Americans do not aspire to be perfect. They aspire, above all, to be happy. And that means that if things don't work out with a new venture, whether it is a marriage or a silver-mining town, Americans are much quicker than people from traditional societies to call it a day and move on, with as few hard feelings as possible.

What Americans are generally reluctant to do—and this is perhaps the most important difference between Americans and Europeans—is to call on the state (or "the government," as Americans prefer to say) to help them out when things go wrong. They do it, of course, and never more readily than in a financial crisis like the one that struck when I was writing this book. But unlike Europeans, Americans feel instinctively that large-scale government intervention is wrong, is at best an emergency measure. In an ideal world Americans would form their families and firms, build their homes and workplaces, buy and sell their goods and services, go to a pizza place on Saturday and church on Sunday, and generally get on with their lives with the minimum amount of state interference.

That makes America a very different target indeed for the biggest challenge since Soviet Communism to confront the Western world: the threat of radical Islam.

CHAPTER 10

Islam in America

The more I traveled around the United States, talking to people about my life, the more I was struck by other differences between the two sides of the Atlantic Ocean. The American audiences clearly felt a sense of outrage at the injustices committed against girls, apostates, and infidels in the name of Islam, just as Europeans did, but Americans seemed much more interested in finding solutions, volunteering, mobilizing—and taking action.

On the other hand, although American audiences were hungry with curiosity—everywhere I went, people had to be turned away because the rooms were too small—they also seemed far less aware than Europeans of the problems that I was talking about.

To take one example: in Europe more or less everyone has heard about Muslim families who punish and murder women who trespass their boundaries of custom and faith. Such stories are featured regularly in the newspapers. People in almost every European audience to which I have spoken had heard of at least one brutal murder of a young girl. Thus most European audiences already understand that Muslim immigrants create specific social problems in their countries and that they often involve the oppression of women on European soil. But in America I was constantly surprised that most people in my audiences perceive Islam as largely about foreign policy—an important question for America's national security, maybe, but essentially about people living *overseas*.

Whenever I spoke, American listeners gasped in indignant surprise at the very concepts of child marriage, honor killing, and female excision. Rarely, if ever, did it occur to these audiences that many women and girls suffer precisely these kinds of oppression in houses and apartment buildings all over the United States.

Roughly 130 million women around the world have had their genitals cut. The operation is inflicted on an estimated six thousand little girls every day. If 98 percent of Somali women are cut, 95 percent of women from Mali, and 90 percent of Sudanese, how many women does that make in every subway car in New York, on every freeway in Colorado and Kansas? If 97 percent of Egyptian girls are genitally mutilated, what percentage of Egyptian girls born in the United States are cut? None? I don't think so.* But my audiences couldn't believe that.

I had encountered this kind of incredulity before, of course. Ten years earlier, when I began speaking out in Holland against genital mutilation, Dutch people were just as horrified as Americans to learn about it. I was constantly told that immigrants to Europe *knew* that this practice was against the law in Europe, so *it just didn't happen* to children once they got to Holland. I did not believe that was true. In fact once I became a member of Parliament and helped to pass a law requiring the authorities to actually look into the situation, we confirmed that little girls' genitals were being cut, without anesthetic, on kitchen tables in Rotterdam and Utrecht.

There are already many genitally mutilated women and girls in America, and many others at risk of mutilation. To take the culture I know best, it is a rare Somali family that will refrain from cutting their daughters, wherever they live. All but the most assimilated parents want their children to marry within the Somali community, and they believe that an "impure" girl, one whose clitoris and vagina are intact, will not find a husband. They may perform the "lesser" circumcision, which involves cutting only the skin of the clitoris, but most of them will do just as our fathers (and mothers and grandmothers) have always done: they will cut off the clitoris and cut the lips of the vagina so that it scars shut, to create a built-in chastity belt. They do not always need to fly back to Africa to do this. Every Somali com-

---

*All figures come from *Integration of the Human Rights of Women and the Gender Perspective/Violence Against Women* (2003), Report of the Special Rapporteur on Violence against Women, Its Causes and Consequences, Radhika Coomaraswamy, submitted in accordance with Commission on Human Rights Resolution 2002/52/.

munity has members who can provide this service close to home, or who know someone, somewhere nearby, who will.

There are already Muslim schools in America where girls learn all day long to be subservient and lower their eyes, to veil themselves to symbolize the suppression of their individual will. They are taught to internalize male superiority and walk very softly into the mosque by a back door. In weekend Quran schools girls learn that God requires them to obey, that they are worth less than boys and have fewer rights before God. This too is happening in America.

But on one point my audiences were insistent. Surely honor crimes, the systematic beatings and even murder to punish a daughter or sister or wife whose "misbehavior" casts shame on the family, could not possibly happen in the United States, the land of the free?

As a newcomer to the country, I had no idea whether that was true. But I was soon to find out that this aspect of Islam's dysfunctional culture had already made its way into the American heartland.

Even though I outraged some Americans with the stories I told about institutionalized Islamic misogyny, I was haunted by the fear that I might instead inspire them merely to pity me. The whole point of my memoir, I tried to explain, is that I have been extraordinarily *lucky*. I managed to make it out of the world of dogma and oppression and into the sunlight of independence and free ideas. I *did* escape, and at every stage of that process of escape I was assisted by the goodwill of ordinary non-Muslims, just like the people in those audiences.

It's true that I have had to pay a price for leaving Islam and for speaking out. For instance, I have to pay for round-the-clock security because of the death threats against me. But because Islam demands that anyone who leaves the religion be punished by death, this constant fear is to some extent shared by *all* Muslims who leave the faith as well as those who practice a less strict form of it.

In my books and talks I want to inspire readers to think of the *others,* those who are still locked in the world I have left behind. I use anecdotes from my life and the stories of women I know or who have e-mailed me or stepped up to speak to me. By drawing verbal pictures of them I try to help audiences relate to them as real people. Behind the veil are human beings of flesh and blood, mind and soul, and once you perceive the suffering that lies behind that veil, it is harder to turn away.

These are little girls who love learning, but who are taken out of school when they begin to menstruate because their families fear that they may meet improper influences in school and sully their purity. Children are married to adult strangers they have never met. Women long to live productive, working lives, but are instead confined within the walls of their father's or husband's house. Girls and women are beaten, hard and often, for a sidelong glance, a suspicion of lipstick, a text message; they have nowhere to turn because their parents, community, and preachers approve of these deadening punishments.

Most American audiences reacted, first, with astonishment, and second with compassion to stories of the routine horrors of a Muslim woman's life, even as they struggled to believe it was happening in their own country. There was one exception to this reaction. This was on college campuses, exactly the kind of environment where I had expected curiosity, lively debate, and, yes, the thrill and energy of like-minded activists.

Instead almost every campus audience I encountered bristled with anger and protest. I was accustomed to radical Muslim students from my experience as an activist and a politician in Holland. Any time I made a public speech, they would swarm to it in order to shout at me and rant in broken Dutch, in sentences so fractured you wondered how they qualified as students at all.

On college campuses in the United States and Canada, by contrast, young and highly articulate people from the Muslim student associations would simply take over the debate. They would send e-mails of protest to the organizers beforehand, such as one (sent by a divinity student at Harvard) that protested that I did not "address anything of substance that actually affects Muslim women's lives" and that I merely wanted to "trash" Islam. They would stick up posters and hand out pamphlets at the auditorium. Before I'd even stopped speaking they'd be lining up for the microphone, elbowing away all non-Muslims. They spoke in perfect English; they were mostly very well-mannered; and they appeared far better assimilated than their European immigrant counterparts. There were far fewer bearded young men in robes short enough to show their ankles, aping the tradition that says the Prophet's companions dressed this way out of humility, and fewer girls in hideous black veils. In the United States a radical Muslim student might have a little goatee; a girl may wear a light, attractive headscarf. Their whole demeanor was far less threatening, but they were omnipresent.

Some of them would begin by saying how sorry they were for all my terrible suffering, but they would then add that these so-called traumas of mine were aberrant, a "cultural thing," nothing to do with Islam. In blaming Islam for the oppression of women, they said, I was vilifying them personally, as Muslims. I had failed to understand that Islam is a religion of peace, that the Prophet treated women very well. Several times I was informed that attacking Islam only serves the purpose of something called "colonial feminism," which in itself was allegedly a pretext for the war on terror and the evil designs of the U.S. government.

I was invited to one college to speak as part of a series of lectures on Muslim women. I was amazed and delighted that an American university would devote an entire lecture series to this subject, but when I received the poster for the series, I was downcast.

> The veil, honor killings and female genital mutilations are now commonly seen, in the West, as signs of Muslim women's oppression.

So far, so good. But then it went on:

> Muslim women's liberation has served as a justification for interventions in the War on Terror. But this is not new. Since the days of British colonialism, the women question has been used to justify rule. This is what Leila Ahmed termed colonial feminism—the selective concern for Muslim women's plight, focusing on the veil rather than education, while opposing women's suffrage back home in imperial England. Why the veil and not education, or health, sexuality, economic and legal rights, religious and gender equality? These latter issues are admittedly messier than a cultural iconic one. They belong to a complex web of historical and political dynamics and interactions, which challenges us to, in the words of Lila Abu-Lughod, "consider our own

larger responsibilities to address the forms of global injustice that are powerful shapers of the world in which [Muslim women] find themselves."

And so on. As soon as it made an interesting point, this little poster veered off into academic nonsense. All its assumptions were either morally or factually empty. First, the term *colonial feminism* carries a snide implication that this alleged brand of feminism somehow subjects women rather than frees them. Concern for the plight of Muslim women was not remotely related to the original European colonization of what is now called the developing world. The scramble for Africa was a brazen competition openly motivated by gold, God, and glory, not a gracious attempt to emancipate little girls.

One great side effect of colonization, however, was that European countries brought their political and legal infrastructure to many Muslim countries, which did improve the situation of women in significant ways. Ignoring this, and beating constantly on the monotonous drum of colonial oppression and bigotry, excuses formerly colonized peoples from scrutiny and criticism for their own failings. For after the colonizers left, many countries reintroduced Shari'a law—always, first, as "Family Law" (in other words, women's law)—and the situation of women in every case became worse.

The idea that something called *colonial* (or sometimes *neocolonial*) *feminism* was a pretext for George W. Bush's war on terror does not stand up to scrutiny either. It is akin to the suspicion that there are Jewish conspiracies: an attempt to displace blame. I was a member of the Dutch Parliament at the time of the U.S. invasion of Iraq, serving a party that was in government, and when we debated the question of whether to vote for or against the war (I voted in favor), the arguments were about weapons of mass destruction and Saddam Hussein's unwillingness to admit international atomic inspectors into the country. Just as with the invasion of Afghanistan, nobody mentioned Muslim women and their liberation as a reason to go to war. Moreover, when the United States put new constitutions in place in both Afghanistan and Iraq, they *indulged* the Muslim clerics, making family law subject to Shari'a.

The argument that by criticizing Islam you defame believing

Muslims is also specious. If I criticize George Washington, I am not defaming Americans; if I deplore Abraham's lying to Pharaoh about his wife being his sister I am not slandering other Jews—or, for that matter, Muslims, who also recognize Abraham as a Patriarch. But a religion, Islam, based on a book, the Quran, that denies women basic human rights *is* backward, and to say so is not an insult but an opinion. If it is a valid criticism, then ignoring the book's view and the practice of victimizing women that stems from it adds to the harming of the victims. My view does not defame Muslims who do not have this belief or do not themselves oppress women.

Similarly, many of the defenders of Islam on campuses also magnified the horror of America's record on civil rights: the extermination and displacement of Native Americans, the slave trade, absurd and cruel laws of segregation. These records are a fact. However, it is also a fact that, especially compared to other developed nations, the United States has led the way in promoting the notion, first at home and to this day in foreign lands, that all people are born free and equal. It is also a matter of record that the American civil rights movement ultimately succeeded in peacefully overcoming the many forms of discrimination against African Americans that persisted long after the end of slavery. From the vantage point of a relative newcomer to the United States, this is not a bad record at all. Yet apparently this was not what many college students were learning.

On campus after campus I would stare in despair at these confident young men and women, born in the United States, who had so manifestly benefited from every advantage of Western education yet were determined to ignore the profound differences between a theocratic mind-set and a democratic mind-set. I once resembled them myself, in the days when I too wore a headscarf and strove to obey and submit with all my mind rather than to question and speak out. But I believe there is a difference between these students and my younger self. These students seemed to lack a basic human empathy for other Muslim women—women who are just like they are but who cannot speak in public or even go to school. If they lived in Saudi Arabia, under Shari'a law, these college girls in their pretty scarves wouldn't be free to study, to work, to drive, to walk around. In Saudi Arabia girls their age and younger are confined, are forced to marry, and if they have sex outside of marriage they are sentenced to prison and flogged. According to the Quran, their husband is permitted to beat them and decide whether they may work or even leave the house; he may marry other women without seeking their approval, and if he chooses to divorce them, they have no right to resist or to keep custody of their children. Doesn't this matter at all to these clever young Muslim girls in America?

I would look around the well-furnished auditoriums of the elite American colleges, rich in so many ways, and think of the many small tragedies they contained. These young people, who had experienced only personal freedom, a liberal education, and economic opportunity, could become the vectors of democratic values, the standard-bearers of a new, more modern Islam, blending Muslim characteristics with Western openness. Yet although they are clearly exposed to education of the highest quality, they refuse to look reality in the face, to see that just because something is written, it is not necessarily right. Instead they insist on a black-and-white view of Islam. They concentrate on defending the image of the Prophet Muhammad, a dead man, from "insults." Why, I asked, did they not organize to defend other Muslims, other women? Even though many were attending colleges where the entire educational ethos was constructed around the need for justice and solidarity with the poor and displaced, the sufferings of women under Islam were simply overlooked.

There are activist groups of every stripe on campus, yet nothing for girls fleeing Islam, no group fighting for the rights of Muslim women. When violence is committed in the name of Islam these student activists are silent. Even when Muslims blow up other Muslims who differ in their interpretation of this supposedly peaceful religion; even when children are used as suicide bombers; even when a devout Muslim woman is raped, goes to the authorities, and is sentenced to be *stoned* on the grounds that she has had sex outside of marriage—even then, these students are silent.

There is a problem with Islam, I would tell the Muslim students who hectored me. By ignoring it, you, student or adult, do a disservice to your community. If your goal is to seek the truth, which education is supposed to do, then we cannot deny that a strict interpretation of Islam is preparation for bigotry, violence, and oppression. You cannot deny that the failure of Muslim societies in the world today to provide peace, prosperity, and opportunities to their inhabitants is linked to these beliefs. Whether your country of origin is Pakistan, Morocco, or Somalia, you are not living there for a reason. Please, embrace what you and your parents bought that airplane ticket to America for: fair justice and a better life, in a place where you can be safe from tyranny, keep the fruits of your labor, and have a say in the running of the country. And if you believe that there should be Shari'a law in America, please, fly back home and take a look at what it's really like.

I would cite the Quran, chapter and verse, where it specifically mandates unequal and cruel treatment of women. For instance, chapter 4, verse 34 instructs men to beat the women from whom they fear possible disobedience. In response, some would become angry and shout that other religions also have passages in their holy books that are not friendly to women. Others argued, absurdly, that beating merely referred to a symbolic tap with a tiny stick the size of a toothbrush. Most would soon segue back into their favorite theme: my exceptionally traumatized youth, my vengeful, personal vendetta against all Muslims.

Such encounters with small but vocal antagonists were seldom fun. But every now and then I realized that my arguments were achieving something. Perhaps I was not changing the minds of the self-appointed defenders of Islam, but I was opening the eyes of the majority of non-Muslim students in the audience. Often I glimpsed the horror on their faces as they realized that these veiled and bearded youngsters, with whom for years they had shared cups of coffee, books, and classes, did not share their most basic values.

At one speech at Scripps College, a women's liberal arts school in Claremont, California, the auditorium was packed, and even before my talk ended a long line of Muslim girls began to form in front of the microphone to ask questions. But before anyone could make the first comment, a girl in a headscarf called out from the audience, "WHO THE HELL GIVES YOU THE RIGHT TO TALK ABOUT ISLAM?"

A red-haired kid standing in the line yelled back, "THE FIRST AMENDMENT!"

That was inspiring.

* * *

In March 2008 the *New York Times* ran a piece headlined "Resolute or Fearful, Many Muslims Turn to Home Schooling." I read, appalled, that 40 percent of Pakistani and Southeast Asian families in the Lodi district east of San Francisco have opted for home schooling for their daughters. Many possible reasons for this decision were listed in the article: so that Muslim children will not be teased or mocked, exposed to pork, "corrupted" by American influences—but mainly so that the girls do not engage in behaviors that would "dishonor" their families and render them unsuitable for marriage.

Smiling, Vermeer-like photos of young girls in veils, reading and playing with their yo-yos, softened the shock that this information might otherwise elicit. But why should American citizens or future American citizens be taught that girls must cover their hair and even their faces? That boys and men are entitled to boss girls around? That loyalty to another, higher law is more important than loyalty to the U.S. Constitution? That a minimal education and an arranged marriage to your cousin is all that a female American Muslim needs? Why live in the United States if you want to keep girls culturally illiterate?

It is important to remember that Muslim schools are different from so-called regular Christian or Jewish schools. By "regular" I mean schools that are Christian or Jewish in identity but have secular curricula. Muslim schools, by contrast, are more or less like madrassas, which emphasize religion more than any other subject. Students are taught to distance themselves from science and the values of freedom, individual responsibility, and tolerance. The establishment of a Muslim school anywhere in the world, but especially in the West, gives Wahabis and other wealthy Muslim extremists an opportunity to isolate and indoctrinate vulnerable groups of children.

When I was growing up in Kenya, my best friend, Amira, was from a Yemeni family. They lived in Nairobi as if they were still in Yemen. Although Amira was at least permitted to attend school—a Muslim school—she had to marry a man from Yemen who couldn't read or write and showed absolutely no respect for her. Her cousin Muna was spectacularly smart—when she was eleven she ranked seventh in a nationwide exam—but when she was fifteen she was married to a pudgy man twice her age who took her away with him to Saudi Arabia.

Amira and Muna, like so many Muslim girls, were seen by their families as little more than incubators for sons. They had no intrinsic value and few choices. That is what lies behind the soft-focus photograph of those three little girls in *jilbabs* on their sofa in America.

Today most Muslims in America are unquestionably different from most Muslims who live in Europe. Because they come mainly through airports, and thus have visas, they have undergone a kind of preselection process based on their educational level, their prosperity, and their language skills. In America this process is far more critical, more attentive to an immigrant's skills and the benefits he will bring to the host country, than in Europe, where the focus is on the benefits the immigrant will gain. Because of simple geographical proximity, Muslims in Europe may arrive illegally and in any case almost always cheaply, looking for menial jobs. This difference doesn't necessarily keep Muslim girls from being oppressed in America, but it does mean that Muslims here are more likely to be middle-class, English-speaking professionals who have made a conscious choice to assimilate some basic American values.

In the United States, because visa requirements are so strict, it is much harder for a male immigrant to later bring in a new bride from his home country, as is commonly done in Europe. So the constant importing of docile, fresh brides from the distant countryside of Morocco or Turkey is less flagrant than in Europe. American Muslims marry other American Muslims; this is another reason why Muslim women's position is better here.

Veiled schoolgirls are one very evident marker of the rise of revivalist, purist Islam, however. They are much less numerous in America than they are in most European cities, but their numbers are visibly growing. And it is now a common sight to see young women in full-length dresses or robes and heavy headscarves, often pushing strollers, in the streets of American cities. The increase in the number of Muslims (whether they are tourists, American residents, or citizens) determined to display their piety is both a measure of their conviction and a measure of growing attempts at social control of those Muslim women who might easily be distracted from the straight path. As more immigrants come to the United States from Muslim countries, they maintain enclaves of tradition that are far stronger than those of other, comparable immigrant groups. And as more *dawa,* missionary work, is done by revivalist groups financed by Saudi Arabia, Muslims in America are becoming much more hard-line.

Probably half the mosques in America have received Saudi money, and many (perhaps most) teachers and preachers of Islam have been supported by Saudi charities such as the Muslim World League. Through the Islamic Society of North America, Muslim student associations, the Islamic Circle of North America, and the Saudi-sponsored World Muslim League, the Saudis have financed summer camps for children, institutes for training imams, the distribution of Islamic literature, mosque building, lectures, and *dawa* work throughout the United States. According to a survey by the Muslim lobby Council on American-Islamic Relations, 33 percent of the mosques in America do not permit women on their governing boards and 66 percent seclude women behind a wall, where they can listen to the sermon through loudspeakers but cannot see the imam speaking. That last figure has actually *risen* since 1994, when it was "only" 54 percent.

I believe it would be a grave mistake to be complacent about Islam in America. According to the Mosque Study Project 2000, regular weekly attendance at mosques almost doubled between 1994 and 2000, and active association with mosques quadrupled. Young Muslims born or raised in the United States are often much more observant of Islamic practice than their parents are. In the United States 50 percent of Muslims age eighteen to twenty-nine say they attend a mosque every week, far more often than the older generations.

And the poll didn't mention what *kind* of mosque. I suspect that, just as I once succumbed to radical Islam when I was a teenager in Kenya, young Muslims in America are drawn to preachers who are young, attractive, intelligent, who seem to echo their sense of being misunderstood outsiders, who give them a shot of self-esteem and the sense of a special purpose in life. They reject their grandparents' Islam of *jinn* and mumbling imams, more folk tradition than quranic dogma, and seek the imagined intellectual purity of the Prophet's true path. At college they join Muslim students associations, which transcend ethnic differences. They are far more likely to worship in an ethnically mixed mosque, one that is not just a kind of cultural club, but that joins together young Somalis and Pakistanis and Yemenis under the banner of the Prophet.

Europeans ignored a similar trend for decades, and young Muslim citizens of Europe were steadily radicalized without any concerted attempt to persuade them into less toxic attitudes. Now they are almost a fifth column.

Can you be a Muslim and an American patriot? You can if you don't care very much about being a Muslim. If you squint and look away, you can avoid thinking about the very basic clashes between the submissive, collectivist values of Islam and the individualist, libertarian values of the democratic West. In a 2007 poll by the Pew Center, 63 percent of U.S. Muslims said they saw no conflict between being a devout Muslim and living in a modern society. But 32 percent conceded that, yes, there is such a conflict, and almost 50 percent of the Muslim Americans questioned in that poll said they think of themselves as Muslims first, Americans second. Only 28 percent, little more than a quarter, considered themselves Americans first.

Asked whether suicide bombing can be justified as a measure to defend Islam, 26 percent of American Muslims age eighteen to twenty-nine said yes. That is one quarter of the adult American Muslims under the age of thirty, and no matter how you count the number of Muslims in America (estimates vary from 2 million to 8 million), that is a lot of people.

We are still at an early stage in the radicalization of Muslim youth in America, but the first symptoms of the disorder are already manifesting themselves, just as they did in Europe. There have already been numerous reports of young American Muslims—many of them Somali, others converts—leaving the United States for training in violent jihad abroad. For example, at least two dozen Somali youths from Minnesota are said to have gone to Somalia to fight in the civil war there. Nothing illustrates more clearly my point that the threat posed by radical Islam is both internal and external.

On a few occasions I was invited to speak at offices of the U.S. government about cultural aspects of Islam, what military people call "cultural intelligence." My questioners wanted to know more about Muslim customs and habits to be able to distinguish traditional and harmless customs from the new practices of politicized Muslims, so they could detect where something dangerous to U.S. interests might be brewing.

They asked me a lot about my teenage years. When I was sixteen my religious studies teacher in Nairobi, Sister Aziza, began encouraging me and my schoolmates to reject our grandmothers' Islam of amulets and superstitious prayers to our forefathers. She introduced us to a literal interpretation of the Quran. Sister Aziza persuaded us to wear the veil and to seek to emulate in all matters the original intention and behavior of the Prophet Muhammad and his followers. The Pentagon wanted to know more about how this movement affected the people around me, how they changed from "normal Muslims" into *politically active* Muslims, actively hostile toward Jews and the West. These military analysts were interested not just in jihadi combatants but also in the process that radicalizes whole communities so that they will aid, abet, support, and accommodate jihadi attackers.

First, I told them how mosques have changed. In the old-style mosques in Nairobi—in Eastleigh, in Juja Road, in Park Road—only men attended and the sermon was chanted once a week in Arabic, which almost no one understood, in a monotonous, almost soporific tone. In the 1980s a new kind of worshipper and teacher infiltrated those old-style mosques and set up new mosques in living rooms and basements. Sermons were not limited to Fridays, and study groups were set up for young people, where we read and analyzed the Quran and the Hadith. The tone of the sermons became shrill and loud, with a revivalist edge and dramatic climaxes and whispers. And their content was political. The vocabulary of the sermons changed; the new imams would shout out words like *Yahud* (Jew), *kaffir* (unbeliever), and *munafirq* (hypocrite), by which they meant Muslims who did not agree with them.

I described a visit I made to Cyprus as a member of the Dutch Parliament in 2006. We visited the office of Archbishop Chrysostomos. Right next door there was a mosque, and hearing these words shouted during the sermon, I knew it was not a "normal," traditional imam who preached there but a political, radicalized Muslim teacher. When

I said this to the archbishop, he sighed and told me that the change had happened years ago. Before that, he said, the sermons were a peaceful drone, but afterward the tone became louder and more hostile.

Another feature of a revivalist mosque, I explained, is that women, who almost never attended the old mosques, now flock there. When I was growing up, women's presence was neither necessary nor particularly desirable, unless it was a special day, such as the Eid festival after Ramadan. But in radical mosques special classes involve women in the lesser and greater jihads for the glory of the Prophet. If you see women flocking to the mosque to pray, perhaps you should be suspicious.

The U.S. government officials to whom I spoke wanted to analyze how Islam is used as a political tool to mobilize masses of young men to do harm; they wanted to understand how proselytizing, *dawa,* operates. Their hope was that I could help them to distinguish a peaceful, regular practice of Islam from something more harmful. It was the same kind of question I had heard in Europe many times before: How do people cross that line? How can you tell when they have done so?

My answer was that they should stop focusing so exclusively on the action of a few proselytizing radicals. By this I don't mean they should no longer pay attention to radical individuals who are preaching Islamism. I mean that, in trying to understand why so many young Muslims are susceptible to the persuasions of the radical agents one must first study the content, the context, and the methods by which almost all Muslims are reared to become practicing Muslims: the agent utilizes an existing memory, reawakens the recollections of the classes from early childhood. At first he or she reinforces those memories, then moves on to the next stage of politicization, and only later violence or martyrdom.

If you are a Muslim, from the time you are born your mind is prepared. You are instructed to submit, not to question. Then, when preachers speak to you about returning to the pure, true path of jihad and personal morality laid down by the Prophet Muhammad, they're not introducing you to something new or alien. They're building on layers of a mental structure that you have imbibed from your parents, your community, your childhood Quran teacher. Thus the stage preceding radicalization in the Muslim mind, the stage when "regular" Islam is taught, is very important. Although the teachings are at first focused on prayer, charity, and fasting, the method by which Muslims learn is rote, and believers are not allowed to question the text or the sayings of Muhammad. After years of an uncritical attitude toward Islamic teachings in general and a demand for obedience, the Muslim mind is ready, prepared when the radical agent shows up. Moreover the mechanism of reward and punishment in Islamic teaching, reinforced by the tribal demand for unquestioning loyalty to the group, makes it difficult for an individual Muslim to resist or even recognize the radical agent as suspect.

All who are concerned with the relative ease with which young Muslims follow the radicals must focus on these preceding stages. Because most politicians and academic researchers define Islam as a harmless religion and view the radicals as deviant, they overlook the importance of delving into the socialization process of the Muslim.

American agencies and academics and social psychologists make a big mistake when they try to understand a brainwashed mind only from the time it becomes radical. Radical Islam is sold in steps, and this is true in America too. At first it is marketed as a program for virtuous behavior, for goodness. Then you are encouraged to seek out other Muslims, to befriend only each other. The whole rancid subject of violent jihad is broached only in the later stages. But the prehistory of radicalism is a soft brainwashing in *submission*—the real meaning of the word *Islam*—from birth.

In early November 2009 I was in New York for a series of meetings. It was exactly five years since the murder of my friend Theo van Gogh by a jihadi youth in Amsterdam. On Thursday of that week I was on my way from a lunchtime meeting when the news came through on the car radio of a shooting at an army base in Texas. American soldiers had been killed in America. There was confusion about the killer's identity: Was he a psychiatrist or a psychiatric patient? Was he killed or still alive? I was intrigued by the combination of his name, Nidal Malik Hassan, and his military rank of major.

As soon as I was done with my meetings I hurried to go online, eager for more details of the story. The television reports I saw clarified a good deal. The killer had been captured and was in the hospital;

he was a psychiatrist and not a mental patient; the number of victims was thirteen. As I watched the clips I couldn't help thinking, *Islamic martyrdom has come to America.* Not only that, but it has penetrated the U.S. military itself.

The story of Nidal Malik Hassan is in many ways similar to that of Mohammed Bouyeri, the murderer of Theo van Gogh. There are also some glaring differences, to be sure. Bouyeri was born in Amsterdam; his father had moved from Morocco to the Netherlands as a guest worker, initially intending to go back home after he earned enough money. Morocco is a poor country but relatively peaceful. Malik Hassan, by contrast, was born in the United States to parents of Palestinian origin, who settled in Virginia and opened a restaurant. The Palestinian territories are in perpetual war, and families are exposed to the upheaval of that war. Malik Hassan's parents had chosen to begin a new life in America and to become Americans.

Bouyeri was only twenty-six when he embarked on his martyrdom mission, while Malik Hassan was thirty-nine. This difference is interesting because it challenges the well-accepted theory that men of Malik Hassan's age are more likely to enable a suicide mission than to take action themselves. Bouyeri's career did not go beyond demanding a government subsidy for a community center where he volunteered, while Malik Hassan made it all the way to the rank of major and earned a degree in psychiatry. Malik Hassan killed thirteen people; Bouyeri poured all his homicidal passion into killing just one man, though he also declared his intention to kill me.

The similarities, however, were uncanny. Both men were introduced to radical Islam not in a Muslim country (Morocco or the Palestinian Territories or Jordan) but in secular democracies: America and the Netherlands. Both came to detest their home nation, to the extent that they wanted to kill their fellow citizens. Both invoked the name of Allah as they killed and said that they were motivated to kill as a service to Allah. Both thought they would be killed in the process and become *shaheed,* or martyrs. But both men woke up in hospitals in the hands of the infidel. One is now in a Dutch prison for the rest of his life, and the other will likely end up on death row.

An even more striking similarity between the two is the astonishing reaction to the incidents in both the Dutch media in 2004 and the American media in 2009—astonishing because it seemed as if all explanations were plausible except the one explicitly stated by the killer, namely his religion.

In both countries the murderers were presented as being fed up with offensive discriminatory behavior. Bouyeri was said to have been compelled to act by Theo van Gogh's reference to Moroccan youth as "goat fuckers." In America a similar significance was attached to the military slang terms for Arabs in Iraq, such as "camel jockeys." In both countries analysts sought answers in the psychological imbalance of the killers. Serious meaning was attached to the fact that just days before Bouyeri committed the murder his mother had passed away of natural causes; the shock and grief he felt at her death were seen as possible motivations to kill van Gogh. Similarly, in the case of Malik Hassan, allusions were made to posttraumatic stress due to combat, until it emerged that he had not been anywhere near combat.

In both countries the debate then turned to whose fault it was that the murderer was not prevented from killing. In Holland the Dutch Intelligence and Security Agency was investigating a radical Islamic cell called the Hofstad Group, but the investigators overlooked Bouyeri's role in that group. It transpired only after the murder that he was in fact the leader. In America there was information that the FBI had intercepted e-mails between Malik Hassan and his mentor, Imam Al Awlaki, but no action had been taken.

Why, I asked myself, was there such a conspiracy to ignore the religious motivations for these killings? And then I began to understand. First, there is a desperate need for intelligence agencies to recruit Muslim agents and sources in order to penetrate the radical Islamist networks. As all Muslims are offended by the charge that Islam is a violent religion, it is official policy not to say so. The same applies to the military: American and allied soldiers do not go into places like Iraq and Afghanistan simply to fight men in uniform whom they can easily identify as the enemy. Their mission is now a complex mixture of fighting, policing, social work, and "nation building." They too are in desperate need of cooperation from the locals, and that overwhelmingly means Muslims. Thus the military takes the same line as the intelligence services: It is not Islamic scripture, the Prophet, or the Quran that presents a coherent argument and activism for jihad, but a misguided few who have usurped the pure and peaceful teachings of Islam.

On the Thursday after the shooting I was catching a flight from New York to Boston. The TV screens at the departure gate were dominated by the image of Nidal Malik Hassan. A woman sitting next to me was staring at the screen.

"Are you worried about terrorism?" I asked.

"I am," she replied, "but this is America they are messing with, and they won't succeed."

"But he was in the military," I said, "an enemy from within."

She fidgeted a little and then gave me a line that I would have expected to hear from a policymaker. "We cherish our diversity in this country," she told me just before we were interrupted by the call to board the aircraft.

Diversity is a wonderful concept, I thought, and *E pluribus unum,* "Out of many, one," is one of the mottos proudly displayed on the Great Seal of the United States (and therefore on every dollar bill). But Americans still have a long way to go before they really understand the challenge posed to their country by radical Islam, a religion that rejects not only those core principles of the Enlightenment that so inspired the founding fathers, but also the very notion that the diverse many should become one united people.

PART III

———◆———

SEX, MONEY, VIOLENCE

CHAPTER 11

School and Sexuality

When I was about five years old, my grandmother would wake me up in the morning, sometimes by prodding me with a stick, other times by yelling out my name. Her aim was to teach me to light the morning fire and make tea for the adults. "Wake up!" she would yell. "At your age my daughters would be milking goats and taking them out to the fields, and you can't even wake up!"

So I would make the fire. I would sleepwalk to the charcoal brazier, which was in a room that my mother had more or less arbitrarily deemed to be the kitchen. With the door and shutters open, the early morning daylight spilled into the room, whose walls were black with soot. I would take my wooden stool and carry it to the stone stove, which was knee-high, shaped like an hourglass, and the size of a large cooking pot. The lower part of the hourglass held the stove up, while the upper part contained a mound of ash, buried in which were burning embers from the night before. My grandmother taught me how to dig out the embers using a pair of metal tongs and a metal dustpan.

She would hover over me, urging me to work quickly, for the longer it took for me to find and pile up the embers, the sooner they died. When there were no more burning embers I would carry the brazier a few feet out of the kitchen and throw out most of the ash. Then I would return it to its corner, flatten out the remaining ash, put some of the burning embers on top of the mound, fill the brazier up with charcoal, and put the remaining burning embers on top. Then I would fan the fire and blow into it. Because it had no chimney or window, the brazier was very hard to light, which is why Grandma would scream that I should be quick before the embers died. I would then pick up an aluminum kettle, fill it with water, balance it precariously on three points of the brazier, and continue blowing and fanning until the water boiled.

As the water came to a boil, I would pick up a packet of Lipton English Breakfast tea and put a scoop of tea leaves into the boiling kettle. Very often the kettle would boil over and kill the fire that I had had such difficulty lighting. The entire time, Grandmother would be cursing and spitting on me for my incompetence. Often she would take over for fear that I would kill the fire or spoil the tea. In fact I was so afraid that the kettle would boil over and kill the fire that I often would put the tea leaves in too soon and spoil the tea.

Grandmother could have done all this on her own, but she was convinced that the oldest daughter should master the skill of making breakfast before she turned six.

Once I was more or less competent at boiling water, Grandmother taught me to milk her goat. First she demonstrated: she leashed the goat and put a wooden stool right behind it, parted its legs, put a bucket underneath its udders, and started pulling at them. But when I first sat on the stool and reached for the udders, the goat kicked me on my forehead, knocking me off the stool. Every day it kicked me again and again, until I had bruises everywhere, including on my bottom, from falling over. On some mornings I refused to go near the goat. Grandmother would pull and prod me and even slap me sometimes, but even that was much more bearable than a kick from that animal.

This was a form of education in subservience. Grandma continually lamented the loss of our nomadic way of life—our soul, as she saw it—and that our culture had begun to give way to a new, decadent way of life. She tried to salvage what she could by making me live according to her wisdom; thus I was required to master all the skills of becoming a good wife. To her, the fact that I cried when the goat hit me, that I made a mess when I tried to light the fire, or that she had a hard time pulling me out of bed were all signs of my corruption, an indication that I was destined for ruin. "Who will ever marry this girl when she becomes a woman?" she would lament. "Ayaan is useless."

All the little girls I knew in Mogadishu had to learn these skills. When we lived in Saudi Arabia, even though the Saudi girls who were our neighbors had servants working for them, they too had to learn to cook. In Ethiopia the Somali girls and women were continuously cooking, cleaning, washing, and otherwise serving. When we moved to Kenya, I was glad to find that the charcoal braziers there were different; they were easier to light and were made of metal and had windows, so I did not have to blow as much. Also, by then I was stronger and more able to snatch the kettle off just before it boiled over, without burning myself or extinguishing the fire.

Sometimes I thought life was hard on me, but then I would look at the experience of girls like Ubah, an orphan who lived in one of the houses on our block in Nairobi. Ubah had been brought to Nairobi from Somalia to live with her aunt, who was pregnant every year and worked Ubah like a slave. Ubah had to sleep on a thin mat in the kitchen that was black with soot from cooking and covered in food stains. She seemed to have only one dress, which was full of holes. All day long Ubah looked after the children, did the heavy grocery shopping, washed mountains of cloth diapers, and was yelled at throughout. My mother and grandmother never tired of reminding me of Ubah's circumstances. "Look! You live in enormous luxury compared to Ubah," they would point out. "Ubah is a slave because she is not with her mother. You are well cared for." More important, I went to school and Ubah did not.

Whenever I hear Westerners today say "Education is the answer," I need only think back to that time to recognize the absolute truth of this statement. The women of the neighborhood would get together and complain that school was corrupting young girls like me and making us rebellious. They saw that Ubah and others who did not attend school simply obeyed. These girls were so accustomed to subservience that they never questioned their status. On a few occasions I caught Ubah trying to stifle the sound of her sobs, because even crying was considered to be a form of protest. The Somali men would also complain, "It's because they go to school that they now talk back to us. It's because they go to school that they are now making all of these demands, trampling on tradition and ignoring religion."

Some girls were pulled out of school just after their first menstruation and kept at home to keep them obedient, or they were forced into early marriages. But for those of us who stayed in school, it was true that education did give us a voice and an awareness of the world outside. My sister Haweya and I spoke to one another in English or

Swahili; both languages were foreign to my mother and grandmother. It gave us power over them that they had not had over their parents.

We also learned something else in our Kenyan schools that girls like Ubah did not learn: sex education. It was nowhere near as open and graphic as that which I later encountered in Holland, but it was enough to intimidate my mom.

Sex education was embedded in our biology book. Actually my teacher, Mrs. Karim, tried to skip the chapter. But like my friends, I skimmed the pages on amoebae, protozoa, and the reproduction of single-celled organisms and went straight to human procreation and the diagrams of fallopian tubes and the uterus, as well as testicles and the penis. It was very scientific, but even so most of the mechanics of sex remained a mystery. Still, at least with this information we began to understand why we were being told to avoid men and the basics of how our bodies worked. Again, this gave us some relative power over our parents. My mother refused to talk about these things and hit me when I first got my period. She hit me out of pure helplessness, for she herself had never been armed with this understanding of how the body functioned, and she feared that my very basic grasp of the simple facts had already in some mysterious way corrupted me.

Like my grandmother, the other Muslim women in my life, mothers of my classmates and of other Somali girls in my neighborhood, felt that the best strategy was to keep girls at home, to cover them, to circumcise them, and, if the girls rebelled too much, to engage their brothers and fathers and even cousins to punish them. These punishments varied from thrashings to forced marriages. We also heard stories of girls who were killed by their families.

Long ago, in the desert, nomads in clan societies bound themselves together by family ties, through old lineages that gave them protection and assistance across great distances. Outside the clan lineage lay danger and chaos, every man for himself. In a clan society, every kind of human relationship turns on your honor within the clan; outside it, there is nothing—you are excluded from any kind of meaningful existence. This was the most precious lesson that Grandma tried to teach her grandchildren.

A man's honor within a clan society—and these societies are, largely, about men—resides in his authority. Men must be warriors; shame consists in being seen as weak. Women are the breeders of men, and women's honor lies in their purity, their submission, their obedience. Their shame is to be sexually impure, and it is the worst shame of all, because a woman's sexual disobedience defiles herself, her sisters, and her mother, as well as the male relatives whose duty it is to control her.

No Muslim man has any standing in society if he does not have honor. And no matter how much honor he builds up through wise decisions and good deeds, it is destroyed if his daughter or his sister is sexually defiled. This can happen if she loses her virginity before she's married, or if she engages in sexual intercourse outside of the marriage—and that includes rape. Even the *rumor* that she may have had sex is reason enough to label her "defiled" and lead to loss of honor for her whole family. A father who cannot control his daughters, a brother who cannot control his sisters, is disgraced. He is bankrupt socially and even economically. His family is ruined. The girl will not fetch a bride-price, and neither will her sisters or her cousins, because the mere suspicion of independent feeling and female action in their family taints them too. Such a man suffers a social death, exclusion from the mutual assistance and respect of the clan—the worst possible fate that could befall a person, whether child or adult, male or female.

Controlling women's sexuality and limiting men's access to sex with women are the central focus of the code of honor and shame. Muslim women are chattel, and every Muslim girl must be a virgin at marriage. Once wed (with or without her consent), she must be faithful to her husband, who, in traditional societies, she will never refer to by his first name but only as *rajel,* my lord. In case of divorce or widowhood, the job of monitoring her sexual activities is assumed by her new guardians: her sons, if they are adults, or her husband's father and his male bloodline. These men may select a new husband for her. Few Muslim women are ever free to choose whom they will have sex with.

An element as powerful and potent as a Muslim girl's virginity also has great commodity value, which means that virginity is above all a man's business. Daughters are bait for attracting alliances, or they can be reserved for the highest bidder. Power, wealth, and the solidifying of clan relations may hinge on marriage alliances, so raising daughters of quality who are modest and docile is important. Using violence to ensure their obedience and to warn them against straying is a perfectly legitimate reminder of the law in a system of values in which women have only a little more free will than livestock. There must be blood on the wedding night from her broken hymen or she will be condemned as a slut.

This ancient code of sexual morality is derived from tribal Arab culture. It dates from long before the Prophet Muhammad began receiving revelations from the Angel Gabriel, which were written down by his disciples on pages that have long since become dust. At that time, in that place—the desert towns of Mecca and Medina, whose distant tribes worshipped many different idols and gods—honor and shame were the central ideas that governed life between men and women. Islam cemented this into an everlasting rule. As Islam grew and spread, it brought its sexual mores to other countries, from Mali to Indonesia. Under Shari'a, a Muslim woman is effectively the property of her father, brothers, uncles, grandfathers. These men are her guardians, responsible for her behavior, in charge of her choices. Above all, she must remain sexually pure.

An inextricable mass of traditional dictates and rituals has been incorporated into Islam, and it is being further amplified by the Islamic revivalist movements that are sweeping through the Muslim world today. The fundamentalists seem haunted by the female body and neurotically debate which fractions of it should be covered, until they declare the whole thing, from head to toe, a gigantic private part.

When and why did Arab, and subsequently Muslim, societies become so obsessed with controlling women's sexuality? Perhaps there was once some logic to it. For a tribe to be strong, its warriors need to be loyal to each other. Maybe independent female sexuality undermined that. Maybe fighting over women was even more divisive to a male society than fighting over camels, and so, once upon a time in the desert, it was resolved to control the women, to confine them to their homes, banishing them from the public sphere, or to veil them so they became invisible, to cut their genitals to limit their sexual desire and sew them shut to make sex unbearably painful.

Grandma did not busy herself with such questions. She understood only that we had to follow the rules as if our lives depended on it—as, perhaps, her own life once had. She explained and enforced that code in our household. As she never tired of saying, "All I am trying to teach you is to survive."

Even today virginity is the linchpin of a Muslim girl's education. Growing up, I was taught that it is more important to remain a virgin than it is to stay alive, better to die than be raped. Sex before marriage is an unthinkable crime. Every Muslim girl knows that her value relies almost wholly on her hymen, the most essential part of her body, far more important than her brain or limbs.

Once the hymen is broken, a girl is a thing used, broken, filthy, her filth contagious. This is how my cousin Hiran felt about herself when she succumbed to desire and then was diagnosed with HIV. This is how Ladan felt about herself and how she lost her self-esteem. She saw herself through the eyes of those closest to her, people like my grandma, and those old ghosts seemed to blame her and scream at her, "Whore!"

Muslim cultures have evolved various means to police and guarantee women's virginity. Many confine their women, depriving themselves of their labor outside the home, and monitor their movements obsessively. This constant whisper of gossip, the continual surveillance of every untoward gesture and raised eye, is also a form of confinement, strangling every movement. When a woman leaves the house, she veils, another form of confinement: every breath of air you take outside your four walls is stifled by a thick, heavy cloth; every stride is hobbled, every centimeter of skin enclosed from the sun. Even out of doors a veiled woman is inside all the time. The air she breathes is stuffy; thick material presses against her eyes, her nose, and her mouth. Everything she does is hidden and furtive. Blindfolded and reduced, erased from public contact, Muslim women often lose confidence in their ability to undertake independent action. Even independent *motion* seems strange. Every woman who has worn such a veil for years and then taken it off will attest that it is difficult to walk at first. It is as if, uncovered, your legs do not work the same way.

After a girl first menstruates, she must have as little contact as possible with men outside the immediate family. In Saudi Arabia women are shut in their homes by law; this is not the case in other countries, but confinement is still common everywhere that there are Muslims. Even after they are married many Arab women are not permitted contact with an unrelated male. It is an offense even to look a man in the eye.

Other societies, too poor to do without their women's labor out of doors, must police their chastity by other means: it must be built into their bodies. This may be the origin of female excision, the only possible incontrovertible proof of virginity. And chastity must be built into their minds. Victims of rape do not report it if they survive it; unmarried women who get pregnant are banished or put to death. Too often girls take their own lives after losing their virginity in a way deemed to be illicit.

Although Muslim doctrine has certainly amplified and confirmed this attitude, the tight web of restrictions on women that characterizes Arab and Muslim clans goes back further than Wahabi Islam, the most common school of Islam in Saudi Arabia. The very word *harem,* the section of the house where the women dwell (in Arabic, *hareem*), is derived from *haram,* forbidden. In most Muslim cultures people still retain memories of the old, pre-Islamic beliefs in *jinn* and ghouls. (This is sharply disapproved of by most Islamic purists, who believe it raises the possibility of deities other than Allah.) Those ghouls are most often withered old women or sexually voracious young women, who inspire fear and disgust in equal measure. Defiled every month by menstruation, the female is naturally closer to evil.

When I worked as a Somali-Dutch translator in Holland, I was often called upon in cases where parents reacted violently to the Westernization of their teenage Somali daughters. I remember one girl at the child protection office close to the city of The Hague. She was about sixteen but looked twenty-five. Her hair had been straightened and colored with red and brown highlights. Her nails were extremely long, curled, and painted in shimmering green. She wore the tightest possible tank top with the lowest possible cleavage and a black skirt that was so short her underwear was visible when she crossed her legs, which were clad in red fishnet stockings and high-heeled ankle boots.

Her father had to be physically restrained so that he would not hit her. He kept screaming, "She looks like a whore! Look at her mouth!

It looks like she fell on the throat of a slaughtered lamb! She has killed me, this girl has killed me!" This was, at least metaphorically, true. I knew that with such a daughter, he was now socially dead to his clan; he had become a thing of mockery and pity. He could leave his house or enter public places only with a bowed head and gritted teeth. But his daughter shrugged in response, waving her hands dismissively.

The Dutch social worker said to the father, "This is what we call self-expression. Your daughter is not doing anything unusual for her age." The girl's mother claimed that her child was possessed, so the social worker added sensitively, "We have done psychological tests on her. She is not mad."

This particular scene ended with the girl being put in a foster home. It was a common conclusion and a very common scenario, not only for me but also for my colleagues who translated between Dutch and Arabic, Turkish, Berber, and Persian. All of us worked a great deal with the child protection services, the police, and other institutions that dealt with Muslim teenage girls who fled their homes because their parents and community would not accept their experimentation with what they interpreted as Western culture.

Later on, when I entered politics and when practices such as honor killings and forced marriages had become public knowledge in the Netherlands, I would often debate with Muslim parents who pleaded with me to understand their perspective. They claimed that Muslim girls dropped out of school so often not because they were forced into marriage, but because they were lured by "lover boys" into prostitution. They argued that child protection agencies could not replace family, because only parents could teach children the difference between right and wrong. At Dutch schools, they said, their children had learned only sin and disobedience. Dutch schools also discouraged them from learning because of their atmosphere of hostility to Islam and discrimination against Muslims, and this was why Muslim students did so poorly and dropped out so often. The solution, these parents reasoned, was to establish Muslim schools so that girls could get an education without learning to disobey.

They were right about the high dropout rate for children from Muslim immigrant families and their often very low success rate in exams. But I didn't think the cause of all this was Dutch discrimination. I thought it lay with the parents' not having properly prepared their children for modern education in a modern country.

Like my mother and my aunts, these immigrants had refused to give their daughters sex education, to talk to them about how their bodies were changing, or to tell them that it was natural to be interested in boys. Unlike Dutch parents, they could not bring themselves to teach their daughters that self-expression is fine but that it has boundaries, so that their daughters might find ways to express themselves without flashing their genitals. They had not taught them how to gradually manage the challenges of independence. And, perhaps just as important, they had not taught their sons respect for women— and in Dutch schools most of their teachers were women.

I didn't think there was anything wrong with Dutch schools, which didn't seem to be preparing *Dutch* girls for lives of debauchery and prostitution. On the contrary, most Dutch teenage girls I knew seemed to be just fine, well on their way to becoming self-reliant, productive, law-abiding citizens, with good humor and grace. But the Muslim parents I spoke to did not agree with me. Often they focused on the sex education classes in Dutch schools. These were not classes on how to understand your sexuality and your body, they insisted; they taught you how to have sex. Teachers would place a large wooden or plastic penis on the table, in front of their daughters, and demonstrate how to cover it with a condom. This was abominable, an invitation to prostitution.

I had not been to schools where they taught sex education, but I had been to asylum-seeker centers where there were programs on hygiene, sex education, pregnancy, prenatal education, and more. I had seen how graphic the Dutch can be, and I had become accustomed to the bluntness with which the Dutch address sexual matters. When the children of my Dutch friends went to their parents to ask about sex—something that floored me at first, considering how unlikely it was that I would have done such a thing—my friends patiently and without panic described sex to the curious child, in detail, using books with very explicit pictures of the body.

Dutch parents approached drugs and alcohol the same way. When a young child asked, "Mom, what's a joint?," his mother would explain what a marijuana cigarette looked like, how it was made, and what it did to your brain. She would talk about the junkies on the side-walk. All this education didn't stop some kids from experimenting with drugs or becoming accidentally pregnant, but the majority of the Dutch population has developed an extraordinarily healthy approach to sex, drugs, and alcohol.

I grew convinced that this calm and very explicit education on the possible dangers of freedom was far more effective in preventing disaster than the mystification that I had been brought up with. This isn't just some biased opinion I developed; it has been empirically proven. The benefit of an enlightened approach to sex and drugs was something that the Dutch never tired of explaining. My colleagues in Parliament, whose responsibility it was to make health care universal, dependable, and affordable, were unanimous in their conviction that prevention was always better than cure.

The spokesperson on health for my political party showed me the number of cases of sexually transmitted diseases, such as AIDS, and which populations they most affected. The gay community was hit hard; so were immigrants. Within the gay community, those who were immigrants were hit the hardest. We looked also at the number of abortions performed every year. The number of native Dutch women who had abortions was declining steeply, except in small pockets of radical Christian communities, whose attitude toward sexuality is somewhat comparable to that of many Muslims. (Although these Christians prohibit both men and women from having sex before marriage, many accidental pregnancies occur and the women have to sneak off to abortion clinics.) The number of immigrant women and young girls having abortions was rising sharply.

Drug usage had a comparable pattern, and in Amsterdam's red-light district it was easy to see with one's own eyes that most of the clients of prostitutes were not tourists but immigrant men. Many, if not most of them, were Arab, Berber, Turkish, and Somali. Most statistics just referred to "immigrants" as a broad category, but if you dug deeper you would find that the health care workers, researchers, doctors, and epidemiologists did not want to be on the record in reports in which "immigrant" mostly meant "Muslim." Non-Muslim immigrants from China or Christian parts of Africa were affected too, but Muslims were affected most.

I did not think that this was just a coincidence. Generally, wherever sexuality is a mystery, where sex and drugs are walled off as unspeakable subjects, people tend to abuse both excessively. Like my cousin Hiran, who became HIV-positive, they cannot face up to what it is they are doing and thus fail to protect themselves from the terrible consequences. For women in Arab Islamic cultures it is a matter of honor, something to boast about, to be able to say, "I do not know anything about matters of sex." Because to know even the most elementary thing is tantamount to sinning.

Muslim parents in Europe are justified in worrying about the future of their children, but for the wrong reasons. They are adamant in their conviction that their own way of life has nothing to do with the terrible fates that they fear for their offspring. They are unwilling to consider changing their views and will not question their insistence on virginity until marriage, their insistence on separating boys and girls and on keeping girls dependent and ignorant, and their penchant for forcing girls into early, arranged marriages and harsh punishments. It is easier for them to blame outsiders than to question the Quran, the example of the Prophet, and long tradition. From their perspective the best strategy is to stifle their daughters' voices, school them in subservience, confine them to their homes, and marry them off as early as possible. This may not make their daughters happy, but family honor is more important than the happiness of children.

I believe that the subjection of women within Islam is the biggest obstacle to the integration and progress of Muslim communities in the West. It is a subjection committed by the closest kin in the most intimate place, the home, and it is sanctioned by the greatest figure in the imagination of Muslims: Allah himself.

Many Muslim parents believe that a Western education corrupts the Muslim way of life. In truth, it does. The education of girls in independent thought *is* a challenge to Islamic teaching, just as it once was a challenge to Christian teaching and Orthodox Jewish teaching. A program of sustained education in curiosity and independent thought is a program of sustained erosion of the Muslim way of life. Developing this program will take a long time in Muslim countries. For Muslims in Western countries, it may not take as long.

We can take hope from the example of other societies. Christianity too once made a magical totem of female virginity. Girls were confined, deprived of education, married off as property. And yet Christian societies today are largely free of this habit of mind. Cultures shift, often very rapidly. They do this under the influence of critical thought, and this can be taught in school.

It is easy to be disgruntled if you are denied rights and freedoms to which you feel entitled. But if you are not coherent, if you cannot put into words what it is that displeases you and why it is unfair and should change, then you are dismissed as an unreasonable whiner. You may be lectured about perseverance and patience, life as a test, the need to accept the higher wisdom of others. This happened to me. When my father decided to marry me to a distant cousin he had just met (and whom I had never seen), he thought he was making a wonderful decision for me. This man, my intended, was a relative (we shared the eighth degree of grandfathers) and thus was less likely to behave abusively (at least this was my father's reasoning); he shared the values of our people (whatever they were) and would keep me safe at a time of civil war and poverty. A match like the one my father found seemed to him to be a blessing.

I, on the other hand, felt that my father had robbed me of my youth and my body, propelling me into the life of a wife and mother—responsibilities I was not ready to assume—alongside a man I found completely repellent. But I did not have the language and logic to persuade my father of the validity of my position. Even though he had sent me to school and I was one of the few Somali girls in my generation who had learned to read and write in English, I didn't have the strength of mind and tongue to muster a coherent argument. The strongest points I could make were that my husband-to-be did not read novels and that he was bald. From my father's perspective, these assertions certified that I needed to be under the authority of someone more reliable and mature.

So I bolted. Only after I had fled and made my way to the University of Leiden, where I took classes steeped in concepts of individual freedom and personal responsibility, was I able to stand up to my father, mind to mind. I managed to articulate to him that by getting a higher education I was only following his example and learning to make my own destiny. To his protests about the disrespect I was showing and my probable erosion of our religion and culture through selfish pursuits, I was able to respond that he himself had paid less attention to such concerns when he was my age. In my conversations with my father in the spring of 2000 in Germany, where I met with him when he was being treated at an eye clinic, I was aware of his grudging respect and maybe even admiration. He was condescending, and he lectured me in his characteristically lightning-fast, long, unstoppable monologues about the hereafter. But he no longer easily dismissed my wishes or protested as he had in 1992.

To resist subjugation and the denial of rights, an expression of resentment and anger are not enough. You must speak the language of the oppressor and have the clarity of mind to identify the principles that justify the oppression and to dismantle them intellectually. Slaves must be aware of the fact that they are slaves, and then transcend anger and pain to convince their master of the wrongfulness of their slavery. If you cannot win by might, you may in the longer term be able to win through an appeal to reason.

Girls like my cousins Hiran and Ladan, who, in a powerful urge for freedom, do manage to shake off the control of their parents often end up in disastrous circumstances because they do not have those vital skills or awareness. Such girls become the examples deployed by traditional Muslim parents when they argue that adopting a Western lifestyle leads to horrific results. Fundamentalists whose agenda is to revive an imagined past of pure Islam win much sympathy from Muslim families when they point to girls like Hiran and Ladan.

If they had grown up in the West, perhaps it could have been different. In all Western countries, laws exist requiring girls to attend school even after they reach the age of puberty; those laws can be enforced. Special programs can be devised to fill the vacuum created by Muslim parents regarding knowledge about sex, drugs, and financial independence. The more Muslim girls do succeed in getting an education, the more likely they are to become financially independent and successful, allowing Muslim parents to see that emancipating their daughters through good schooling is in their material interests, even if it collides with their traditional values.

*   *   *

One final point needs to be made on the subject of the sexual complexes of Muslim immigrants. To claim that the oppression of women has nothing to do with Islam and is "only" a traditional custom is intellectually dishonest, a decoy. The two elements are interwoven. The code of honor and shame may be tribal and pre-Islamic in its origins, but it is now an integral part of the Islamic religion and culture. Honor killing asserts what Islam also asserts: that women are subordinate to men and must remain their sexual property.

In the text of the Quran and in Shari'a law, men and women are self-evidently not equal. Muslim women are considered physically, emotionally, intellectually, and morally inferior to men, and they have fewer legal rights. The Quran decrees that daughters inherit half a son's share: "Allah prescribes with regard to your children: To one of masculine sex falls [in the division of an estate] just as much as to two of the feminine sex" (4:11). The value of their testimony in a court of law is fixed as half that of a man's. Even in the case of rape, the victim's testimony is worth half that of her rapist..

The Muslim father's authority over his daughters is comparable to that of a feudal sovereign over serfs. Marriage transfers that authority to the girl's husband, and ultimately to his father. A wedding is a pact between men, implying mutual assistance and debts in the future. It can be a significant financial transaction and an act of alliance to solidify clan relations. The bleating of the reluctant bride delivered to the hands of a stranger is an incidental annoyance. The Quran and the Hadith (the sayings of the Prophet, considered scripture) concur that a woman's consent to marriage is not essential; only her guardian's consent is.

The Quran teaches that a husband may confine his wife within the home—even until she dies there, if he so wishes it: "And if some of your women do something despicable, then summon four of yourselves as witnesses against them; if they give testimony to this, then shut them up in the houses until death overtakes them or Allah gives them an escape" (4:15).

Women living under Islamic law cannot travel, work, study, marry, sign most legal documents, or even leave their home without their father's permission. They may not be permitted to participate in public life, and their freedom to make decisions regarding their private life is severely, often brutally curtailed. They may not choose with whom they have sex nor, when they are married, when or whether to have sex. They may not choose what to wear, whether to work, to walk down the street.

The rule is that a woman must obey her husband, unless, of course, he asks her to leave the Muslim religion. He is her guardian, and if she disobeys he may beat her: "As for those from whom ye fear rebellion, admonish them and banish them to beds apart, and scourge them" (4:34). It is always instructive to read transcripts of televised discussions by imams on exactly what kinds of punishment (such as beating on the limbs, or only with a small stick) are acceptable when husbands chastise their wives.

When well-meaning Westerners, eager to promote respect for minority religions and cultures, ignore practices like forced marriage and confinement in order to "stop society from stigmatizing Muslims," they deny countless Muslim girls their right to wrest their freedom from their parents' culture. They fail to live up to the ideals and values of our democratic society, and they harm the very same vulnerable minority whom they seek to protect.

CHAPTER 12

Money and Responsibility

The challenges of becoming a citizen are different from the challenges that a member of a tribe faces. In many ways, the challenges of citizenship are far easier than managing the complexities of traditional societies' taboos and superstitions. But what makes modernity so elusive, even treacherous to some, is precisely that it looks so easy. It isn't. If you are not prepared—if no one teaches you a fair approach to sexuality, for example, or new ways of dealing with aggressive impulses short of violent revenge—then naturally you will fall back on what you know. Your habits and attitudes have been ingrained by clan and faith. But these values of the bloodline are not compatible with those that underlie citizenship in the modern world. If one is to succeed in modern society, one must unlearn anachronistic, out-of-place attitudes. This unlearning applies to money as much as it applies to sex.

In 1992 I lived in an asylum-seeker center in Lunteren, a small village in the heart of Holland. It's mainly farmland. The people are staunchly Protestant, of the Dutch Reformed Church. I felt I had been honored with the greatest gift that I could ever receive: I had been granted permission to stay in the Netherlands with what is called the A status. It permits you to move freely in the country, to worship freely any religion you choose, to profess any political creed you want. It meant I could escape the marriage that my father had contracted for me against my will. It also gave me access to the Dutch welfare state.

Once I had received the A status, I had to go to the city council, meet a social worker, fill out forms, and be registered for an identity card. I could also apply for housing and to receive an unemployment allowance of 1,200 guilders per month. That seemed to me to be an enormous amount. (It was at the time roughly equivalent to $800.) It seemed a lot because money was something I didn't know much about. Before arriving in Europe I had never managed money of my own.

In the asylum-seeker center where I had lived while waiting to learn whether or not I would be granted refugee status in the Netherlands, I was given 150 guilders every three months to buy clothes, in addition to a stipend of 20 guilders per week. Every Tuesday I stood in line in the center, showed my pink card to the man or woman behind the counter, received two bright blue notes equal to 10 guilders each, and then waited for my girlfriends to do the same. We would then walk to the village of Lunteren, where, within minutes, my money would evaporate. Instead of two bright blue notes I would now be holding a plastic bag containing a jar of body lotion, perhaps shampoo, a bar of chocolate, and some oranges. The 20 guilders was meant to last me a week, but it was gone. Yasmin's allowance would be gone too, and so would Dahabo's. We were astonished that those 20 guilders, which were worth so much in the places we had come from, were not worth all that much in Holland. We gathered in new groups from many parts of the world and lamented about how little 20 guilders could buy.

When I was given my 150 guilders to buy clothes, I bought a telephone card for 50 guilders, which seemed like a truly serious amount. I called my sister Haweya. Within minutes I heard a click and then a long tone indicating that my card was finished. At the time, the cost of an international call from Holland to Kenya was 4.95 guilders per minute. We had not even finished discussing the weather by the time my card ran out.

Now that I had received my A status I would no longer have to live in the asylum-seeker center. I registered with the Ede City Council to be allocated an apartment where I could live with Yasmin, who had told the authorities that she was a minor. (This gave her an advantage when requesting residency.) I too had lied on my refugee application, and I was nervous about it. Not only had I invented a story of my involvement in the civil war in Somalia and neglected to point out that my sojourn there was brief, but also, in order to conceal my whereabouts from my relatives, I had altered my name and date of birth.

While waiting to be allocated an apartment, I decided that I wanted to work. I found temporary jobs as a cleaner and in factory assembly lines. For every job I had to inform the center authorities that I was working and being paid for it. As a result I was not given any pocket money, and I was even supposed to give back some of the money I made, so that no matter what, even if I had worked five or six days a week, I had only 20 guilders per week of my own. I asked one of the social workers, "Why, when I work all day, am I not allowed to keep my money?"

She patiently explained to me that I was receiving food and boarding and that those things were costly. So it wasn't as if the authorities were confiscating my money, she said: I was contributing to my upkeep. The reward I got from working was that it fought back boredom, taught me Dutch, and helped me feel as if I were doing something useful. But there didn't seem to be any connection between the hours I worked and the money I made. Surely my upkeep cost far more than the few guilders I earned doing odd jobs.

Finally a letter came in from the housing agency informing me that I had been assigned an apartment and that the minor, Yasmin (who was actually my age), would be released to live in my care. For the first time in my life I had to deal with paying rent and utilities, cable, and telephone bills. I had to find furniture for the house. I hadn't grown up in a country where the temperature was different between winter and summer; here, you paid for heating, so life in the winter months was more expensive than in the summer.

I went to the social security office, where people were taking turns talking to the civil servants, who stood behind a long counter. After a little while I realized that I was supposed to pull a small piece of paper with a number on it from a pole at one of the two corners of the waiting room. As people finished their business with the civil servants, new numbers would appear on a screen, and each time the number changed I heard a loud ping. I was fascinated by the ingenuity of this. People did not have to line up as we did in Africa; they did not have to cut in line, shove, or otherwise act in aggressive ways to defend their place in line. You could take a seat while your piece of paper stood in line for you. It was even more impressive to me that the civil servants worked at such a speed that you never waited longer than ten or fifteen minutes.

"Next!" called a blonde woman with a scarf around her neck and a tight smile on her thin lips.

I went rushing to the counter. I said, "That's me, Ali!"

"Show me your ID," she said.

I was wearing a jacket with five pockets. I opened the zipper of my right-hand pocket and shoved my hand in, but the ID wasn't there. I tried my left-hand pocket; my ID was not there either. I looked into the breast pockets, and finally found it safely tucked into my sleeve pocket, where always I kept some coins and a 10–guilder note for the bus in case my bicycle tire ran out of air. My jacket sleeve pocket was to me what a safe-deposit box was to the Dutch and the pillowcase was to my grandmother. I deemed my ID and my 10 guilders the most precious things I had on me, so that's where I kept them.

Always nervous before a government agent, I half expected the woman to tell me to go back to my country. I imagined her losing her temper and snapping, "What are you doing here? Get back! Go back home, go back to your parents." Or that she would say in a conspiratorial tone, like so many officials I had encountered in Africa, "Have you got a present for me?"—meaning *Give me a bribe.*

Instead she waited patiently for me to find my ID and hand it over to her. She looked at me, at the picture of my ID, at me again, and at the papers she had in a file that seemed to hold all the details on my case from the time I had asked for asylum. "Tell me your first name," she said.

"Ayaan."

"And your last name?"

"We don't have last names," I said. "I can tell you my bloodline."

"Is it Hirsi?" she asked.

"Yes," I said. "He is the son of Ali."

"Ali?" she asked, and nodded her head. "Good, come with me, please."

I walked around the counter and she led me into a small office. She took a seat behind a desk and asked me if she could fetch me tea, coffee, water, or anything else to drink. My nervousness must have shown on my face.

"I am getting coffee for myself," she said. "I don't mind getting one for you."

"All right," I said. "Coffee, please."

When she came back she smiled and said, "Congratulations, you now have an apartment in Ede. In order to furnish your place you'll need some money. Do you have any savings?"

"Savings?" It was probably the first time I heard the word. My grandma used to sew into her pillowcase money that she was given by my mother, her son, or my father. She never seemed to spend it. "What is that?" I asked.

"Have you put any money away to spend later?"

"We get only twenty guilders a week," I said, "and mine always vanishes the day I get it." This was how I felt about it. It wasn't that I *chose* to spend the money; it just walked out of my pocket.

"So you haven't saved any money?" she said.

"No," I murmured. I felt ashamed, although I didn't know exactly what caused the shame. Everyone seemed to talk about money very bluntly in Holland, but it always made me uneasy. I was further embarrassed by the fact that I didn't know the meaning of words like *savings* or anything at all about bank accounts or any of the related jargon she began using. The idea of setting aside money in a bank account that collected interest was completely foreign to me.

"Okay," she breezed. Her attitude toward me remained polite, warm, and friendly. She was not judgmental. But her next question almost made me choke on my coffee. "Did your parents save any money for you?"

This was an incredible question that fully laid out the vast differences between Holland (and the West in general) and where I came from, the nomad culture. This woman took it for granted that most parents are able to save money for their children, putting it in a special bank account in their child's name. "P-p-p-parents?" I spluttered.

"Don't you have parents?" she asked. "Where are they?"

I was sweating; I could feel the sweat in my armpits. The more I tried not to be nervous, the more I thought it showed. I had told a lie when I asked for asylum, and it seemed to have gone well, because I received the A status. But I thought this was another test. At the time I did not realize that different agencies of the Dutch government do not communicate on these things.

"Where do your parents live now?" she continued. "I see you have an A status. I know there is war in Somalia, that must really be bad for you."

I felt a sense of relief and delved into the story that I had rehearsed for months now about the civil war. She stopped me and said, "Let's continue with the application."

"Application?" I asked, confused. I thought I already had an A status.

"Yes," she said, "I'm talking about the application for a loan. You need a loan to furnish your apartment."

"Oooh!" I exclaimed. "I need to furnish my apartment." *Furnish . . . my . . . apartment.* Three huge separate concepts were thrust at me all at once.

"How much do you need?" she asked.

"Just enough," I answered warily.

She said I could borrow anything from 1,200 to 5,000 guilders. "You don't know what things cost, do you?" she went on.

"No," I agreed. "I don't know how much things cost."

"Well, do you have friends?" she asked. "They could take you to the cheap stores." At the word *cheap* I felt a deep sense of dishonor, a sense that I now was at the lowest rung of this society, that I had fallen low.

"Yes, yes, I have friends," I said. I couldn't bear to say that I didn't have friends.

She continued to fill out the application. "When do you think you are going to pay back the money?"

"Do I have to pay it back?" I asked. "I thought you were giving it to me."

"No, I am not giving it to you. It is a loan. L-o-a-n. It is a loan."

"What is a loan?" I asked. "Oooh, you mean a *debt*?" I was disturbed at the idea of owing a debt to an infidel. That would surely mean I would have to pay interest, which is un-Islamic and wicked. This was certainly an infidel trick.

"Yes," she said. "You would have to pay interest."

"But in my religion that's forbidden!" I squawked.

"You don't *have* to do it," the social worker counseled me. "In fact you should not take a debt at all, it's not good for you. Your religion is wise. But you don't have any furniture and you have an empty house and it will get cold soon after the summer. Do you want to think about it and come back sometime next week?"

I said no, I did not want to think about it. I felt that this additional sin of participating in usury would not truly make any difference. I had already sinned so much. I had taken money from the infidel, I had slept in their camps, I had disobeyed my parents, I hadn't been praying much, I had cut my hair short, and I wore trousers just like a man. I was certainly damned in any case. And it *was* cold, and I *did* want a nice apartment, and this lady was offering me a truly alluring amount of money, over $4,000. "I would like to continue with the application, please," I said.

"Good," she said. "The payback plan is this: as long as you have no job, you receive an unemployment payment of twelve hundred guilders. Every month we will subtract one hundred guilders from your unemployment allowance to cover the debts. We will do this for five years, until it is paid back. If you find a job, I or a colleague of mine will sit down with you and we can arrange for you to make a new payment plan. Do you understand?"

"Yes," I said, feeling a little stupid.

"Then sign here, please. And the date, then you are all set."

"But how do I get the money?" I asked.

"Open a bank account and then let us know the account number."

I had never had a bank account. A volunteer caseworker from the Dutch refugee assistance organization had to take me to a bank to open one. The woman at the bank asked me if I wanted to deposit any money. I offered her the 10 guilders in my jacket sleeve. "Oh no, you can keep that," she said. "It's okay."

I received a little shiny blue card that said *Giro*. It didn't work in cash machines—it was just a record of my account number—but I thought it looked terrific.

The volunteer caseworker was very kind and very precise. He advised me that I should get a wallet instead of putting my money and documents in my jacket pockets. I was too embarrassed to ask him what a wallet was. We were speaking English, but *wallet* wasn't a word I had ever looked up.

Two weeks later, two good things happened. My 5,000-guilder loan arrived in my brand-new bank account, and the bank sent me a debit card. I could get money out of a machine in the wall along the road any time I felt like it!

Yasmin and I were jubilant. I suppose we had both dreamed of becoming rich. Grandma and Ma used to allude to the possibility for my sister and me. But getting rich to us meant that we would marry wealthy men who would take care of us, as well as provide for Ma and Grandma. Thus becoming rich was connected to luck (you were lucky if a rich man proposed to you) but also to impeccable behavior as a very docile, *baarri* girl and a virgin whose honor and purity would stand above that of all other women.

Now, thanks to Allah, Yasmin and I were rich. We talked about decor, about curtains and carpets and furniture. We said "pretty" and "beautiful" a lot, but never anything specific. The last time I had lived in a decorated house was in Addis Ababa when I was eight. Other than that, my mother's idea of decor was to unpack our squat *gambar,* which are Somali wooden stools with cowhide seats, and lay thin mattresses on the ground. They were all-purpose: we sat on them and slept on them, and we ate on the floor. (In one house in Kenya we had a dining table and four chairs, but Ma broke them in a fit of anger.) Ma covered windows with sheets or long cloths from the street market.

My family led a nomadic life even when we lived in cities. We moved often, and each time we rented a new house, finding windows was like a revelation. "Windows," my father would say, pleased with himself. "Lots of windows. *Noor.* Light, lots of light, lots of light."

My mother would cut him short. *"Daah, daah, daah,"* cover, cover, cover. We would need curtains. My father would grimace. There would be a fight.

"Why do you choose a house with so many windows if you don't want to pay for the curtains?"

"Why do you want to plunge us into darkness? What do you need curtains for? We have nothing to cover up. We are pure, we are Muslim, we are the children of Magan."

So curtains had always been an issue.

Yasmin wanted deep burgundy, silk brocade curtains. She wanted lush carpets, sofas with cushions you could sink in so deep, chandeliers. Her wealthy urban grandmother had brought her up in Nairobi— Yasmin was also a Somali exile—and her situation had been the very opposite of my relatives'. She would invest a lot of money, energy, and time in getting the right tint of curtain to match her upholstery.

Brocade. Upholstery. What did I know? These were words from

Jane Austen, and I was already living in the Alice-in-Wonderland world through the looking-glass, with a *bank card* and an *apartment*.

A security guard who worked at the asylum-seekers center offered to drive us to furniture stores after his work hours. He asked us what our budget was, and when we told him he said he would take us to stores that were cheap. But we didn't want to go there. Yasmin and I held our noses and said, "Oh, no, this is not who we are, we would like something more upscale."

He tried to reason with us: "You can't afford it. You're wasting your time."

"No, no," we said. "That's what we want, please take us to the upscale stores." I had never been to any kind of furniture store, but I wanted brocade, upholstery, quality—nothing nasty and cheap; that would be *low*.

So this dear man drove us from one store to the next, and at one point we settled on a sample piece of wall-to-wall carpeting that was black, pink, and purple. A salesman informed us that it would cost us 110 guilders per square meter.

We were euphoric. "Yes," we said in chorus. "This is what we want, this is what we want."

The expression on the face of our Dutch friend was incredulous. He just stood there, frozen.

Then we fell in love with some wallpaper. It was white, with a pattern on it. There was no real need for it—the walls of our apartment were not falling apart—but I was genuinely fascinated by the idea of wallpaper. It reminded me of covering our textbooks in school. It seemed so grown-up, so *rich*.

The man in the store who took our bank card was happy. He said there had to be someone at home when the carpet was delivered, that they would remove the old floor materials and put the new carpet in. We loaded the rolls of wallpaper into the car. We spent four days with our Dutch friend peeling off the old paper and pasting up the new one in our living room, hallway, and two bedrooms. A week later our new wall-to-wall carpet was installed.

And here is the surprise: we had 400 guilders left from the loan of 5,000. In other words, we had a carpet, wallpaper, and nothing else. No curtains, nothing to sit on, no beds, no chairs, no dishes.

Yasmin and I were at first baffled.

The money was worth nothing here. Was the whole loan about just a carpet? We quickly decided it was God's will. There was no need to quarrel: Allah had willed it thus.

The carpet had been cut to fit and glued down. We had no choice but to pay.

The following week, Gerda, a volunteer teacher of Dutch as a second language, came to see us. As soon as she was inside she exclaimed, "Ooooh, you have a nice carpet!" Her expression, however, could not have been more different from her words. She seemed horrified.

We urged her to come in and sit down with us on the floor. We patted our carpet.

"How did you get this . . . this . . . carpet?" she asked.

"They brought it," I said.

"Who is 'they'?"

"The store."

"And who picked out the colors?" she asked. "If you want any help from me to return it, all you have to do is say so."

"But we want to keep it," I said.

Gerda's father rang the doorbell. She had brought him so he could help us fill out forms to settle down in Ede; he was retired, she said, and would enjoy it.

"What a cheerful carpet," he said, when he came in. "Did you find this in the house? If you want, I can take it out. I can get a couple of young men to remove it."

"Oh no," I replied. "The carpet is new, it is ours, we want it."

We showed her father our bookkeeping, which was in envelopes that we kept in a plastic bag. He brought out two huge files and a perforator and proceeded to show us how to make holes with it and how to file our papers. I had been to a Kenyan secretarial college, so although I had very little practical experience of filing, I did understand what he was trying to teach us.

Next he took a look at our receipts. He saw the bill for the carpet and exclaimed, "It is your entire loan, except for four hundred guilders!" He was visibly upset. "This is wrong!" he said. "A scandal. The salespeople have taken advantage of you. I will write them a letter that this is indecent and should not have happened. We have to reverse this."

I was speechless. Yasmin thought she would rescue the situation by serving mountains of cookies and tea.

"Uhmmmm," I stammered. "Uhm uhm uhm, but we like the carpet."

"But now you don't have anything else," he said.

"More tea?" I asked, hoping to change the subject.

Gerda and her father spoke in rapid Dutch. Yasmin and I looked at each other helplessly. Then Gerda saved the day. "Okay," she said, "if you really like the carpet, then keep it. We will get you some furniture. You need beds, you need chairs, and you need a table, a desk, a TV."

Within a week she and her father had mobilized their old but incredibly fit retired friends and relatives to help us. They brought furniture, beds, curtains, plates, forks, and knives. Because I spoke English (I did not yet speak Dutch), my role was to answer the phone and open the door. For a couple of weeks, all that came out of my mouth was "Yes, thank you. Of *course* we like it. Thank you very much."

Kind volunteers walked in carrying more chairs, side tables, little ceramic statuettes, even gnomes, and every time I opened the door I said, "Yes, yes, yes, come in, please, thank you."

We had four beds, three televisions, two sofa sets, two tables, and more than a dozen chairs; on one of them sat a pile of various sizes of lacy acrylic curtains. Our airy three-room apartment resembled a furniture storage room. I was sneezing from all the dust.

One day Yasmin started crying. She hated living this way. So we took everything we hated down three flights of stairs to the basement. When Gerda or her father came by, they always called in advance, so we would spend a couple of hours bringing everything back upstairs.

We still hadn't put up curtains. Neither of us knew how, and we didn't really like any of the ones we'd been given; they looked like nasty cast-offs. One day when I came home from Dutch-language class Yasmin said she'd found a perfect answer to the curtains. She had a large glossy catalogue on her lap with lots of photos in it and a great big smile on her face. "Ayaan, look, we can throw out all the rubbish!" she cried joyfully. "We can get fresh new curtains, furniture, anything we want!"

In that catalogue were clothes, shoes, gadgets, utensils, everything you could ever wish for. "But how are we going to pay for this?" I asked.

"You don't have to pay for it!" cried Yasmin. "You buy and you pay later." She told me about visiting some people she'd met at the asylum center. They had also found an apartment, but, she said, unlike us, they lived in beautiful surroundings—and they didn't pay.

"Okay," I said, "let's order curtains." So we ordered thick, beautiful curtains, gold and brown with a satin-like surface and a thick cotton lining. They arrived twenty-four hours after Yasmin ordered them, in boxes that were delivered right to the door of our apartment. That was another magical thing about the buy-now-pay-later stores: instant gratification.

Yasmin seemed to know exactly what to do, and began fitting little pieces of bent metal into pockets in the curtains. It took us half a day to hang them all up. But when we were done they were much too long, leaving a lot of textile curled up on the floor along the wall. Yasmin said that if we had chosen the shorter measurement that was available in the catalogue the curtains would have been too short. So we left them too long, again thanking Allah and agreeing that it was his wish.

A week later a letter informed me that I was now another 4,000 guilders in debt. Four months later, Yasmin disappeared. A short time later I received a bill from the telephone company: she had run up 2,500 guilders in phone calls.

A number of helpful Dutch people assisted me in applying for various long-term payback plans. In the following months my friend Johanna, a lovely woman who had offered to teach me Dutch, showed me how to shop in large, cheap supermarkets and tried to teach me how to budget. In 1995, as my Dutch-language skills improved, I got a job as a translator and interpreter. I made more money this way than through other odd jobs.

I began to avoid friendships with my fellow Somalis in Ede, although many of them would invite me over so that I could translate for them into Dutch. They continued to buy from various mail-order catalogues that gave you the option to pay in the distant future. Others borrowed money from banks and the social services, which they then sent to their relatives in Somalia or in the Somali diasporas of Africa. I translated for several people who had taken out the same 5,000-guilder loan that I had, and who had sent it all to relatives so that they could pay the entire sum to someone who would smuggle them into Europe.

To pay back these loans, some Somalis took on occasional jobs, but they usually neglected to tell the social services that they were employed. This meant they could continue to receive an unemployment allowance as well as their salary. But it was considered fraud, a felony that could get you in a great deal of trouble. If you were discovered you had to pay back the excess money you had received, plus a fine. This meant more loans, and sank you ever deeper into debt. You might also lose your job because you now had a criminal record, so you had to go back to welfare. In such cases, the authorities would retain part of your unemployment allowance to cover your debts, paying out only enough to cover essential monthly expenses, such as rent and utilities. Many people neglected to pay those bills and became locked into insurmountable debts. I heard of several people who absconded to England or Scandinavia to try to avoid paying back the debts they owed to various banks and agencies in Holland.

Practically everyone I knew had built up overwhelming debts. They applied for credit cards, magical pieces of plastic that meant you could just sign a tiny piece of paper and walk out of any shop with whatever you wanted. They received endless stipends from the social services—for unemployment, for child support, for various medical benefits—and yet in almost every conversation they would lament the miserly amount of money they had to live on, wholly oblivious to the sacrifice of the society that was paying for it all.

They had no idea, in other words, of the obligations of a citizen, let alone the complexities of the welfare state.

*   *   *

As an interpreter for the Immigration and Naturalization Services, I translated for men and women who pleaded desperately to be allowed to live in the Netherlands. The civil servants who interviewed them asked them the same questions that I was asked when I applied for asylum: Had they been persecuted? How did they get to Europe? Had they resided in any country other than Somalia before reaching Holland? Had they ever committed any criminal act?

All these questions were about the past. None of the applicants was asked what he or she expected once admitted into the country. Their skills were not tested. They were not questioned about their values, customs, practices, or their knowledge of Dutch customs and laws.

Like me, some of these applicants were granted residency. But none of us had been *citizens* before, in the modern sense of citizenship. We had never felt a participatory loyalty to any government. We remained loyal to our bloodline.

In a tribal culture everyone is required to share his earnings with family members and extended family, who take happily. The obligation is also emphasized in the Quran. A poor member of the family who wants help from a well-off member will cite verses from the Quran and sayings from the Prophet to induce his relative to give him money. The tribal code of honor and shame does the rest.

The pressure felt by most immigrants, even second- and third-generation immigrants, to share their earned income with family members living in their country of origin is admired by some development economists and aid workers, but it is part of what keeps people poor. They never save enough money for themselves or for their offspring.

To my fellow Somali refugees, admission into Holland meant, above all, material gain. Some of it—money, clothes, and other luxury items—could be shared with relatives back home or flaunted in front of other Somalis to distinguish oneself from lower clans. My motivation to become a refugee was slightly different: I did not want to be married to a man I did not choose. But none of us was driven by a motivation to become Dutch citizens. Our arrivals were random, an accident or coincidence, depending on one's perspective.

Imagine you are a Somali who escaped the civil war and you are now in Nairobi. Kenya is considered by most Somali refugees a port of transition to the rich West. So you go to see a smuggler of people, whose business is making fake passports, visas, and other immigration documents. The smuggler, like any other businessman, will show you his wares: entry to the United States costs (say) $20,000; Canada, $15,000; Germany, $10,000; Scandinavia, anywhere from $5,000 to $10,000. Switzerland is really expensive. If you can raise enough money, usually with the help of your relatives already in one of these countries, then you belong to the lucky few who will have access to a life without hunger and with free health care and housing and the opportunity to smuggle in more of your relatives now in refugee camps or some other limbo land.

Most people in this situation never get out of limbo. They court and marry and have children and survive as best they can. Some go back to Somalia and then back to Kenya; some give up in defeat. Those who can afford the smuggler will get a choice of all the countries they can ask for asylum. Some smugglers will provide more than just papers, if you pay for the extra service; they will give you an entire fictitious life story based on the questions that various immigration and naturalization bureaucrats will ask you.

Very often, of course, the scam doesn't work. Some who pay a smuggler to deliver them to the United States are detained in a European port. Some are deported straight back. Yet many manage to linger on by following the instructions given to them by the smuggler: "Tear up all documents that you have on you with any personal information on them if you are caught anywhere at a transit point. Flush them down the toilet. Upon landing as you approach passport control, put your hands up and ask for asylum." In this way, as European airports are pressured by the United States to more closely control travelers transiting from Africa and the Middle East, more and more would-be migrants end up in destinations they have not chosen, often in Europe.

A long process follows after they ask for asylum. A lucky few, like me, are allowed in and eventually become citizens through naturalization. But they ask for asylum, which means they apply to the state to be recognized as refugees. Refugee status, if given at all, is given to those who can convince the state that they would be persecuted if returned to their home country. In return, the host country demands that they never go back to their country of origin. If they do go back, their refugee status is nullified, as they no longer meet the condition for protection. People who come to Europe this way end up settling in Europe, not because they desire or even understand what it means to be a citizen but purely for the sake of convenience or because they genuinely do need protection from persecution. These people are therefore not the slightest bit motivated to adopt the values and customs of the countries they flee to.

None of us was remotely prepared to adopt new values. Nearly all of us got in trouble in the society of milk and honey to which we had serendipitously been admitted. And of all the challenges we faced, the biggest was money.

Once in a while I socialized with my colleagues who were translators in Arabic, Farsi, Dari, Berber, Turkish, and other languages, and we would share our experience with the clients from our respective countries. Money was the number one problem. Refugees borrowed too much, were unable to pay back loans, abused credit cards, didn't pay their taxes, and sent money abroad to relatives rather than caring for their own financial well-being. Our clients all seemed trapped in a cycle of poverty, overwhelmed in a swamp of debt so deep that, even if they acted responsibly for the rest of their lives, it would take almost a generation to work their way out of it.

None of us was prepared to grasp the very sensible and frugal Dutch mantra *Earn, save, invest, and reinvest.* All of us lived beyond our means. In later years, as I began studying public policy, I came to see that this pattern of debt was clearly related to the enduring poverty of immigrants as a class. Debt perpetuates poverty. When I looked into the causes of debt among Moroccans and Turks—who, unlike refugees from Somalia, Iraq, and Afghanistan, had come to Holland to work—I found that their attitude toward money (borrowing it, failing to save, remitting large amounts of money back home, spending to show off, buying from catalogues, overusing their credit cards) was roughly the same as mine, Yasmin's, and other Somalis'.

All of us came from countries that were broken-down or corrupt, with a massive gap between the rich and the poor. If you were wealthy, you lived lavishly, owned cars and homes and had expensive jewelry and other rich man's accessories. Others lived off their wealthy relatives. Then there were the poor: those who lived as servants, beggars, or thieves.

*   *   *

As a child I learned Arabic, Amharic, and English with no pain, no stress; I have no memory of ever working hard to learn them. One day I didn't speak them, and the next day I did. Learning Dutch was different. I remember every single effort: the irregular verbs, the exceptions in rules, the verbs at the ends of sentences. I remember working at memorizing the vocabulary.

Clearly, even if you have a knack for it, learning a language as an adult is more arduous than imbibing it as a child. And so it is with regulating your personal finances. I simply didn't learn how to do it. It sounds pathetic, but nobody ever taught me the difference between ten cents and twenty-five cents, the denominations of coins. I was amazed to find out that Dutch *children* receive pocket money, not as a gift to spend on whatever they want, but as a deliberate method to teach them how to budget and deal with finances.

Late in life I discovered that money matters. If you don't deal with it, it will hurt you. It involves choice and planning. Tearing myself away from my father and the man he chose for me had opened up a huge world of freedom, but it also forced me to think about new kinds of limitations to freedom: health insurance, taxes, rent or mortgage payments. I had to have priorities: how much to spend on what. I was bewildered, insecure, confused.

In 1997 I moved in with my Dutch boyfriend, Marco. He was appalled to find that I, a woman who appeared to be independent and relatively prosperous, was in fact a financial child. He would find damp little wads of guilders (notes of ten guilders, or twenty-five or fifty or even a hundred) in the pockets of my shirts or jeans after washing them. After months of explaining that the cloth wasn't worth the money that it had been washed with, he tried to explain why it was important to carry a separate accessory just for money. So he bought me one exactly like his. Unaware that what Marco called a *portefeuille* had a male and a female version, I found myself carrying a man's wallet, and I was constantly surprised by the number of tiny women's purses (which I later learned were simply women's wallets) I was given as gifts.

I still struggle to manage even everyday transactions of money.

Because I have been brought up to say yes, I cannot say no to sales-girls. All my life I have signed things, and sometimes bought things, just to please a merchant. I lie to get out of conflict situations rather than tell the truth. If a real estate agent shows me a rental, I'm embarrassed beyond words to say I don't like it; I invent ridiculous stories to explain my way out of this rather routine and obvious situation, then take the agent to an expensive lunch to apologize.

In a very slow and painful process I stumbled forth and discovered the intricacies of financial responsibility. What I did not know, I learned. Based on that experience, I believe it would be prudent to teach refugees a few basic skills *before* giving them loans and presenting them with credit cards and furniture catalogues, *before* they get sucked into a subculture of borrowing and fraud.

In a modern, Western society, citizens' financial ethics, like their sexual ethics, are based on individual responsibility. Within the tribe, ethics are about obedience to clan values, and because of the obligation to assist impecunious family members, those who are irresponsible with their money get away with it. Loyalty to members of the tribe in faraway countries requires borrowing money to send to them. This makes it hard to see the country of your new citizenship as "home"; it has a cost too in terms of your own prosperity. At face value, it may seem very generous to share your money with your extended family, but when this involves taking out loans it has a serious long-term cost.

Skills of earning, budgeting, and saving are indispensable for citizens. But we are not born with them. Muslim girls and women, in particular, are not trained to have such skills. Their ignorance of all things money-related affects them personally, of course, but it also perpetuates the poverty of their families. These girls become mothers too soon, and as mothers they fail to teach their children what it is to be financially responsible. They fall prey to easy credit and fantasy spending. This breeds dependence on welfare states that are already overstretched.

There is growing disaffection in Europe with immigration, a feeling that many immigrants do not deserve the help they receive from generous welfare states. It is said that immigrants disproportionately abuse the system, behaving like parasites. It is important to take this disaffection seriously as the demographic share of people from a tribal background grows.

My proposal is not to kick out the immigrants and their children, as some populist politicians suggest, or to recommend that Western societies shut their borders or stop welfare altogether. But my own financial learning process and knowledge of the struggles of clients for whom I translated, as well as the many studies of poverty and debt of immigrants I read as a member of Parliament, suggest that many people who share a background with me are not familiar with the prevailing morality of money in the countries they have adopted. Rather than respecting their culture, Westerners who feel compassion for the poverty of immigrants need to encourage them to learn new attitudes that will enable them leave that poverty behind.

CHAPTER 13

Violence and the Closing of the Muslim Mind

I don't remember my first day in Quran school in Mogadishu. I was probably three or four. The room had a thatched roof and a sand floor covered with papyrus mats. It was surrounded by a wall made of twigs and woven dried grass. Most of the children were my age; some were a little older. There were both boys and girls. A teacher with a long thin stick in his hand herded us into the room. He shouted, "In the name of Allah, most Gracious, most Merciful," and we shouted after him. He shouted verses from the opening chapter of the Quran and urged us to repeat them in chorus. We recited the text in Arabic, a language that we did not speak. The imam probably also did not speak much Arabic. He was teaching us to recite a text whose meaning was unknown to us all. And no one explained why.

We were to learn to recite four or five verses by heart and then write them down on a wooden board. It was in that madrassa that I learned how to make ink from charcoal, water, and milk. We were given little sticks, just like the ones we used to clean our teeth. We chewed on the stick until the tip was soft like a brush. If the brush became too long as we chewed on it, then cut the extra bit with our teeth and spit it out on the floor. Then we dipped the stick into a large inkpot. I learned to write *alif*, the first letter of the Arabic alphabet.

Everything we wrote down on our wooden boards, we were told, was holy. We washed the boards with special water that had been blessed; it was a sin to put the boards on the floor.

In the middle of the madrassa was a large book on a wooden lectern: the Holy Quran. It was open, but it was so sacred that we were not allowed to touch it; only the older children, advanced in learning, were allowed even to approach the book. Not only the content of the Quran but the physical book itself was holy. The older children knew what it meant to purify themselves and make their ablutions. They knew how to recite many verses by heart. We younger ones were ignorant of purity, so we were not allowed anywhere near the book. Learning the Quran at that time meant growing up to be old enough to perform your ablutions, learn many suras (chapters) by heart, learn the Arabic alphabet, and write down the Quran.

After many hours of such learning we were released to go home. We had lunch, we were put to bed for a nap, and when we woke up we sat under the talal tree in front of our house and prayed for my father to be released from prison. If during those supplications I managed to recite some of the quranic verses that I had learned, I was praised.

The Quran was used for other purposes. My auntie Hawo was sick with breast cancer. Once in a while my mother hired a number of Quran scholars. They would sit around my auntie in a circle and recite the Holy Quran and after a few verses would lightly spit on her. The Quran was medicine: it could cure.

The Quran was also used as punishment. At the entrance of the madrassa hung a hammock, tight between two poles. I was told, "If you are naughty, if you misbehave, if you are disobedient, you will get the *Itha Shamsu* treatment." I had no idea what that was until one day I saw our teacher lift one of the little boys into the hammock. It was strung so high that if he fell out he would certainly hurt himself on the hard ground. The teacher then instructed the older boys and girls to each pick up a long, thin stick from a stack in the corner and to stand around the hammock and, to the cadence of a chapter in the Quran that we call *Itha Shamsu Kuwirat*, to flog the child. I have never been so terrified.

Itha Shamsu Kuwirat means "The sun is folding up," although I did not know that then. The chapter is a description of the punishments of the Last Judgment, but this meaning was not revealed to us. In the madrassa, questions were not welcome; they were considered impertinent.

*   *   *

Violence, as you will have guessed by now, was an integral part of my upbringing. But this was not because I was the victim of a uniquely abusive family or series of schools. My experience was typical of the way most people from all over the non-Western world grow up with violence as a social norm. In one of my experiences as an interpreter in Holland, I was called to an elementary school in The Hague to translate for a couple whose seven-year-old firstborn son, Mohammed, had beaten Mark, another child about his age. Both sets of parents were upset and felt misunderstood; they had been yelling at each other for days, and now the school was trying to resolve the conflict by bringing in a translator: me.

The teacher, fixing a firm and disapproving gaze on Mohammed's parents, began by saying, "Mohammed is very aggressive. He hit Mark. He kicked him, punched him in the face, and threatened to kill him."

Mohammed's mother responded, raising her voice and waving her hand at the teacher, "It is Mark's fault. He provoked Mohammed by a calling him names, by making humiliating gestures at him and by laughing at him."

"That is right," the teacher interrupted. "But it was Mohammed who hit Mark first!"

Then Mohammed's mother and father raised their hands over their heads and cried in unison, "Of course, you don't wait to be hit first. We taught him to punch any child in the face who so much as gives him a wrong look."

The Dutch teacher, stunned and almost speechless, looked at the parents, then at me, and asked in disbelief, "Are you rearing him to believe that violence is the way to solve conflict?"

Given the mutual bewilderment of both my clients as they looked at each other, I asked if I could step out of my neutral role as an interpreter of text alone and venture into cultural interpretation.

I explained to the parents that, unlike in Somalia, the way to resolve conflict in Holland was by learning to talk, to talk until you drop, in search of a compromise solution—or, if that fails, to go to court, where a lot of talking is done by people called lawyers who represent you. All the talking ends in a settlement pronounced by a judge. No special skills in punching, kicking, biting, stabbing, or shooting are needed. Besides the normal curriculum of math, language, and geography, kids are taught the skills of talking one's way out of problems and into college, into jobs, into love, out of love, and so on.

To the Dutch teacher I explained that, in Somalia, strong clans teach their children, both boys and girls, the merits of physical aggression: how to be the first to deal a blow; how to respond if you are surprised with a blow; the art of deception in aggression; how to pretend you are down and then strike; how to pretend to apologize and then regroup, change your tactics, and hit back. My older cousin used to take me to "fighting practice" after school when I was about five or six. I was encouraged to pick a fight with a classmate, who was encouraged to pick a fight with me. We poked out our tongues at each other, made faces at each other, and called each other names. We said things like "You are low, accursed, shameful, dishonorable, *kinteerley*." Then, surrounded by cheering older relatives, we went at each other. We kicked, scratched, bit one another, wrestled until we were covered in bruises, our little dresses torn, our knees scraped from all the falling. You were defeated if you gave up first or if you cried or ran away. In all three cases you would undergo a severe verbal and physical beating from your fighting coach. In my case my coach was my older cousin, the only daughter of my mother's twin sister.

Throughout the first two decades of my life I got used to the practice of violence as a perfectly natural part of existence. At home Ma hit me and my siblings. My father, whenever he was with us, beat my brother with slaps and shoves and then in long thought-through whipping sessions with his belt. In turn, Mahad beat Haweya and me, sometimes to aid Ma in her crusade to teach us manners and break our spirit for being so disobedient, sometimes as a way of showing us that he was the boss, the vice head of the house, replacing my father's authority with his. For Haweya and me to take him seriously and acknowledge this authority, he had to use physical violence. This we regarded as quite normal. All of my girlfriends at school feared their brothers and fathers. We whispered about the different punishments we were subjected to. All of them involved corporal punishment of some sort.

In school the teachers also had the right to cane us. In my class Mrs. Nziani used what was known as a *black mamba,* a hard black pipe. The impact from that hurt depending on where she hit you and how much force she used. As a math teacher her favorite way of stimulating us to get our sums right was by hitting us on the head for every sum we got wrong. Sometimes I would get only five sums right out of thirty. That meant I got twenty-five strokes of the pipe.

Some teachers used the pencil-and-ruler method. A pencil would be wedged between the index finger and the ring finger, holding down the middle finger. Then the teacher would take a ruler and hit you as hard as she could on the knuckles of the fingers holding the pencil.

Bullying was another nightmare in school. Some of the older children would gang up on the younger ones or weaker age-mates, forming a circle around the poor child and then beating the hell out of him or her. There were times I used to think that children were more cruel than adults. Every week teachers would preach about why bullying was bad and how the bullies would be punished—violently, of course—if caught.

Violence seemed to follow me around. One day in the beginning of 1989 the Kenyan government decided to carry out a large-scale rounding up and deporting of illegal Somali immigrants into Kenya. In practice this meant that police were to stop anyone who looked like a Somali and demand their ID. If you did not have one, you went to a police cell. My mother and I went to buy an ID for me in a neighborhood called Pangani, about a twenty-minute walk from our neighborhood on Park Road. We left the house without IDs and, predictably, were stopped by two policemen. We might have been released had we given them the money that we had for our groceries. Instead Ma decided to get all principled and refused to bribe them. We were escorted to the Pangani Police Station, where we spent two nights. Even though the conditions were abysmal—hard cement floor, urine and excreta on the ground, and about forty people in a 13-by-16-foot cell—we were not physically harmed.

However, in that jail I saw the utmost cruelty. Kenyans charged with mostly petty crimes such as stealing spare tires were brought in. Five uniformed and armed policemen pummeled an alleged criminal. With their heavy boots they kicked him in the head and in the belly and they kicked all his limbs. It was a ghastly sight. I will never forget the crack of bone as his kneecap was shattered.

In Kenya that was the most common form of state violence. In all the countries where I lived before coming to the West, the use of torture and corporal punishment was so normal that people were surprised if you questioned it. This habituation to violence poses real problems when people from such societies move to the West, as I soon discovered.

My work as a translator frequently took me to the courts and prisons of Holland. Almost all these cases involved assault and murder. All the perpetrators were male. There was one case of a Somali man who neglected to pay his rent for months. One day the landlord came to demand payment and threatened the tenant with eviction. In response the Somali walked into his apartment, grabbed a thick wooden stick, and hit the landlord on the head as hard as he could. The victim survived, but the impact was so hard that the Somali was charged with attempted murder. In court, defended by a pro bono lawyer, the Somali first denied hitting the landlord, then blamed him for making him lose his temper. The lawyer put forth a strong case in his defense, citing the civil war and the psychological toll it had taken on her client. She had lined up all sorts of experts, psychiatrists and sociologists who testified to all the possible causal links between that war and the reason the Somali man attacked his landlord.

The Somali's extended family, neighbors, and friends all testified that the defendant was a good, polite, charitable man who under normal circumstances would not harm a fly. They agreed that, if the landlord had not provoked him, the whole episode would not have happened. The defendant himself showed no remorse of any kind and was sentenced to a year in prison.

In my time as a Dutch MP I heard numerous possible explanations for the disturbing level of violence among immigrant families. These families came from Turkey, Morocco, Somalia, Afghanistan, Iraq, Egypt, Sudan, and Nigeria; people from the Antilles and Surinam were also overrepresented in violent-crime cases. There were first-generation and even third-generation citizens among them. All who were suspected or convicted of actual or attempted terrorist violence were Muslims. Aside from terrorism the list of indictments was topped by assault, sometimes with firearms, sometimes with knives and other sharp objects, often with bare hands.

I tried to explain to my colleagues why this was. In some Muslim families—though not all—the barrier between violent and nonviolent behaviors is very thin and fragile. In some families it simply does not exist. Children are groomed into unquestioning conformity. Disobedience—especially by boys—is punished with a series of severe reprimands. If these fail, physical punishment soon follows. Husbands who fear disobedience from their wives are permitted to beat them. In school, particularly in the madrassas, mistakes are punished by beatings. Boys may receive lashes and hard slaps across the face; girls may be lashed but more often are slapped or pinched, or their hair is pulled.

The Westerner is surprised to hear a suicide bomber described by all his neighbors and relatives as quiet, charitable, polite, friendly, and smiling. How can a man go from helping an old woman cross the street to plotting or even committing a mass murder? The answer is that, in the Muslim family, politeness, friendliness, and charity are regarded highly, and all families aspire to instill in their children these ideals of universal good behavior, but conformity to Allah's will is held in even higher regard. And violence is regarded as a legitimate means of enforcing that conformity.

In saying this, I don't want to create the impression that all people from Muslim countries or tribal societies are aggressive. They are not. But whereas physical violence is now regarded in the West as barbaric, most commonly associated with drunken football hooligans or gangs of drug dealers, in Islamic culture it remains an integral part of the system of social discipline.

If there is an infallible mark of an advanced civilization it is surely the marginalization and criminalization of violence. In order to understand why Islam promotes violence, and indeed terror, as a political tool, we can look a little more closely at my own religious education.

After we left Somalia, my next Quran school was in Mecca, in Saudi Arabia. Held in a large room with a blackboard, it was for girls only.

We sat on cushions on the floor, a cement floor this time, not sand. There was no spitting; we did not write on wooden boards; we didn't chew sticks into writing implements; and we didn't have to make our own ink. But here we were required to cover ourselves from head to toe, and we were not asked about ablutions: it was assumed that our parents had prepared us. Purity was a concept and a practice that was ingrained in even the smallest child. But the biggest difference was that we each had a copy of the Quran.

It was not the whole Quran, just the thirty shortest chapters, which are known as suras. These booklets we called *Juz Amma*, after the longest chapter that they contained, and they came from a high shelf. We were not allowed to put them down on the counter that sat in front of us; they too were holy. We all opened to the same page, and collectively we chanted, slowly, following the teacher's lead. We spoke each word with reverence, but, as in Somalia, no one bothered to explain the meaning of what we were saying. And again, any impertinence or questioning was punished severely. Before we replaced them on their special shelf we kissed the books and touched them to our foreheads.

My family lived in Saudi Arabia for one year. In the regular school, which was also for girls only, we also learned to read the Quran, and there we attended a class where we learned something about the meaning of what we were reading. Most of what we learned had to do with the hereafter and with rewards and punishments. Another class in regular school taught us about the Hadith, the sayings of the Prophet Muhammad. As Muslims we were required to follow his example, but as girls we were required above all to follow the examples of his many wives.

After Saudi Arabia we lived in Ethiopia, which is a Christian country. There my mother was convinced that we would not get enough religious schooling. My father reassured her that we would, and he was right. We had an extra class in school that was like madrassa, although we sat on chairs and at desks. Using small Qurans, we learned verses by heart, chanting them slowly. In this school too there was no discussion of their meaning.

In Kenya, where we lived for ten years, we attended another Quran school, where we placed the Quran on our laps and continued to learn it by heart. But this Quran school was for boys and girls together, which troubled my mother. After I began menstruating she decided to hire a private Quran teacher, who was Somali. He took us back to the old method of making our own ink and writing on wooden boards. Although I rebelled against these tedious old-time practices, I didn't rebel against the Quran. Our teacher severely beat me for my rebellion; once he fractured my skull against the wall of our living room.

Then the school that I attended hired a new Islamic studies teacher, Sister Aziza. Her method of teaching was much kinder. She didn't hit us and she didn't yell at us. She discussed the content of the Quran and urged us to understand its meaning. Sister Aziza was what Europeans and Americans would now call a fundamentalist or an Islamist. At the time I didn't realize it, but I was undergoing what specialists would now term a radicalization process.

Sister Aziza did not force us to pray or to fast or to cover ourselves in robes that would hide our (more or less theoretical) womanly attributes. Instead she inspired and stimulated us to what she called "the inner jihad," a constant struggle to fight temptation and distraction by worldly things, such as listening to music and hanging out with friends. Our struggle was to observe all five daily prayers and to fast for all of the thirty days of the holy Ramadan, compensating for the five days when we were not allowed to fast because of menstruation.

Sister Aziza allowed us to ask questions. I wanted to know why I couldn't be friends with non-Muslims. It was an inconvenient rule because it meant cutting ties with some of my best friends. I also wanted to know why men were allowed so much freedom, whereas we girls and women were so constrained. Sister Aziza simply told us, "That is Allah's wisdom. Allah is all-knowing." So although we were allowed to ask questions, we did not in fact receive answers.

Persistent questioning was itself considered to be sinful, a sign that you were under the influence of Satan. You could of course ask for clarification about the exact distinctions of what was acceptable or forbidden, the so-called gray areas between *halal* and *haram*. You could ask, "Is it permissible to marry a cousin if your mother suckled him when he was an infant?" You could say, "Today I fasted, but just before nightfall my period came. Is that day of fasting valid, or do I have to repeat it?" The Ramadan fast generated what seems to me now a neurotic amount of such specific queries, such as "As I was brushing my teeth the tiniest amount of water slipped down my throat. Did I violate my fast?" The fear of accidentally swallowing water compelled many of us to avoid brushing our teeth in the morning for the whole month and led others to spit on the ground all day, lest they swallow their saliva.

Thus my personal experience of what I call the closing of the Muslim mind involved not only fundamentalist individuals such as Sister Aziza and Boqol Sawm (another of my quranic tutors in Kenya), who themselves had been radicalized in Saudi schools, but also non-radical, "regular," or what some would call "moderate" teachers. Both these groups discouraged meaningful discussion of the Quran; they would just say "Do this" and "Refrain from doing this. It's in the Quran." There was absolutely no criticism of the text, no reflection on why we should obey the rules, and certainly no exploration whatsoever of the idea of *not* obeying one or another of the rules that were dictated in the Quran by the Prophet fourteen centuries ago. Moreover, most people I knew when I was growing up either did not read the Quran or knew it only in Arabic, which very few of them could understand. It is a holy artifact, holy in its totality, even in its language. You approach it not with a spirit of inquiry but with reverence and dread.

This is the biggest misunderstanding between Muslims and non-Muslims. Anyone who identifies himself as a Muslim believes that the Quran is the true, *immutable* word of God. It should be followed to the letter. Many Muslims do not actually obey every one of the Quran's many strictures, but they believe that they *should*. When non-Muslims see Muslims dressed in Western clothes, listening to Western music, perhaps drinking alcohol—people who, in their social lives, are not very different from Westerners—they assume them to be moderate. But this is an incorrect assumption, because it posits a distinction like that between fundamentalist Christians and moderate Christians.

Moderate Christians are those who do not take every word in the Bible to be the word of God. They don't seek to live exactly as Jesus Christ and his disciples did. They are actually critical of the Bible, which they read in their own language and have revised several times. There are parts they find inspirational and parts they deem no longer relevant.

That is not what a moderate Muslim is. A moderate Muslim does not question Muhammad's actions or reject or revise parts of the Quran. A moderate Muslim may not practice Islam in the way that a fundamentalist Muslim does—veiling, for example, or refusing to shake a woman's hand—but both the fundamentalists and the so-called moderates agree on the authenticity and the truthfulness and the value of Muslim scripture. This is why fundamentalists manage, without great difficulty, to persuade Muslims who don't practice much of Islam to begin engaging in the inner struggle, the inner jihad.

I have heard from so many people, both in Holland and in America, "So-and-so was a good friend of mine. We used to go out together. She had a great job. Sometimes she would drink alcohol. She was just like us, but now she wears the headscarf. She stopped eating pork and drinking wine. She doesn't want to be friends with us anymore." Or "We always knew he was a Muslim, but now he has become more pious. He has grown a beard, he dresses differently, and now he distances himself from us." In the past decade, as fundamentalist Islam has grown exponentially, many Muslims who weren't strictly observant have suddenly changed. Fundamentalist preaching has turned them around very easily, because those nonobservant Muslims do not have the intellectual tools to refute what the fundamentalists say, which is, basically, *If you are a true Muslim and you believe what is in the Quran, then start practicing it.*

Some Muslims do not belong to either one of these categories; they are slightly observant but not extreme in their beliefs. And some of them have made attempts to modernize Muslim scripture through a process of interpretation and reinterpretation. This is an exercise that is encouraged by Western non-Muslims, mostly people in academia.

I have read books written by Muslim "feminists" who seek to reinterpret the Quran. I have read all sorts of papers and listened to discussions of Muslims trying to reinterpret the fundamentals of Islam, such as jihad, the treatment of women, the rejection of science. The fundamentalists refer to these modernizers as heretics and infidels, confused and corrupted by the West. A famous example of this group is Nasr Abu Zayd, an Egyptian scholar. He has suggested that parts of the Quran could be interpreted in such a way that it would be compatible with modernity. But he was attacked by fundamentalists, labeled an infidel, and forcibly divorced from his wife, a professor of literature, on the basis that he was an apostate (although he insisted that he remained a Muslim), and a Muslim (such as his wife) cannot be married to a non-Muslim. Ultimately Abu Zayd was forced to flee to the Netherlands.

An Iranian American Muslim woman, Laleh Baktiar, wrote a new translation of the Quran. This was not a work of critical reexamination of the Quran but a polishing up of some of its more cruel and inhuman passages by deliberately losing their meaning in translation. She too was ridiculed by fundamentalists and threatened with death.

Yet the works of these so-called moderate interpreters of the Muslim faith are not helpful in their attempt to present a moderate Islam. Reading them is like putting on a blindfold and trying to find your way around your apartment after someone has rearranged the furniture: everywhere you go, you hit an obstacle. The language is very difficult to understand, the reasoning unintelligible. Clear-cut quranic commands such as "Beat the disobedient wife" and "Kill the infidel" are made obscure, and a lot of fences are built around them. Their reinterpretation is something like "Don't beat her on the face. Don't beat her to break her bones. Use only a small stick"—none of which is present in the original Arabic. In one text the word *tharaba* is interpreted to mean "leave her," not "beat her," if you fear she will be disobedient. This "improvement" from *beating* to *leaving* is presented solemnly, without a hint of irony. (The translator, so focused on unsaying the word *beat,* is oblivious to the consequence of the newfound translation *leave* and its ties to the Muslim man's breezy right to divorce his wife at any time simply by crying out three times in the name of Allah and in the presence of two male witnesses "I divorce thee.")

What is striking about this tortuous struggle to reinterpret Muslim scripture is that none of these intelligent and well-meaning men and women reformers can live with the idea of rejecting altogether the troublesome parts of scripture. Thus, in their hands, Allah becomes a God of ambiguity rather than of clarity. From an articulate transmitter of Allah's Word, Muhammad is turned into someone who left behind an incoherent muddle of rules. Ironically, this was the position of the Christian and Jewish critics who first heard Muhammad. They found that he stole whole passages from the Old and New Testaments and Jewish scriptures and reshaped them into a contradictory muddle that he claimed to be original. This vision of Muhammad is not at all what the reformers seek. According to them, Muhammad was good; he sought to liberate women, for example, but his words were turned and twisted and now must further be twisted and turned in order to create a semblance of tolerance and equity.

Fundamentalists do not take kindly to these attempts to reshape the Holy Quran into a modern document; to them, this is a clear degradation of God and Muhammad. And here, I believe, the fundamentalists win, because they are not suffering from what psychologists call cognitive dissonance. The fundamentalists' God is all-powerful; he dictated the Quran, and we must live as the Prophet did. This is a stance that is clear. It's the Westernized theologians who are trapped in confusion, because they want to maintain that the Prophet Muhammad was a perfect human being whose example should be followed, that the Quran is perfect scripture, and that all of its key injunctions—kill the infidels, ambush them, take their property, convert them by force; kill homosexuals and adulterers; condemn Jews; treat women as chattel—are mysterious errors of translation.

It is not only the prohibition against criticizing the Quran and the Prophet that closes the Muslim mind, and not only the life-long socialization of learning by rote. It is also the continuous construction of conspiracy theories about enemies of Islam who are determined to destroy the one, true religion.

The chief enemy is the Jew.

When I was a pious Muslim in my teens, I made my regular ablutions. In those days, with every splash of water I cursed the Jews. I covered my body, spread a prayer mat, faced Mecca, and asked Allah to protect me from the evil that is spread by the Jews. I hurried to our local mosque and joined the crowds in prayer. We lined up—in the women-only section—and followed the instructions of the male imam, who was invisible to us. We cried in unison *"Amin"* to all his supplications to Allah, and when he called Allah to destroy the Jews, I also fervently said *"Amin."*

When I was in secondary school I pored over magazines published in Iran and Saudi Arabia that contained graphic photographs of men and women covered in blood. The captions always identified the dead as victims of the Jews. Even though I was a curious child, and as a teenager was an even more curious student, I never questioned the veracity of the pictures, the captions under them, or the stories of how the Jews killed and maimed Muslims like me.

In Nairobi after school I attended classes in Islamic centers generously provided to the public by wealthy men from Mecca and Medina. I believed that these wealthy men had built these centers out of kindness and goodness; they were practicing *Zakat,* or charity, the third pillar of Islam. I listened to one teacher after another talk about how the Jews had declared war on Islam. I learned that the Prophet Muhammad, the holiest of all holy men, in whose footsteps we Muslims all aspired to follow, had warned of the treacherous and evil ways of the Jews. They had betrayed him and tried to kill him, for wherever there is a Jew he plots and plans to destroy Islam. He smiles at the Muslim, but deep inside he hates him. He extends his hand to the Muslim in pretended peace, all the while enticing him toward a trap of debt, debauchery, and sin.

I swallowed all this propaganda as the whole truth and nothing but the truth.

The other students who joined those lessons were as diverse as any group of students in a city like Nairobi; their families were from Yemen, Somalia, Pakistan, Sudan, and various Kenyan regions. But we identified ourselves first and foremost as Muslims; ethnicity was no barrier to our deeper loyalty to our faith. In the name of Islam we digested the anti-Semitic propaganda that was offered to us. It came to us in the mosque, in our religion classes at school, in Islamic centers, and from Islamic radio, magazines, pamphlets, television stations, and audiocassettes (and later, videos, DVDs, and blogs and other online instruments). Jews were bloodsucking, lethal enemies of Islam.

Some of my fellow students, selected on the basis of their piety and loyalty to Islam, were offered special scholarships to further their study of religion in Mecca and Medina, the holy cities of Saudi Arabia, or in Lahore or Teheran. They came back to Nairobi after a few years and, like Jehovah's Witnesses in the West, went from door to door in their respective neighborhoods. They preached Islam, of course: prayer, charity, fasting, and the pilgrimage to Mecca (if you can afford it). But they also made thousands of believers aware of an enemy that lurked in the shadows, ready to attack them: the Jew.

When I reflect back on this particular strand of anti-Semitism, I see three distinct features. The first is demographic power: increase the number of people who believe that Jews are their enemies. The second is to use Islam as a vehicle to promote anti-Semitism. The third is psychological: present the Muslim as an underdog fighting a powerful and ruthless enemy.

A Somali woman poet, Safi Abdi, who is clearly immersed in this same propaganda, recently published a poem in English that is a perfect illustration of this strategic triangle:

Hamas is a victim of U.S. policy.

Hamas is Palestine, Palestine is Hamas.
Hamas was born under Israeli siege.
Hamas was born at the foot of a Zionist boot.

In this poem the Jews are a scapegoat for evil and Islam is a unifying force against evil. Muslims are called upon to ignore their local problems of war, poverty, and tyranny and to unite against Israel, the Zionists, the Jews. This is the anti-Semitism of the twenty-first century. A Muslim who questions the existence of this enemy or his motives is either a fool or a traitor and a heretic.

Europe's long tradition of Christian and pseudo-scientific anti-Semitism was taken to its logical conclusion by Hitler and the Nazis, with the willing help of many other Europeans who participated in his program of Jewish annihilation. The evil of this "Final Solution" was exposed after the defeat of the Third Reich and combatted thereafter by the reeducation of ordinary Germans, the memorialization of the Holocaust, and the stigmatization or prohibition of neo-Nazi groups. As a result, by the end of the twentieth century most civilized people in the West believed that European anti-Semitism was a thing of the past.

But it is not. It has mutated into something new: Arab Islamic anti-Semitism has replaced European anti-Semitism. The new anti-

Semites have borrowed a few tricks from the Nazis. They employ propaganda tools, such as the counterfeit *Protocols of the Elders of Zion*, that were developed by the Nazis. However, they also have something that the Nazis did not have: a world religion that is growing faster than any other religion, a warrior faith that is espoused by over one and a half billion people. Hitler had *Mein Kampf* and the might of the German Wehrmacht; today's anti-Semites, like the Iranian leader Mahmoud Ahmedinejad and Osama bin Laden, have a holy book, a far greater demographic power, and a good chance of getting their hands on a nuclear weapon.

Despite outer appearances, the conflict between the Israelis and Palestinians in the Middle East is no longer about territory. It may seem to be so to Jews and Americans, but from the Arab Islamic perspective it is a holy war in the name of Allah, and victory will come only if the Jews are destroyed or enslaved, if all the infidels are killed, converted, or "dhimmified" into the status of submissive, second-class citizens.

Wars are never fought only on battlefields with military means. Israel, America, and Europe may have stronger armies, but Islam has the numbers. The targets of Muslim propaganda—women, gay people, infidels, Christians, atheists, and Jews—are divided among themselves. The more these groups in the West are divided, the better for Islam. Shia and Sunni Muslims may hate one another; Arab Muslims may degrade African Muslims as slaves; Turks and Persians may look down on Arabs. But at the end of the day, when an imam calls for *Tawhid,* unity in the oneness of Allah, and performs the *takbir,* "*Allahu Akbar,*" nearly all Muslims unite.

For Muslims to stay united, however, Islam needs an enemy, conspiracy theories, and a rival creed. Jews are the best of scapegoats, for the conspiracy theory that claims they control the world is believed by many. I have heard a Muslim theologian in Holland preach that all evil has been brought to humanity by the Jews. According to him these evils are communism, capitalism, and individualism. He pointed out that Karl Marx was a Jew, Milton Friedman was a Jew, and Sigmund Freud was a Jew. Marxism is an atheist creed and therefore an enemy of Islam. Free enterprise is a distraction from prayer; it involves the ungodly pursuit of earthly wealth and a system of lend-ing and borrowing with interest (usury), which is forbidden by Islam. So capitalism too is an enemy of Islam. Acknowledging individual urges, dreams, consciousness, and layers of subconsciousness replaces a focus on the hereafter; virtues and vices are not seen as tensions between following the straight path of Allah and that of Satan but as the result of natural and psychological causes. Thus Freud and his followers are also enemies of Islam.

Islam is not just a belief; it is a way of life, a violent way of life. Islam is imbued with violence, and it encourages violence.

Muslim children all over the world are taught the way I was: taught with violence, taught to perpetrate violence, taught to wish for violence against the infidel, the Jew, the American Satan.

I belong to a small group of lucky people who have escaped the permanent closure of my mind through education. I have learned to drop the prejudices that were ingrained in me. In school and in university it was hard sometimes when I learned things that were contrary to the teachings of Islam. I was always aware of a nagging sense of guilt and sin. Reading political theory in Leiden, I felt as if I had been transported to Sodom and Gomorrah. Everything seemed to contradict the political theory of Muhammad. But slowly I learned the new rules of a free society, new ideas that have replaced the old set of values that my parents gave me. The crucial question is whether or not there is a way to help many more young people achieve this opening of the Muslim mind.

Time and again in the past few years I have been asked by Americans who have heard my warnings about the increasingly dangerous impacts of Islam on Western societies: What can be done? Is there anything can we do? It is now time to address the all-important question of *remedies*.

PART IV

REMEDIES

CHAPTER 14

Opening the Muslim Mind
An Enlightenment Project

The Muslim mind needs to be opened. Above all, the uncritical Muslim attitude toward the Quran urgently needs to change, for it is a direct threat to world peace. Today 1.57 billion people identify themselves as Muslims. Although they certainly have 1.57 billion different minds, they share a dominant cultural trend: the Muslim mind today seems to be in the grip of jihad. A nebula of movements with al Qaeda–like approaches to Islamic precepts has enmeshed itself in small and large ways into many parts of Muslim community life, including in the West. They spread a creed of violence, mobilizing people on the basis that their identity, which rests in Islam, is under attack.

A person with a mind that has been closed unquestioningly listens to and absorbs the teachings of the fanatics who claim that it is God's law that Muslims should join the struggle. A person with an open mind—one that is empowered, that has shaken off the fear of hell—can tell the agents of al Qaeda *Yes, it is true that what you say is in the Quran, but I disagree with it. Yes, you ask me to follow the example of the Prophet, but I believe that parts of his example are no longer valid.* A person with an open mind is not immune, but he is armed.

I believe that it is possible for the Muslim mind to be opened and that it is crucial that the closing of so many young minds in the name of Islam should be prevented. But I think there is a much easier and more direct way of opening the Muslim mind than by reinterpreting the Quran so as to tone it down, and that is by a campaign of *enlightenment*.

The intellectual tradition of the European Enlightenment, which began in the seventeenth century and produced its greatest works in the eighteenth, is based on critical reasoning. It employs facts instead of faith, evidence instead of tradition. Morality in this worldview is determined by human beings, not by an outside force. It is a worldview that came into being mainly in reaction to a particular religion, Christianity, and a particular institution of Christianity, the Roman Catholic Church. The process of reaction was very arduous, and actually began centuries before the Enlightenment, when the Catholic Church did not just excommunicate people who disagreed with its worldview but persecuted them, banished them from their homes and communities, threatened them with death, and sometimes killed them.

The Muslim mind is not a monolith, but Muslims share common ideas and reactions that, in the age of jihad, are indispensible to know. For instance, I'm intrigued by the fact that hundreds of thousands, maybe millions of Muslims felt compelled to protest against a cartoon of the Prophet Muhammad. Regardless of where they are born, what language they speak, whether they are male or female, rich or poor, Muslims very often refer back to the teachings of the Prophet Muhammad. The reason most often given by the agents of radical Islam to mobilize the Muslim masses is *It is in the Quran, the Prophet Muhammad said it.*

There is an enormously important scholarly movement under way to explore the nature of the historical Quran. How did the Quran come to us? When was it written, and who wrote it? What is the origin of the stories, the legends, the principles in the Quran? How do we determine its authenticity? This movement, which is largely an enterprise by secular, non-Muslim academics, seeks factual answers. Their project is not to discredit or attack Islam, or even to enlighten Muslims. These scholars have no political or religious agenda, only a classical academic approach, just like the one that has long applied historical analysis to the Old and New Testaments. Some of them fear for their lives, however, and have to write under pseudonyms. Their work is vital because, if the Muslim mind can be opened to the idea that the Quran was written by a committee of men over the two hundred years that followed Muhammad's death, the read-only lock on the Holy Book can be opened. If Muslims can allow themselves to perceive the possibility that a holy book was needed to justify the Arabs' conquests, every kind of inquiry and cultural shift is possible.

If the Muslim mind is opened, will there still be religious practice—prayer, pilgrimage, dietary laws, a fasting month? Quite possibly. There might even be anti-Semitism, veils, and domestic abuse. Tradition and habit are powerful forces. But behind the veils and beards would be minds asking questions. The possibility of legitimate, individual, critical review of Islamic dogma would at long last exist.

This can be an uncomfortable and painful possibility. Personally, I felt a sense of intense relief when I accepted the possibility that there is no life after death, no hell, no punishment, no burning, no sin. But for others, this insight can lead to misery and emptiness. My sister Haweya and my friend Tahera, whom I knew in the Netherlands, lost their fear of guilt and sin and the terror of everlasting punishment. But their sense of doom in the afterlife seemed to transfer itself into their own lives right here on Earth. I too still sometimes feel this pain of separation from my family and from the simplicity of Islam. It is like the pain of growing from childhood to adolescence or the pain of letting go of parents when they age and die. It is the pain of standing on your own two feet. It is not easy to adapt, or to make good choices; it can be a harsh, harrowing business. Enlightenment thinking will not necessarily bring happiness and ecstasy to the Muslim mind. But it will put the individual firmly in control of his or her own life. Each of us will be free to navigate our way through life, make our own wrong choices, recalculate, and choose again. We will make mistakes, but we will have a chance of overcoming them rather than just fatalistically succumbing to them as Allah's inscrutable will. Muslims will become true individuals: free, and responsible for their own beliefs and acts.

Let us imagine two teenage friends, Amina and Jane. We meet them just after the Mumbai attacks in November 2008, when Pakistani fundamentalists killed almost two hundred people.

JANE: You are a Muslim. What do you think of the men who killed people in the Taj Hotel in Mumbai? It was a hotel, people were having dinner, they were happy and innocent of wrongdoing.

AMINA: Why are you asking me this question?

JANE: The killers were Muslim and they called out "Allah is great!" when they attacked. They obviously thought they were doing this for Islam. You're a Muslim too.

AMINA: What has that got to do with anything?

JANE: It is your God.

AMINA: People kill in the name of your God too.

JANE: Yeah, hundreds of years ago.

AMINA: No, now, in Afghanistan, and in Iraq and in Chechnya.

JANE: That's not being done in the name of Christianity. Maybe Christians support those wars and maybe they don't, but they're not being fought in the name of the Bible.

AMINA: Yes they are. George Bush is a Christian. It says on the dollar "In God We Trust." The American military prays before they go on a mission. All of this is done in the name of Christ, it is a Christian war against Islam.

JANE: But these Muslim men who killed in the name of Islam in India, they did not distinguish between military and civilians. Their victims were just tourists, they were having dinner.

AMINA: Indians are killing Muslims in the name of their Hindu religion.

JANE: Would you kill for your God? Would you kill me, your friend?

AMINA: What a weird question. Why do you ask?

JANE: Because you say Christianity makes people do this, Hinduism makes people do that, Muslims defend themselves in the name of Islam, whatever. Would you kill me? If a Muslim wanted to kill members of my family, would you stop him?

AMINA: I don't like where this conversation is going. I want to stop talking about this.

JANE: Would you kill me? Would you stop a Muslim from killing me or my family?

AMINA: Would you stop a Christian killing me in the name of Christianity?

JANE: Well, yes, actually. In a nanosecond. And you know, I'm not a Christian. I don't believe that we should take orders from an outside force. Life is my religion.

AMINA: I really don't want to talk about this.

JANE: You don't want to talk about it because you would not save my life or because . . .

AMINA: (close to tears) I don't know. I want to do what is right. Allah tells me what is right. I just want to be a good Muslim, I don't want to kill people, I don't want people to be killed, I just want to be a good Muslim.

JANE: Are you sure you want to be a good Muslim? Here! (She takes the Quran out of her bag and puts it on Amina's lap.) Have you read the Quran? Do you know what it says? Look on this page: It says "Kill the infidels." Look, here it promises eternal punishment for all unbelievers, here, I marked it for you. And here it says "Beat the disobedient wife." Here, turn this page, look, it says "Flog the adulterer." Are you sure that you want to do what Allah wants you to do? Are you sure?

AMINA: (now in tears, desperately crying) I really don't want to talk about this.

Faced with this imaginary scenario, one group of people would say that Jane is too cruel, too insensitive, that she seeks to drive poor help- less Amina over the edge. It's not Amina's fault that some Muslims act badly in the name of their shared religion. Amina needs to protect her identity and her traditions; Jane should be more tolerant, more polite. Muslim organizations would charge Jane with Islamophobia. On all sides there would arise a chorus of pity, treating Amina as a victim.

But this is exactly how minds are opened: through honest, frank dialogue. Tears may be shed, but not blood. Amina's feelings may be hurt, she may be upset or confused, but perhaps she will begin thinking, questioning her unspoken assumptions in the light of her own, real experience. It is a myth to think that people's minds will be opened by their government or some higher authority; even teachers in school are not as effective as peers. Classmates like Amina and Jane ask each other questions in the schoolyard. Colleagues confront each other on the work floor, neighbors in each other's kitchens.

My first encounter with the Enlightenment as a movement, a coher- ent set of ideas by philosophers who have enthusiastic supporters as well as passionate enemies, was in 1996. I was then twenty-six years old, attending the University of Leiden, one of the first great beacons of the Age of Reason. I was living among students for whom these values and ideas were so familiar that they were unaware of them. My own naive discovery of them made people react to me with a mixture of surprise, amusement, and even alarm.

The first value of the Enlightenment was one I had already encountered in the Netherlands and had taken to immediately: encouragement and reward for asking questions. The adults in my life (my mother and grandmother, other relatives, and teachers) had systematically rejected and punished inquisitive behavior as insolence toward authority. In Holland I was permitted to question authority and was entitled to an answer. This very simple attitude was to me a revelation. It reflected an attitude in which all problems had physical causes and possible solutions. Afflictions of all kinds were not simply handed down by Allah as a curse for unknowable reasons that could be lifted only by prayer. If the causes were not known, then it was a noble exercise to pursue knowledge of them; inquiry was not a blasphemous or insolent act.

I secretly used to watch a children's TV program called *Willem Wever*, presented by a man of that name. Children would write in questions on issues they were curious about. (This was before Google.) Their parents would assist them—*assist them!*—in posing the question in a clear way. Two or three questions would be selected every week, and the children would be invited onto the show to elaborate on what they wanted to learn. Then they would go on a journey to find the answer. Why do fireflies have lights in their body? Why do planets move clockwise around the sun? Why do people in England drive on the wrong side of the road? Mr. Wever and the child would visit experts and build models and put together the pieces of the puzzle; the riddle would finally be solved.

When some of my friends found out that I actually stayed at home to watch this, they treated me as if I were a child in an adult's body. But to me it was a revelation. By asking questions, you got not a scolding but answers!

This brings me to a second value of the Enlightenment that was new to me: learning is a life-long experience and it is for *everyone*.

Acquiring knowledge is not reserved for adults only, or men only, or a certain clan or class only; everyone is assumed to be capable of acquiring knowledge.

The third value, individual freedom, is related to the second. If you assume that everyone, regardless of descent, sex, ethnicity, or religion, can increase his knowledge via the simple process of asking questions and seeking answers, then you have already accepted that individuals are free, because this freedom is inseparable from a life of curiosity. If the rest of the group does not like your questions, or the answers that you found, or what you did with those answers, or if you develop the annoying habit of posing more questions and chasing their answers, no matter how annoying or disrespectful they are, you run no risk of being punished.

Nobody in Leiden understood why I found this so odd, so new, so revolutionary.

A few years later, because of my research (asking questions) and my statements about Islam (the answers that I had found), I was threatened by Islamic fundamentalists. Many people, some of them the same professors and fellow students I had known in Leiden, were just as surprised then as they had been when I was a student. How could this be happening? How could it happen *anywhere* in the world, but especially in Holland? Surely this reactionary, violent attitude was from the Middle Ages?

It is hard for Westerners today, inheritors of the legacy of rational thought, to comprehend the phenomenon of group thinking, the claims and constraints that groups lay on their members' conscience, time, money, sexuality, loyalty, and even life. For the fourth value of the Enlightenment (though it was not quite so clearly formulated until Max Weber put it this way in the late nineteenth century) is that the state has the monopoly on violence in society. If individuals are free to seek answers to any question, they may come up with answers that are unacceptable to some of the members of the society to which they belong. These groups may attempt to silence the questioners. They may even use violence. It is the state's responsibility to deal with outside aggression and also with cases of violence between citizens. Checks and balances bind the state to rules that counter the potential for abuse of its enormous power. If a church wants to silence a believer, the Enlightenment state stands by the individual believer, for articulate and well-educated adults may say and do what they please, so long as they bring no harm to others. Thus the thinkers of the Enlightenment devised a dynamic framework of legal and community instruments to help people resolve conflict without resorting to violence.

A fifth appeal of the Enlightenment is the idea of property rights as the foundation of both civil society and the political system. As a child, if you succeed in working your way out of a miserable parental environment, succeed in making money and buying property, the rule of law will protect you and your property.

So this, in a nutshell, was my Enlightenment: free inquiry, universal education, individual freedom, the outlawing of private violence, and the protection of individual property rights. It did not take me long to see that the very novelty of these concepts made me treat them with much more respect than many of the people living around me in the Netherlands, who took them entirely for granted.

Social workers in the West will tell you that immigrants need to maintain group cohesion for their mental health, because otherwise they will be confused and their self-esteem destroyed. This is untrue.

The idea that immigrants need to maintain group cohesion promotes the perception of them as victim groups requiring special accommodation, an industry of special facilities and assistance. If people should conform to their ancestral culture, it therefore follows that they should also be helped to maintain it, with their own schools, their own government-subsidized community groups, and even their own system of legal arbitration. This is the kind of romantic primitivism that the Australian anthropologist Roger Sandall calls "designer tribalism." Non-Western cultures are automatically assumed to live in harmony with animals and plants according to the deeper dictates of humanity and to practice an elemental spirituality.

Here is something I have learned the hard way, but which a lot of well-meaning people in the West have a hard time accepting: *All human beings are equal, but all cultures and religions are not.* A culture that celebrates femininity and considers women to be the masters of their own lives is better than a culture that mutilates girls' genitals and confines them behind walls and veils or flogs or stones them for falling in love. A culture that protects women's rights by law is better than a culture in which a man can lawfully have four wives at once and women are denied alimony and half their inheritance. A culture that appoints women to its supreme court is better than a culture that declares that the testimony of a woman is worth half that of a man. It is part of Muslim culture to oppress women and part of all tribal cultures to institutionalize patronage, nepotism, and corruption. The culture of the Western Enlightenment is *better*.

In the real world, equal respect for all cultures doesn't translate into a rich mosaic of colorful and proud peoples interacting peacefully while maintaining a delightful diversity of food and craftwork. It translates into closed pockets of oppression, ignorance, and abuse.

Many people genuinely feel pain at the thought of the death of whole cultures. I see this all the time. They ask, "Is there nothing beautiful in these cultures? Is there nothing beautiful in Islam?" There is beautiful architecture, yes, and encouragement of charity, yes, but Islam is built on sexual inequality and on the surrender of individual responsibility and choice. This is not just ugly; it is monstrous.

No doubt there was once poetry in Somali clan culture; people dressed in colorful garments; they had a dark and biting sense of humor; they knew strategies for surviving a harsh desert environment that perhaps the world could have learned from. But the multiculturalist belief that Somali clan culture should somehow be preserved, even when its products move to Western societies, is a recipe for social failure. Multiculturalism helps immigrants postpone the pain of letting go of the anachronistic and inappropriate. It locks people into corrupt, inefficient, and unjust social systems, even if it does preserve their arts and crafts. It perpetuates poverty, misery, and abuse.

Instead of affirming the value of tribal lifestyles, people in the West—activists, thinkers, government officials—should be working to dismantle them. At least they should encourage individuals to escape them, perhaps even by providing specific incentives to those who do. Liberals should be engaged in an active campaign of civilizing—not by colonizing people, but by vigorously trying to educate them, by making freedom attractive to all, as it was conceived in the Enlightenment.

In the West, individuals free their imagination from the fear of superstition and direct their energies toward the pursuit of their own happiness. This is a great achievement. Of course there are many complacent followers of habit in the West, but individuals who want to pursue happiness on their own terms may do so. Yet Western governments also practice a racism of low expectations: they presume that people from traditional countries are like toddlers who will freeze in growth, who cannot evolve, who will never be able to let go. But I know that they can, for I have done it myself.

I strongly believe that the Muslim mind can be opened. Yet when I have criticized the teachings of the Quran, as Enlightenment thinkers once challenged the revealed truths of the Bible, I have been accused of blasphemy. Muhammad says my husband can beat me and that I am worth half as much as a man. Is it I who am being disrespectful to Muhammad in criticizing his legacy, or is it he who is disrespectful to me?

Every important freedom that Western individuals possess rests on free expression. We observe what is wrong, and we say what is wrong, in order that it may be corrected. This is the message of the Enlightenment, the rational process that developed today's Western values: Go. Inquire. Ask. Find out. Dare to know. Don't be afraid of what you'll find. Knowledge is better than superstition, blind belief, and dogma.

If you cannot voice—or even consider—criticism, then you will never see what is wrong. You cannot solve a problem unless you identify its source. And if you cannot look at the root of what is wrong with Islam today, then in a very real sense Islam has already defeated the West.

The Enlightenment honors life. It is not about honor after death or honor in the hereafter, as Islam is, but honor in individual life, now. It is about development of the individual will, not the submission of the will. Islam, by contrast, is incompatible with the principles of liberty that are at the heart of the Enlightenment's legacy. Yet more and more people are coming to the West from countries where life is organized according to tribal custom and increasingly subjected to radical Islam. They introduce customs, practices, and dogmas that preceded the Enlightenment and are indeed clearly anti-Enlightenment.

Some people in Western society—not only multiculturalists but socialists and Christians who feel there is too much freedom in Western society—admire what they see as the innocence of these immigrants from far away, their purity, their seeming commitment to family values and cultural traditions. When the multiculturalists use the word *diversity* they assume that immigrants will somehow maintain their traditional culture within the Western way of life and the Western value system, like an exotic exhibit of primitive carving in a smart new museum. Unfortunately for the West, radical Islamists reject diversity, for Islam justifies the oppression of women as well as all kinds of violence, including child marriage and marital rape. The West should eliminate such practices from its own societies and condemn them wherever else they occur across the globe. We cannot do so, however, without acknowledging that there is something wrong with the religion that justifies them.

Besides being accused of blasphemy, I have been accused of bad manners. But good manners should not be confused with free speech. Having good manners means that when I meet a closet Islamist like the Oxford professor Tariq Ramadan, I don't pour my glass of water on his head and call him names. Exercising free speech means that I can call his book, *In the Footsteps of the Prophet,* a badly written piece of proselytism and say that he doesn't deserve the title of professor or a university chair from which to propagate his program of medieval brainwashing. All this will no doubt offend Ramadan, but you cannot subject Karl Marx to scrutiny and give the Prophet Muhammad a free ride.

Free speech is the bedrock of liberty and a free society. And yes, it includes the right to blaspheme and offend.

The Muslim mind *can* be opened. Hard-line Islam offers an ideal of martyrdom and a lifestyle of self-denial that is difficult to maintain. Many people, perhaps especially girls, feel trapped in the web of rules and strictures that extreme Islam demands. It is difficult to pray five times a day, to marry a man you have not chosen, and to live a life of continual self-denial. Over the long term it becomes unbearable.

Many Muslims recognize the weaknesses in Islam. For example, a significant proportion of the mail forwarded to me is written by Muslims who agree with what I say. But they will not join me in atheism, because they still believe there must be a God. This is not easy for an atheist like me to admit, but it appears that the painstaking construction of a personal ethic is not enough for many people.

An Afghani living in California wrote me recently, "I support you and your mission. The only difference between you and me is that I covertly fight the religion of Islam and you, openly. . . . Please know that you are not alone. There is a silent crowd who agree with you and who are fighting Islam. I have my family to look after, but you're giving me the courage to speak up openly."

A Muslim woman in Canada wrote, "I have struggled with the belief system of my people for some time now, yet I am so afraid of speaking out. Speaking out comes at a price, doesn't it? I wish I was able to just disbelieve in silence and shut out the xenophobia, the homophobia and the irrationality of my people, but the hypocrisy of it all is a pain that eats away at me daily. Surely you were informed, the price one loses for disowning Islam is grave."

A woman from Sudan living in Virginia e-mailed me, "I felt what was required of me as a Muslim woman was to hate your book but then I read it and I identified with you. Every emotion that you tried to bring to words in the book, I have felt. Every mental conflict that you had within yourself I have felt. . . . I find myself wanting to understand Islam but not being able to do so. What is it that makes Islam so enticing and perfect to my parents but so flawed to me?. . . . I don't denounce Islam because I believe there is some truth to it—and if I were to renounce Islam, where would I go?" She continues, "Am I destined to hell because I did not accept what my parents destined for me?" And yet she concludes, "I don't think I have the courage to do what you have done, to question Islam as you have."

Such letters show that I am not the only Muslim woman who has dared to challenge her upbringing and faith. But there has never been a clear-cut attempt to win the hearts and minds of Muslims to the idea of critical thinking. Close textual analysis of the Quran is a start, because it will feed doubt, but it is only a start. Novels, musicals, comedies, short stories, comics, cartoons, and movies that are critical of Islamic dogma can be made. But hardly any are actually being made because of the fear of sparking violence. Take the case of Kurt Westergaard, the Danish cartoonist who drew the cartoon of Muhammad wearing a bomb in his turban. Since the cartoon was published in the fall of 2005 he has survived two attempts on his life. In the most recent one, a Somali man carrying an axe and a knife broke into his home. Scooping up his five-year-old granddaughter, Westergaard ran into a bathroom that had been transformed into a secure area and alerted the police, who came in time to catch the perpetrator. This incident, like the fatwa against Salman Rushdie, the assassination of his Japanese translator, and the attempted murder of his Norwegian publisher, is bound to discourage Muslims with doubts about Islam and Westerners who want to take on the principles and icons of Islam. Terror is effective.

In recent years the persecution of people in Western societies for their ideas has become a part of our mental landscape. Salman Rushdie has lived under a sentence of death by fatwa for twenty years. Taslima Nasreen, who was brave enough to say that Islam doesn't permit democracy and violates human rights, now lives in hiding, without even an apartment to call her own. Irshad Manji in Canada and Wafa Sultan in the United States, women who have dared to criticize Islam in public, now require protection, as I do, and an intellectual like Ibn Warraq, the author of *Quest for the Historical Muhammad* and the impressive *Why I Am Not a Muslim*, must publish under pseudonyms.

It is not a trivial thing to know that, even in the West, if you criticize or even analyze a particular religion you may require protection for the rest of your life, that if you speak out about Islam you may start a riot or a massive international campaign, and that perhaps you yourself will become a target, stalked, ostracized, even murdered. It is an unpleasant option. Most people, consciously or not, seek to avoid it. Fear has an effect.

Thus slowly, and sometimes not so slowly, people begin to get used to *not* saying certain things, or they say them but certainly won't write them. The thin fingers of self-censorship begin to tighten around individual minds, then groups of people, then around ideas themselves and their expression. When free speech crumbles in this way, when Westerners refrain from criticizing or questioning certain practices, certain aspects of Islam, they abandon those Muslims who seek to question them too. They also abandon their own values. Once they have done that, their society is lost.

CHAPTER 15

Dishonor, Death, and Feminists

On New Year's Eve 2007, in a suburb of Dallas, an Egyptian man, Yaser Said, shot his nineteen- and seventeen-year-old daughters in the back of his taxi. He then parked in the driveway of a hotel and absconded, leaving their bodies in the cab.

Amina, the older girl, had been awarded a $20,000 scholarship for college; she had dreamed of becoming a doctor. She told her friends that her dad was angry because she had refused to marry the man whom he had chosen for her, who lived in Egypt. Her father, who came to America in 1983, was enraged to learn that both his daughters secretly dated American boys, Eddie and Eric, whom they had met in school.

Yaser Said was known to be fanatical about his daughters' virtue. He made them stop working at a local grocery store after months of monitoring their movements; their former coworkers said he had watched the girls clock in and out like a stalker. He had physically hurt both girls before. There were reports by family members that he had threatened to kill them for going out with boys. Their mother, an American woman from a troubled family, who married Said at the age of fifteen, told police that on Christmas Day she and the girls had fled their home in Lewisville because she feared he would kill them. "Me Mina and my Mom r running away!" Sarah Said texted a friend. "My dad found out abt Mina and is goin to kill us."

But a few days later their mother relented. She took Amina and Sarah back to Lewisville and persuaded them to go to a restaurant

219

with their father, so the three of them could talk. About an hour later the younger girl, Sarah, called 911 from her cell phone and said she was dying.

I found all this out on the Internet. The story filled me with pity and rage. These girls were so promising, cut down so senselessly. Both of them were good at sports, popular; their MySpace pages, which I pored over, showed they were striking beauties, bright-eyed, taking funny poses, though I thought I saw a sadness in Amina's eyes.

I had had to flee my family, to escape my fate as a Muslim girl. Alone in Europe, I cast aside a destiny of confinement and threats. I severed the bloodline that my grandmother imprinted in my mind. I rejected the notion that I was intended only to serve and honor others all my life, and in time I will cease to feel the pain of being called a traitor. But these teenagers were born in the United States. It should have been easy for them. They had told their friends how frightened they were; they predicted what was going to happen. But nobody took them seriously, because nobody believed it could happen in America.

I was scheduled to go to Texas in February 2008 to give speeches at the University of North Texas and at a meeting of the World Affairs Council in a Dallas hotel. I thought that I would learn something about the murders; I assumed that people would be talking about them, since they had happened barely ten miles from the hotel where I was staying. Everywhere I went I asked about them. But almost no one seemed even to have heard about the killing of Amina and Sarah Said. To my relief a lone journalist nodded at the mention of it. But others were perplexed. An honor killing? In Dallas? In Texas? In America? They didn't know. They were earnest, horrified at their ignorance. (Americans, if they don't know about something, will often just say so, with great innocence and frankness, which still surprises me. As a Somali I was brought up to feel ashamed if I didn't know something and to try to hide it.)

The murder of the Said sisters had in fact received very little attention in the local media. Almost all the articles that were written were careful to state that it hadn't been an honor killing, and that, even if it had, honor killings had nothing at all to do with Islam. Every article quoted Amina and Sarah's brother, a scrawny nineteen-year-old named Islam Said, who said, "Why is it every time an Arab father kills a daughter, it's an honor killing? It didn't have anything to do with that."

This was apparently enough for the reporters to dismiss the notion that the girls' murders represented an honor killing. Even the FBI shied away from the term, at first stating on its website that Yaser Said was wanted for an honor killing, then withdrawing the term after criticism by Muslim groups.

This, of course, is just how self-censorship works. We do not wish to offend. We fear the perception that we might be acting disrespectfully. And we fear the possibility of retaliation.

But you will never solve a problem if you don't look at it clearly. Ignoring the role that honor—and Islam—almost certainly played in the Said sisters' murders will only allow more murders to happen. If you don't talk about it, other people won't be able to spot the signs. Insight into the pattern that eventually leads to murder is an aid to educators, social workers, law enforcement officials, and neighbors and friends of potential victims.

So what exactly is an honor killing? An honor killing happens when a girl shames her family's reputation to the point where the only hope for them to restore that honor is to kill her. Her offense almost always relates to sex. She has been alone with a man who is not a relative, or she has resisted a forced marriage, or she has been going out with a boy of her own choice. The offenses can be even more trivial. Possibly she is completely innocent and is simply suspected of having violated the clan's code of honor. In August 2007, a Saudi man beat and shot his daughter to death for going on Facebook. The event was publicized only seven months later, when a cleric cited it as evidence that the Internet was damaging Islamic morals. (He showed no concern for the victim.) The father is unlikely to receive any significant punishment for murdering his daughter. In July 2008, a Saudi court sentenced a female chemistry student to 350 lashes and eight months in jail because she had a "telephone relationship" with one of her professors.

The killer is usually the father or brother, someone the girl has grown up with and knows well. Imagine the skulking, fearful life of a girl who knows that if she so much as meets a boy she likes without a chaperone, this may be her fate. Imagine the terror of seeing your own father walk up to you with a gun, a knife, or a cord. Imagine the killer: a man tortured so powerfully by his daughter's shame that in order to live up to his clan's twisted sense of right and wrong, he takes up a gun or a knife and kills the girl he has raised, whom he once dandled on his knee and helped to take her first steps.

This is not an ancient custom, long forgotten, like medieval witch burning. Every year at least five thousand honor killings are committed around the world, according to the United Nations Population Fund, which adds that this is a conservative estimate. Most of them take place among communities from or in Pakistan, Saudi Arabia, Syria, Iran, Iraq, Jordan, Turkey, Egypt, Algeria, and Morocco, all of them Muslim countries. Not all the victims are Muslim—honor killings do also occur among Sikhs and non-Muslim Kurds—but most of them are.

This is the crucial element in honor killing, what distinguishes it from random, individual crimes of passion: it is most often approved by the wider community. As a parent, you will be excluded from society if you "permit" your daughter to "misbehave"; mothers will be sneered at, fathers will be seen as impotent, weak, freakish. You will be redeemed only if you put an end to your daughter's misbehavior.

In 2006, in a BBC poll of five hundred young immigrants in Britain (many of them Muslim, but also some Hindus and Sikhs), one in ten said honor killings could be justified. No such poll has been taken in America, and I am not trying to say that Muslims who live in the United States necessarily would say the same. But the fact remains that honor killings do happen in America.

Five months after Amina and Sarah Said were killed, in the town of Henrietta in northern New York a twenty-two-year-old Afghan man stabbed his nineteen-year-old sister because she had disgraced their family and was a "bad Muslim girl," according to court documents. She was going to clubs and wearing immodest clothing, and planned to leave the family home. As I read more about it, I learned that the case was the second in four years in the same county in which a Muslim man had killed or tried to kill a family member in order to restore his own honor. In April 2004 Ismail Peltek, an immigrant from Turkey, stabbed and beat his wife to death and wounded his two daughters at their home in Scottsville, five miles from Henrietta. He told investigators that he was attempting to restore his family's honor after his wife and one daughter were sexually assaulted by a relative and the other daughter was "sullied" by a medical examination.

In July 2008 in Jonesboro, a suburb of Atlanta, police investigators reported that Chaudhry Rashad, a Pakistani man, who owned a pizza parlor, admitted to strangling his twenty-five-year-old daughter, Sandela, with the cord from an iron, because she wanted to leave the husband he had arranged for her to marry in Pakistan. According to the police, Sandela had refused to continue living with her husband in Chicago and had returned to her parents' house, where she told her father she wanted a divorce. According to one report, "When the police arrived, he stated that he did nothing wrong." A photo of the victim posted on the Internet showed a pasty-faced, uncomfortable-looking girl with a look of anguish in her eyes.

In February 2009 in Buffalo, New York, a forty-seven-year-old Muslim businessman who had set up a cable TV station to "promote more favorable views of Muslims," beheaded his wife, who was seeking to divorce him. Muzzammil Hassan had previously been very violent, and Aasiya, the mother of his two young children, had just obtained a protection order banning him from their home.

In every case American police, officials, and reporters seemed to bend over backward to avoid the heinous words *honor killing*, as if a change of label could transform these horrific killings into ordinary domestic crimes. It made me wonder: Were there no organizations in the United States that could look at these issues? Not that I planned to start one at that time—I had had my fill of politics. But, I thought, someone needs to do something; there should be some kind of activism under way, some kind of visibility, some kind of group.

Honor killing is not a random expression of a personal madness. The murders of Amina and Sarah Said in Irving, Texas, were punishments for those two girls' perceived infringement of a cultural order. Although that order is old and brutal and comes from far away, it can operate in Dallas or Henrietta or Atlanta as lethally as anywhere else.

* * *

When I read about honor killings I am haunted by the certitude that something, many things, could have been done. There were plenty of signals that, in hindsight, could have set alarm bells ringing in Irving long before Yaser Said picked up his gun. A clear and well-established pattern of beliefs and behavior is involved in all these cases. Is there an urgent need to try to recognize this pattern and prevent these killings? Yes. Are we talking about how to do this? No.

Why not? Why the hell not?

When Muslim women face not just oppression but violent death, why aren't the feminists out protesting these abusers? Where are the great European and American campaigners who powered the contemporary movement for women's equality in the West? Where, to take just one example, is Germaine Greer, author of such classics of Western feminism as *The Female Eunuch*? Greer believes the genital mutilation of girls needs to be considered in context. Trying to stop it, she has written, would be "an attack on cultural identity." She goes on:

> The African women who practice genital mutilation do so primarily because they think the result is more attractive. The young woman who lies unflinching while the circumciser grinds her clitoris off between two stones is proving that she will make a good wife, equal to all the anguish of child-bearing and daily toil. . . . Western women, fully accoutered with nail polish (which is incompatible with manual work), high-heeled shoes (disastrous for the posture and hence the back, and quite unsuitable for walking long distances over bad roads) and brassieres . . . denounce female circumcision without the shadow of a suspicion that their behavior is absurd.

What, you may wonder, does Greer have to say about honor killing? In December 2007, at a lecture she was giving in Melbourne, Australia, on Jane Austen, an Australian writer named Pamela Bone asked Greer if she saw any parallels between the concept of family honor in Austen's *Pride and Prejudice* and the concept of family honor in Middle Eastern societies today. She then asked why Western feminists seem so reluctant to speak out against things such as honor killings. According to Bone, Greer answered, "It's very tricky. I am constantly being asked to go to Darfur to interview rape victims. I can talk to rape victims here. Why should I go to Darfur to talk to rape victims?"

When Bone answered, "Because it's so much worse there," Greer asked, "Who says it is?"

Bone explained that she had been to Darfur and assured Greer that the situation there was worse. Greer responded, "Well, it is just very tricky to try to change another culture. We let down the victims of rape here. We haven't got it right in our own courts. What good would it do for me to go over there and try to tell them what to do? I am just part of decadent Western culture and they think we're all going to hell fast, and maybe we are all going to hell fast. But we do care. We do oppose these things. We are all wearing white ribbons this week [a reference to an international campaign to eliminate violence against women], aren't we? A lot of good that will do."

In her article about the incident in *The Australian,* Bone shrewdly observed, "Behind Greer's enthusiastically received comments is the dreary cultural relativism that pervades the thinking of so many of those once described as on the Left. We are no better than they are. We should not impose our values on them. We can criticise only our own. . . . Odd that so many old feminists think racism is worse than sexism."

I read and reread the piece, which a friend forwarded to me, and thought, *Tricky? "It is very tricky to change another culture"?* What has happened to Greer and her core values? It is truly absurd for someone like Greer, who is schooled in philosophy, not to see that the element of choice is crucial to distinguish between the behavior of an adult "victim" of the pain of fashionable shoes and the pain of a child who is truly a victim of violence. It is unconscionable for her to refrain from speaking out against honor killing because it would be "tricky" to challenge the culture that condones it.

Feminism developed in the West. It is a child of the Enlightenment, the period that developed ideas of individual liberty. But even before the Enlightenment, even at its darkest, Western culture was kinder to women than the tribal Islamic culture of the Arabs. To be sure there were practices in Europe and America such as labeling women "witches," then torturing, drowning, or burning them. Domestic violence, stigmatization, and the exclusion of women from public roles and participation in government were also common. Reading the lives of the women of the past frequently makes me speechless with rage and pity. The belief that women are fickle, irrational, and unreliable appears to have once been almost universal, as was marriage as a practical business transaction between families, conducted by male guardians. Western history is full of the tragic stories of child brides.

But there are differences between Western culture and that of other civilizations. Women and men in Arabia, China, India, and Africa may have dreamed of liberation from their respective shackles. Perhaps they discussed ways of changing the minds of their oppressors and even organized and rebelled against subjection. But it was only in the West that the ideas, words, organizations, and successful revolutions of liberty actually saw the light of day.

The story of feminism, or at least feminist thought, is also, at first, largely a story of aristocrats. Young men and women were permitted to mingle (although under strict rules and with chaperones). In many European societies following the Middle Ages daughters were permitted to learn to read and write, to study history, music, even philosophy, if only to be capable of conducting witty conversations on social occasions. Rather than memorizing traditional stories and poems, which was my grandmother's and her grandmother's education, with the rigid moral aim of preserving the habits and customs of our forefathers, Western women could go one decisive step further: they could construct logical arguments and ideas of their own.

Western women during and after the era of the Enlightenment were able to lament their inferior position. They were able to do this in a language and a manner that made perfect sense to some of the men of their time, notably John Stuart Mill. Daughters of the Enlightenment, like the English Mary Wollstonecraft and later the American Margaret Fuller, were pioneers of feminism in the West. Among the original feminists' first demands was the plea that the institutions of higher learning be open to women, or at least that colleges be established and reserved for women.

Sadly, some Muslim women who are now lucky enough to benefit from a high-quality education at these same institutions choose to defend the image of Islam over the rights of women. Such educated women (and I have met many) are still the lucky few. High-quality education is closed to millions of their fellow countrywomen. They boast of their privileges: their university education, their experiences with liberal fathers and brothers, their designer accoutrements, and their freedom to travel without the watchful presence of a guardian. But they ignore those underprivileged masses with whom they purport to share a religion and a culture. Some take it one step further: they claim that the subjugation of Muslim women is "folklore," that it happens only in remote, obscure villages, in just a few countries. All this, they claim, is on its way out, a leftover from history, nothing serious, nothing to worry about.

When slavery divided their nation, American feminists grasped the immorality of the arguments used by the slaveholders. They denounced slavery, but they took their reasoning one step further to also indict the values that justified the treatment of women as property. It is ironic that many educated Muslim women are so well able to condemn the principles used by foreign imperialists a century ago to dominate colonized countries but shy away from addressing the moral framework that underpins injustices against their own Muslim sisters.

The civil rights movement in the United States provided another opportunity for American feminists to side with African Americans who were denied their rights because of the color of their skin. And again these feminists stretched the argument beyond discrimination on the basis of color. They stood up to their husbands, fathers, brothers, teachers, and preachers; they argued that, if discrimination on the basis of color was wrong, then it was equally wrong to discriminate on the basis of sex. If the laws of the land were going to be changed and policies adopted that protected the civil rights of blacks, then the laws should be changed and new policies adopted to protect the civil rights of women too.

In passionate debates on decolonization in Europe, many European feminists stood alongside the "freedom fighters" who strove for nationhood and independence. The reasons for self-rule were clear to them. And they did not waste the opportunity to point out that, if once-colonized people could be trusted to govern their collective destinies, then so could women be trusted with their individual destinies.

All these were conflicts of principle. All of these struggles addressed the consequences of denying men and women their freedom. All these struggles were won essentially by revealing the immorality of the opposing arguments, whether they invoked the Bible or long-held feudalistic traditions. (Those who wanted slavery, civil rights abuses, and misogyny to continue all used religious arguments.) These arguments were revealed, reviled, and ridiculed, and eventually the laws that institutionalized inequality were repealed.

Yet, paradoxically, because these struggles were all fought against white men they helped fix in the minds of most people the simplistic notion that blacks, women, and colonized peoples can be victims only of white male oppression. Having sided with other movements of social revolution, such as the movements for national independence in Southeast Asia and minority rights of all kinds, particularly the fight against apartheid and for the Palestinians, feminists began to define white men as the ultimate and only oppressors. White men had engaged in the slave trade, apartheid, and colonialism as well as in the subjugation of women. Nonwhite men were, almost by definition, seen as members of the oppressed.

As a result, the plight of Muslim women—indeed all third-world women who are oppressed in the name of a moral framework of custom or creed created and maintained by men of color—has largely gone unchallenged. A few nonprofit organizations address it, to be sure; the World Bank, for one, has grown more self-confident in condemning the subjugation of Muslim women. But the massive public effort to reveal, ridicule, revile, and replace old views has not yet begun.

In fact a certain kind of feminism has worsened things for the female victims of misogyny perpetrated by men of color. My colleague at the American Enterprise Institute, Christina Hoff-Sommers, calls this "the feminism of resentment." This is the position of "feminists [who] believe that our society [read, Western society] is best described as a 'male hegemony,' a 'sex/gender system' in which the dominant gender [read, white male] works to keep women cowering and submissive." These feminists of resentment refuse to appreciate the progress Western women have made, from the right to vote to the punishment of those who try to harass women at work. They see only the iniquity of the white man and reduce such universal concepts as freedom of expression and the right to choose one's own destiny to mere artifacts of Western culture. They thus provide the men of color with an escape route. If the king of Saudi Arabia is questioned about the laws in his land pertaining to women, he merely demands respect for his faith, culture, and sovereignty, and apparently this argument suffices.

Because these Western feminists manifest an almost neurotic fear of offending a minority group's culture, the situation of Muslim women creates a huge philosophical problem for them.

There are 13.5 million women in Saudi Arabia. Imagine what it's like to be a woman there: you are essentially under permanent house arrest.

There are 34 million women in Iran. Imagine being a woman there: you may be married legally when you are nine; on the order of a judge, you may be lashed ninety-nine times with a whip for committing adultery; then, on the order of a second judge, you may be sentenced five months later to death by stoning. This is what happened to Zoreh and Azar Kabiri-niat in Shahryar, Iran, in 2007; after being flogged for "illicit relations" they were then tried again and found guilty of "committing adultery while married." The punishment they were to receive for adultery was death by stoning. Their sentence was recently confirmed, on appeal.

There are 82.5 million women in Pakistan. Imagine being a girl there: you grow up knowing that if you dishonor your family, if you refuse to marry the man chosen for you, or if someone thinks you have a boyfriend, you are likely to be beaten, ostracized, and killed, probably by your father or brother, who has the support of your entire immediate family. You're also liable to be jailed on the grounds of the Huddud, laws of Islamic transgression.

Imagine being a girl in Egypt, Sudan, Somalia—any one of twenty-six countries around the Middle East, Africa, and the Pacific. Your clitoris has been cut, as well as your inner labia, and the opening of your vagina has been sewn together. Even though excision is not mentioned in the Quran, most of the 130 million women alive worldwide who have undergone this brutal ritual are Muslim women.

Virginity is the obsession, the neurosis of Islam. Wherever there is a

Muslim community, forced or coerced marriage, even child marriage, is common, even in families who are relatively educated. Like domestic violence, most people consider it normal. Men are the guardians of their daughters. A girl is therefore the property of her father, who is entitled to transfer that property to the husband he selects. Child marriage is also a logical outgrowth of the Muslim fixation on female purity: if you marry her off early, as soon as possible after menstruation, she won't have time to damage your reputation and devalue your goods. The reality of this can be extremely bitter: imagine a thirteen-year-old girl transferred to the arms of an old man she has never seen before.

Child marriage is illegal in Western countries, of course, but other aspects of the Muslim oppression of women can readily be imported into both Europe and the United States. The fact that honor killings can occur in Texas, New York, and Georgia makes the virtual silence of Western feminists on this subject all the more bizarre and deplorable.

Western women have power. They are now firmly established in the workforce. They have access to contraception, to their own bank accounts, to the vote. They can marry the men they choose, or choose not to marry at all, and if nature allows it, they can have as many or as few children as they want. They can own property, travel wherever they choose, and read any book, newspaper, or magazine they wish. They can have an opinion on the moral choices of others and express that opinion freely, even publish it.

In the West the notorious glass ceiling within most professions has been cracked, though not altogether removed; we can now surely make time for some more vital issues. If feminism means anything at all, women with power should be addressing their energies to help the girls and women who suffer the pain of genital mutilation, who are at risk of being murdered because of their Western lifestyle and ideas, who must ask for permission just to leave the house, who are treated no better than serfs, branded and mutilated, traded without regard to their wishes. If you are a true feminist, these women should be your first priority.

We women in rich countries have an obligation to mobilize to assist other women. Only our outrage and our political pressure can lead to change. We need to push the situation of Muslim women to the top of the agenda. It's not enough to say it's shocking, it's appalling, and to condemn only individual acts. We need to challenge and bring down the tribal honor-and-shame culture as codified in the Islamic religion.

Organizations from within those communities will lobby and litigate to change the subject, then will plead vulnerability and victim-hood. Their advocates among the multiculturalist intellectuals and appeasing politicians will support them. It's essential that we maintain awareness that what we women advocates are talking about are two distinct value systems between which there is no possible compromise.

Muslim women are not the only group of women who are oppressed. As I wrote in 2006, in an article for the *International Herald Tribune*, between 113 and 200 million women around the world are demographically "missing," and every year between 1.5 and 3 million women and girls lose their lives as the result of violence or neglect because of their sex. Female babies and young girls in many parts of the world, not only Muslim countries, die disproportionately from neglect. The brutal international sex trade in young girls kills uncounted numbers of women. Roughly 600,000 women die giving birth every year, and domestic violence is a major killer of women in every country on the globe. "Gendercide" takes many forms, but for most of these suffering women, the major issue is poverty.

The subjugation of Muslim women, by contrast, is a matter of principle.

What can be done? First, we need a worldwide campaign against the values that permit these kinds of crime. Cultures that endorse the denial of women's rights over their own bodies and fail to protect them from the worst kind of physical abuse must be pressured to reform. They should not be treated as respectable members of the community of nations. Today human rights activists are frustrated in their work; they are denied access to data and are intimidated or ignored. A serious international effort must be made to record and document violence against girls and women, country by country, and to expose the reality of their intolerable suffering.

But the more pressing business is what feminists can do now to prevent an alien culture of oppression from taking root in the West.

In America too Muslim girls may be pulled out of school by their parents, violently punished at home on a routine basis, obsessively watched over and forcibly married and even murdered in the name of honor. Such basic, brutal violations of women's rights must be confronted head-on and effective measures to protect Muslim girls urgently devised. Ignoring the problem means abandoning the next victims to their fate; even worse, it means abandoning the core values that sustain Western society. This is what Americans can learn from Europe's experience with Muslim immigration: we simply cannot compromise our own principles by tolerating honor killing, female genital mutilation, and other such practices.

In Holland and the United Kingdom organizations have been set up to educate the police, schools, and other government agencies about this specific type of domestic violence. However, citizens and officials still find it difficult to talk about these issues without being accused of Islamophobia and racism. In Holland, for instance, I called for a control system on female genital mutilation to be put in place. Such a system was developed, but on a voluntary basis, which is absurd, because a mother who is convinced that she is doing what's right according to the sacred custom of her heritage will not come forward and say, "I've just committed an act that will send me to prison for fifteen years."

Well-meaning people sometimes look at me kindly at this point and perform the emotional equivalent of patting my hand. They are rarely impolite enough to actually say so, but they clearly believe that this battle is a hopeless one: there is no way that half the current Muslim population around the world can be freed.

I choose not to adopt this defeatist approach. I believe the honor-and-shame culture can be discarded. To think otherwise is to define Muslims as incapable of growth and adaptation, and I can't think of anything more pejorative and racist. To effect real change will undoubtedly require massive shifts in attitude, the dismantling of a whole infrastructure of religious thought and tribal values. But in order to achieve this we desperately need a new feminism that will attract Muslim women. The militant anti-male discourse of some feminist leaders is abhorrent to me and, I think, a perversion of the message of Mary Wollstonecraft. Feminism in the twenty-first century needs to move on, to bridge the gap between Western women and those they've left behind. Just as the world's free thinkers and lovers of liberty once banded together to support the fight against apartheid, we should be banding together to support the rights of women in Islam.

As I watched the 2008 presidential and vice presidential election campaigns of Hillary Clinton and Sarah Palin on TV—both of them contending for two of the most powerful offices in the world—I eagerly waited for the moment when they would talk about what they planned to do for other women, longing for the moment when someone would ask the question, demand a serious debate on the rights of Muslim women. It never happened.

Now Hillary Clinton is secretary of state; before her, Condoleezza Rice and Madeleine Albright held that office. It appears a silent consensus has emerged in Washington that the Department of State should be headed by women. Some people complain that this is a half measure, to placate us women, because what we really want is the presidency. But I disagree. I believe having a woman as secretary of state represents a huge chance. It means that an American woman will sit down with the leaders of the rest of the world, including the Arab world, the Muslim world, and be treated not merely as an equal but as the representative of the world's only superpower.

The liberation of women is like a vast, unfinished house. The west wing is fairly complete. Most of us who reside in this corner enjoy privileges such as the right to vote and run for office. We have access to education, and we may earn our own living if we choose to. We have managed to convince most legislators on this side of the house that domestic violence, sexual harassment, and rape are crimes for which the perpetrator must be punished. We have reproductive rights over our bodies and our sexuality; although a girl's parents and teachers and community leaders may coach her, they make no attempt to coerce her into or out of a relationship with a man (and recently, even with another woman). Prospective mates may woo and worship but must swallow their pride if a girl rejects them.

Like all homes, the western side of the house is not always run smoothly. In some cases, the house rules are not enforced. Girls' complaints of domestic violence are ignored or denied or the perpetrator gets off with a warning or a punishment far less severe than the harm he has inflicted. Other women may feel that they do not receive equal compensation for doing the same jobs as their male colleagues; still others find themselves hitting a glass ceiling. Thus some women seek to furnish the house with more rules and to smash all the glass ceilings.

Go to the east wing, however, and what you find is worse than unfinished. Parts of it have been started, then abandoned, and are now falling into ruin. In other parts, every time a wall is put up someone comes and bulldozes it down. In what would have been beautiful courtyards there are shallow graves of nameless girls who died because they were not seen as worth feeding or treating for a common, curable illness. In the east wing girls are transported as property by their parents, often when young, to gratify the sexual urges of adults. There are girls working the land, fetching water, tending to livestock, cooking and cleaning from dawn to dusk with no pay for their labors, while others are beaten by their closest family members with impunity. Young women die while giving birth because they lack the most basic hygiene and medical care.

In some corners of the east wing mothers are not always delighted when they learn they are pregnant. A doctor will check whether the unborn child is a girl or a boy; if it is a girl he accepts the wretched mother's payment and removes it, and if she cannot afford the abortion, the child, once born, is suffocated or left alone to die. This abortion of girls is so systematic in some rooms of the east wing that you will find numerous boys without mates to marry them.

Closer to the middle of the east wing most women are banished from the public rooms and hallways, and if they can be glimpsed at all they are covered from head to toe in dark and ugly garments. Many never learn to read or write; they are forced into marriage and seem to live pregnant ever after. They have no reproductive rights. If raped, they must shoulder the burden of proof, and in some rooms women and girls as young as thirteen are flogged and stoned to death in public for their disobedience in sexual matters. In the eastern side of the house some people are so terrified of a woman's sexuality that they cut the genitals of girl children, mutilating and branding them with the mark of ownership.

These days many people from the east wing find their way to the other side of the house, even if it is only to the cramped servants' quarters. Here in the west wing the fate of girls in the east wing seems far away. And while the girls in the west wing remain preoccupied with creature comforts like the shade of paint, the size of the chandeliers, and the shape of the hedges in the garden, not to mention that bothersome glass ceiling, men from the east wing claim western rooms for themselves, where they can practice eastern habits.

I was sitting in my office in New York, high above the great, intense hub of the west wing, fantasizing that the wealthy women of the West would one day band together to make the liberation of the hovels of the east wing their greatest priority. They would surge forward to build a new edifice of freedom, strength, and plenty for the East, knocking down the old hovels and opening the visible and invisible prison doors to allow their sisters to see the light of day.

That is my dream. But frankly, I do not know if Western feminists have the courage or clarity of vision to help me realize it.

CHAPTER 16

Seeking God
but Finding Allah

One June evening in 2007 I had dinner in Rome with Father Antoine Bodar, a Dutch priest who had been recommended to me by a mutual friend. I found him to be rather inspiring, a peaceful, intellectual, and yet also very worldly man. The restaurant that he had chosen for us was just behind the Vatican, and as we sipped our wine I found myself genuinely enjoying the evening. Night was drawing in, the Renaissance buildings were lit up and became almost surreally majestic and beautiful, and I was struck by the idea that we were seated in a place of great power: the Hejaz of Christianity.

And yet, how are the mighty fallen, I thought to myself—or not fallen exactly, but faded. While Islam is rising across Europe, Christianity appears to be in decline in Muslim lands. Churches are falling empty, converted into apartments and offices, even nightclubs, or razed, while mosques are sprouting from the ground. The magnificent cathedrals of France are deserted; some people have even suggested that small disaffected chapels and churches should be modified into mosques in order to give the booming French Muslim communities space for prayer. This would also be a way to distance Islam from the hard-to-monitor garages and basements where young people are radicalized at a rapid rate.

As we sipped coffee, I tried to imagine having a meal in Mecca with a member of the 'ulema, or with any imam for that matter, almost anywhere. It seemed another demonstration of fundamental differences: Islam and Christianity are *not* the same.

I explained to Father Bodar why I had asked him to meet me. "I'm not a Christian, and I'm not here to ask you to help me convert and become one," I told him. "But I think the Christian churches should begin *dawa* exactly as Islam does. You need to compete, because you can be a powerful tool to reverse Islamization. You should start with Muslim neighborhoods in Rome. Europe is sleepwalking into disaster—cultural, ideological, and political disaster—because the authorities of the church have neglected the immigrant ghettos.

"The churches could go into Muslim communities, provide services just as the radical Muslims do: build new Catholic schools, hospitals, and community centers, just like the ones that were such a civilizing force under colonialism in Africa. Don't just leave this in the hands of governments—take an active role. The churches have the resources, the authority, and the motivation to convert Muslim immigrants to a more modern way of life and more modern beliefs. Teach hygiene, discipline, a work ethic, and also what you believe in. The West is losing the propaganda war. But you can compete with Islam outside Europe and vigorously assimilate Muslims within it."

Father Bodar positively beamed with happiness. He said he had been trying to achieve just this for years and that he had often been mocked for even suggesting it. The Roman Catholic Church has a long history of resisting religious challenges from inside and outside what used to be called Christendom. All kinds of heresies have been combated successfully from the earliest times. The Counter-Reformation saw the Church vigorously reassert itself against the teachings of Martin Luther and the other Protestant reformers. And, of course, the Church had fought against Islam not only in the time of the Crusades but also when, as recently as 1683, Muslim troops of the Ottoman sultan menaced the Holy Roman Emperor's capital, Vienna.

But what about the challenge facing Christian civilization today—the challenge of radical Islam that is already inside Europe's supposed fortress?

Islam claims to be the fastest-growing religion in the world today. This expansion is achieved partly through the relatively high birth rates of Muslim societies but also through *dawa,* by which people are persuaded to adopt its values and its outlook. Millions of Muslims now live in the West; clearly it's not enough to assume that the allure of the material plenty around them will sway these Muslims to relax into a Western value system of tolerance and individual rights. Some of them may, but the evidence is all around us that many will remain sympathetic to a worldview that is steeped in conspiracy theories and blames all Muslim failures on outsiders. Moreover some non-Muslims in the West will be attracted to that worldview and become converts.

You can (and must) fight violent jihadis with military might. But military means are just one element of war. Although it is important to stand your ground and deploy weaponry, you can't use military means to affect the larger mind-set that supports the Muslim warriors. Propaganda is a powerful tool of war geared to win over the masses, persuade them to defect, break their morale or their trust in their own ideology.

Some Westerners have a vision of Muslims as a mass of unbending, irrational, unthinking beings, incapable of calmly examining new ideas on their merit. But a Muslim's mind is just like anyone else's and is capable of absorbing new information. If Muslims can be helped to reexamine the bedrock ideas of Islam, they may then admit that the Prophet Muhammad's example is fallible, that not everything in the Quran is perfect or true, and that this doctrine can be adjusted so that the mental pain that comes of trying to apply it in the modern world is diminished.

I have a theory that most Muslims are in search of a redemptive God. They believe that there is a higher power and that this higher power is the provider of morality, giving them a compass to help them distinguish between good and bad. Many Muslims are seeking a God or a concept of God that in my view meets the description of the Christian God. Instead they are finding Allah. They find Allah mainly because many are born in Muslim families where Allah has been the reigning deity for generations; others are converts to Islam or the children of converts.

My theory is based on two observations. One is the fact that many Muslims—some pundits would say most—are instinctively appalled by the violence committed in the name of their faith. Their reaction to terrorism is always the same: *No, it cannot be. The terrorists have hijacked my religion. I think it is wrong to kill and maim people. My religion stands for peace; it tells me to be compassionate.* "Unto thee thy faith and unto me my faith," they quote from the Quran, thus proving to themselves that Islam promotes freedom of religion.

My second observation is that most Muslims do not know the content of the Quran or the Hadith or any other Islamic scripture. The much-quoted edict promoting freedom of religion is indeed in the Quran, but its authority is nullified by verses that descended upon the Prophet later, when he was better armed and when his following had grown to great numbers.

The Muslims who say that Allah is peaceful and compassionate simply do not know about other concepts of God, or the concepts they do have are wrong. They have been told that Christians have misunderstood the real God, Allah, that they are guilty of *shirk* (an unforgivable sin) by associating the one true God with the Holy Ghost and Jesus, a mere prophet, they argue, whom Christians wrongly put on the throne as the son of God.

The Muslims who hear all this (and worse) about Christianity hardly ever make an attempt to find out more. Meanwhile Christians have stopped teaching people in Muslim countries because the bitter resistance from the local Muslim clergy and political elites made it harder and harder to do so. In short, the Muslim masses are insulated from all alternative religions.

To change this, I have in mind a kind of spiritual competition. This was my question for Father Bodar in Rome: If Saudi Arabia invests millions of dollars in madrassas and a systematic campaign of *dawa*, taking advantage of all the institutions of freedom in the West, why should the Catholic Church, with its financial resources and its millions of steadfast followers, not do the same?

I hope my friends Richard Dawkins, Sam Harris, and Christopher Hitchens—the esteemed trinity of atheist activists in Britain and the United States—will not be dismayed by the idea of a strategic alliance between secular people and Christians, including the Roman Catholic Church. I concede that the idea is a little paradoxical. For centuries the proponents of the scientific revolution and the Enlightenment saw the Vatican as their archenemy. The Church persecuted and in some cases executed those it condemned as heretics. My atheist friends are right to point out that many Christians have abandoned biblical literalism only because of the constant criticism by such freethinkers. It is also true that there is no shortage of misogyny in the Judeo-Christian tradition. Contempt for women is inscribed in the works of Saint Paul.

But the modern Catholic Church is a very different and more tolerant institution. Christians in more recent times must be given some credit for heeding a least some of the critiques advanced by the thinkers of the Enlightenment. That very openness to criticism is what makes Christianity different from Islam.

Nor is Christianity riven as it used to be by bitter sectarian conflicts dating back to the Reformation. Today the relationship between the Catholic Church and the mainstream Protestant denominations, the Anglicans and Episcopalians, the Presbyterians, Unitarians, and Universalists, is peaceful. In most of the Western world these churches and their congregations either leave one another alone or have good ecumenical relations. Finally, the Christian churches have put behind them the centuries of anti-Semitism that so stained their reputation.

It is true that on a wide range of issues the Roman Catholic Church takes positions with which I, along with most liberals, disagree. On questions such as abortion, birth control, and women priests there are deep divisions within the Western world. Many American Protestants as well as Catholics are deeply opposed to abortion, a polarizing issue particularly in the United States. But all these differences are matters of debate and not matters of war. Debate, however bitter, takes place within Western societies in a peaceful if sometimes heated exchange of words. The occasional madman who blows up an abortion clinic or murders physicians who provide legal treatments to women whose pregnancies are unwanted is the exception that proves the rule.

The clash between Islam and the West is different. All possible means are used by the agents of radical Islam to defeat the West. Even though most of our attention is consumed by those Muslims who are willing to blow themselves up in the name of their religion, we cannot ignore the more subtle campaign of conversion and radicalization. For too long the West has sat back and allowed Islam to make a run at people who are susceptible to conversion. Sometimes I feel as if the only people in the West who really get this are Jews, who are far more exposed to the workings of radical Islam because of their contacts with the state of Israel.

Take a look at the institutions of the Enlightenment, the schools and universities established throughout the Western world on secular principles. To defend the values of the Enlightenment from the encroachment of Islamist thought they must wake up and see how effectively they have been infiltrated. Their resources are limited, and large donations from Saudi princes and Qatari sultans come with strings attached. Their curricula are increasingly politicized, and they tolerate and even encourage the rise of all kinds of anti-Enlightenment movements based on feelings of group grievance and victimhood. Some teachers even encourage their classes to wallow in self-flagellation over the misdeeds of Western history. Eastern, Middle Eastern, and African cultures that see compromise and conciliation as manifestations of weakness interpret all this as a sign of their own impending victory: it emboldens them.

In this clash of civilizations the West needs to criticize the cultures of men of color too. We need to drop the ethos of relativist respect for non-Western religions and cultures if respect is simply a euphemism for appeasement. But we need to do more than criticize. We need—urgently—to offer an alternative message that is superior to the message of submission.

When I'm told to be careful not to impose Western values on people who don't want them, I beg to differ. I was not born in the West and I did not grow up in the West. But the delight of being able once I came to the West to let my imagination run free, the pleasure of choosing whom I want to associate with, the joy of reading what I want, and the thrill of being in control of my life—in short, my freedom—is something I feel intensely as I manage to extricate myself from all the shackles and obstacles that my bloodline and my religion imposed.

I am not the only one who feels and thinks this.

The multiculturalism and relativism so rampant in Western institutions of learning remind me of my aunt Khadija's imposing and beautiful polished antique cabinet in Mogadishu. One day, when she moved the huge wooden cupboard to clean behind it, the whole thing came down with a shocking crash. An infinite army of termites had ensconced themselves in the rear of the cabinet and had slowly, inch by inch, eaten almost the whole thing. No one had suspected it, and now only the exterior skeleton of the frame was left.

I want nothing more than that pro-Enlightenment, free-thinking atheists should spontaneously organize themselves to combat the comparable gnawing threat of radical Islam. But the likelihood of such an organization attracting significant support seems remote because the children of the Enlightenment are hopelessly fragmented in their views about how to deal with Islam. Many contemporary Western thinkers have unconsciously imbibed the toxin of appeasement with the ideas of equality and free speech. They give chairs in the most distinguished and best institutions of higher learning to apologists for Islam. There is no unity, no shared view of how to deal with this threat. Indeed, those of us who clearly see the threat are dismissed as alarmists.

That is why I think we must also appeal to other, more traditional sources of ideological strength in Western society. And that must include the Christian churches. There are people in Europe and America who maintain that it is secularism that has made us defenseless against a Muslim onslaught. But it is not only leftists who appease Islam. Afflicted with similar pangs of white guilt, many prominent Christian theologians have also become accomplices of jihad.

When I came to the West what I found truly amazing was the fact that believers, agnostics, and unbelievers could debate with and even ridicule one another without ever resorting to violence. It is this right of free expression that is now under attack. And in time of war, internal feuding in the ranks—between atheists and agnostics, Christians and Jews, Protestants and Catholics—serves only to weaken the West. So long as we atheists and classical liberals have no effective programs of our own to defeat the spread of radical Islam, we should work with enlightened Christians who are willing to devise some. We should bury the hatchet, rearrange our priorities, and fight together against a much more dangerous common enemy.

Given the choice, I would by far rather live in a Christian than a Muslim country. Christianity in the West today is more humane, more restrained, and more accepting of criticism and debate. The Christian concept of God today is more benign, more tolerant of dissent. But the most important difference between the two civilizations is the exit option. A person who chooses to opt out of Christianity may be excommunicated from the Church community, but he is not harmed; his destiny is left to God. Muslims, however, impose Allah's rules on each other. Apostates—people, like me, who leave the faith— are *supposed* to be killed.

Christians too killed blasphemers and heretics, but that was long ago, during the dark days of the Inquisition. On September 12, 2006, at the University of Regensburg, Germany, where he had once taught theology as a professor, Pope Benedict gave a wide-ranging lecture, titled "Faith, Reason, and the University—Memories and Reflections." In it he proclaimed that any faith in God must also obey reason; God cannot ask you to do something unreasonable, because God created reason. Islam, he pointed out, is not like Catholicism: it is predicated on the idea that God may *overturn* law and human reason. Allah may demand immoral or unreasonable behavior, for he is all-powerful and demands absolute submission.

In spite of the pope's invitation to dialogue with people in other cultures, his speech unleashed Muslim protests around the world, and several churches were fire-bombed: more evidence of the intolerance of criticism of Islam by Islamists. This speech was still very much present in everyone's mind during my visit to Rome eight months later. Indeed, Father Bodar and I discussed it.

Pope Benedict XVI, the Vicar of Christ, Successor of the Prince of the Apostles, Supreme Pontiff of the Universal Church and Servant of the Servants of God, heads the world's strongest system of religious hierarchy. No other spiritual authority can claim to control such a well-structured network. I'm sure that his pyramid of priests, bishops, and cardinals has kept him fully aware that another spiritual potentate, King Abdullah bin Abdul Aziz al-Saud, feudal ruler of Saudi Arabia and Custodian of the Two Holy Mosques, has for years been investing in *dawa*, in unifying peoples of different languages and geographies into a powerful body called the Organization of the Islamic Conference, a formidable and wealthy body that has transformed the United Nations Human Rights Commission into a sad comedy, organized the Muslim boycott of Danish companies after the publication of cartoons depicting the Prophet Muhammad, and sought to influence the domestic policies of several European nations. Members of the OIC, for instance, mounted a well-organized campaign of global condemnation against Switzerland when a majority of voters supported a ban on the building of minarets on Swiss soil. However, members of the nations of the OIC pay only lip service to protect Christians living in their own countries from persecution.

The pope also knows that wherever radical Islamists become a majority they oppress other faiths. In Muslim countries there is no equal competition for souls, hearts, and minds, because atheists and missionaries and communities of Christians are forced to operate in an atmosphere of physical menace. And although there are plenty of mosques in Rome, not a single church is permitted in Riyadh.

Imagine if the pope were to organize some fifty nations as the "Organization of the Christian Conference." They could dispatch deputations of ambassadors every time construction of a church was banned in a Muslim country. Where the OIC seeks Islamic dominance and the erosion of human rights, an OCC would aim for the defense of Western civilization and the advancement of human rights.

A confrontation between the values held by Islam and those of the West is inevitable. There *is* already a clash, and we *are* in some sense already at war. That Western civilization is superior is not simply my opinion but a reality I have experienced and continue to appreciate every day. I assume that the West will win. The question is how.

Can the various churches of Christianity help stem this rising tide of violent Islam? Can today's Christianity play a role in preserving the values of Western civilization? Can the Vatican join in this campaign, if not lead the way—or is it doomed to become a decorative relic, like the European royal families and the fish fork? Can the Established Churches of Europe heed my call—or will the cultural and moral relativists prevail, Christian leaders like the Archbishop of Canterbury, who professes to have an "understanding" attitude toward Shari'a?

*   *   *

Globalization is not just an economic process, moving jobs to countries that have cheap labor, bringing goods to countries with money. It's also about people. The commercial unification of the world during the West's long boom following World War II brought millions of people from historically Muslim countries to live in Europe with extraordinary speed, far quicker than the process of establishing Christianity in Europe's colonies or the march of Muslim armies from the Arabian Peninsula to the heart of Europe in the century that followed the death of the Prophet. These millions of modern Muslims brought their medieval social mores with them.

At first they were guest workers who intended to work in Europe only temporarily. They left their families in the distant villages of Berber Morocco or Anatolian Turkey. Their belief in Islam was mostly like my grandmother's, a diluted, superstitious tradition, more a set of cultural rituals than a rulebook, and they had few mosques in Europe to sustain or harden their observance of the faith. Many of them drank alcohol and adopted other Western habits, and only intermittently observed such Muslim rules as praying five times a day.

But in the 1980s Islam was resurgent again following the siege of Mecca and the revolution in Iran, and many *families* began arriving in European neighborhoods such as Whitechapel and Amsterdam-West. They congregated in geographically separate communities. And, particularly when there was no colonial history with their host country (and thus no common language), as those communities grew larger they kept more and more to themselves. They shopped at their own shops and watched television from Turkey or Morocco by satellite. And then the imams arrived.

Just as European governments and other civil society groups underestimated the intentions of the radical expansionist agents of Islam, the churches, both Catholic and Protestant, neglected to offer the new Muslim immigrants the spiritual guidance they sought. To be sure, many Christian volunteer aid workers offered immigrant communities neutral and pragmatic advice along with social assistance. Islamic charity is conditional on your beliefs; these Christians were ecumenical to the point of making no attempt to convert those they sought to help. Ecumenism for most Christians is a measure of progress, allowing a choice of faiths and forms of worship while establishing peaceful relations between them. Islam is quite different. It was started by a warrior who conquered faster than he could think through a theology or political theory. Islam since his death has been plagued by a crisis of authority, leaving an everlasting vacuum of power that, throughout the history of Islam, has been filled by men who seize power by force. The concepts of jihad, martyrdom, and a life that begins only after death are never challenged. The Christian leaders now wasting precious time and resources on a futile exercise of interfaith dialogue with the self-appointed leaders of Islam should redirect their efforts to converting as many Muslims as possible to Christianity, introducing them to a God who rejects Holy War and who has sent his son to die for all sinners out of love for mankind.

Perhaps if volunteers had more actively preached to these early immigrants and actively sought to convert them to Christianity, the tragedy of the unassimilable Muslim might have been avoided. Converts to Christianity would have recognized the radicals when they arrived and resisted the siren song of jihad.

By the 1990s, however, radical Muslim preachers were going door to door in the tower blocks of Leeds and Lille and Limburg. Indeed, in some of those cities—historically the heartland of Christianity—it seemed easier to find Allah than the Christian God. Despite the enormous potential for assimilation offered by a European urban environment—free schooling of a quality that was certainly much better than that in most immigrants' home communities, free health care, plentiful consumer goods and trinkets, and a powerful cult of material well-being—startling numbers of European-born children began turning toward the Saudi-trained imams and their extremist revival of Islam.

This is a tragic story of countless missed opportunities. How is it possible that a man who has grown up in Scotland and has trained there to become a doctor could become so devoted to a violent interpretation of Islam as to want to blow himself up at an airport along with countless women and children? How could this happen, after so much potential acculturation, so much potential contact with the values of tolerance, secular humanism, and individual rights?

Part of the answer is that out of a misplaced respect for the immigrants' culture, no real, concerted attempt has been made to shift their traditional ways of mind. Despite high rates of crime and unemployment and low rates of success in schools—all indicators of a failure to integrate large numbers of Muslim immigrants into European society—there has not been a deliberate drive to urge immigrants to adopt Western values. The other part of the answer is the willful denial by Westerners that there is a clash of values between the West and the rest, and particularly between Islam and the West.

For decades European leaders, including Christian leaders, neglected to bring the newcomers into their fold. They unthinkingly supposed that the buffet of material pleasure and individual freedoms on offer in European cities would be sufficient to lure immigrants from Muslim countries into adopting modern lifestyles. They assumed that, along with pop music, denim jeans, and the legal right to have sex at age sixteen, the values of individual rights and individual choice, intellectual freedom, and tolerance would entice Muslims into accepting modernity in every sense. Christian leaders assumed the passive position that people will be attracted to the church on their own and that the church had no business trying to persuade them of the superiority of the Christian God.

Muslim Brotherhood members, by contrast, are tireless in their efforts. A Muslim preacher working in a neighborhood in Glasgow or Rotterdam sets up sports clubs, classes, and discussion groups for children and teenagers, works with criminals and drug users, creates networks to maintain order in his community. In immigrant neighborhoods across Europe so-called Brotherhood Women—young and single and bursting with the energy of the born-again—work their way through the housing projects asking how they can help harried mothers. They clean house and offer tape-recorded cassettes of sermons, along with DVDs of desperate martyrs. They counsel on parenting, on employment benefits, on what to do with wayward kids. They give money and bring medicine. There is no end to the kindness; they are doing this for Allah.

But Allah wants something in return for all this charity. He wants submission of will, mind, and body so total that those kids who are saved from the streets and drug addiction are persuaded to commit to the jihad against the infidel.

As a result the people who live in these ghettoized communities no longer feel alone and alienated. Feelings of social rejection, unemployment, poor educational performance, and, perhaps most urgently, the fear of what a modern value system may do to their daughters—all of these draw people to the Brotherhood's message of an alternative, pure, and good life. Return to the ways of Islam, and everything will be better: this is religion as a dream of returning to the old, sure ways.

For the younger generation, who feel no roots in their parents' home countries, the Brotherhood's focus on the global community of Islam also makes it a powerful force. Its simple message of unity in a movement of anti-Western jihad is the teenage dream: rebellion *with* a cause. All over Europe such young people live in what were once Christian neighborhoods. These places had churches, with congregations, priests, and ladies who put flowers in the chapel every Sunday. But far too few people crossed the tracks and stretched a hand out to the Muslim families who moved into the housing projects of Europe. No priest matched the efforts of the Moroccan imam with the box of cassette tapes. The random messages of Nike advertisements and pop culture were not enough to anchor this new, disoriented immigrant population into a sense of citizenship and community with Europe. The jihadis didn't have any real competition; of course they spread.

The churches must have seen this happening, and yet for some reason didn't seek to raise the alarm. They did not try to fight either the massive wave of conversions of traditional Muslims to fundamentalism or the smaller wave of conversions of people from historically Christian communities to Islam. The reason seems clear: the Vatican and all the established Protestant churches of northern Europe believed naively that interfaith dialogue would magically bring Islam into the fold of Western civilization. It has not happened, and it will not happen.

Right now there are three kinds of messages being disseminated in many immigrant communities in European cities: the traditional, more dilute Islam that is mainly a kind of cultural habit; strong, radical Islam, which is clearly on the rise; and the get-rich-quick scams offered by the lords of organized crime who deal in the trafficking of women, weapons, and drugs.

I would prefer, as a fourth option, to offer Muslims who cling to the idea of a creator and eternal life a religious leader like Jesus, who said, "Render to Caesar the things that are Caesar's, and to God the things that are God's," rather than a warrior like Muhammad, who demanded that the pious seek to gain power by the sword.

To help ground these people in Western society, the West needs the Christian churches to get active again in propagating their faith. It needs Christian schools, Christian volunteers, the Christian message. The Saudis have no hesitation in converting Jean-François and Gustav to become "born-again" Muslims. The pope should be spreading his faith too. For Islam isn't a genetic inheritance. A child born in Holland is not bound to be a Muslim just because his parents come from Morocco.

In the blighted neighborhoods of Europe where the jihadis currently have free rein, there is no special reason why Christians should not set up after-school programs, peer programs for teenagers, sports clubs, and homework help. Religious people are generally more effective than state-salaried caseworkers because they give more time, and when the beneficiaries of this kind of very practical help realize that it is coming from volunteers, that in itself is impressive. For a Muslim housewife who feels her family is falling apart, who has no idea how to bring up teenagers in a modern society, whose child has begun stealing or breaking windows, and who receives constant demands and reprimands from social workers, teachers, and policemen, for such a woman it is an intense relief to have a volunteer who comes to help with cleaning, who says, "I know what you're going through," and who comes back again and again. The housewife no longer feels alone.

In the same way, I believe, we now need a Christian school for every madrassa, the Quran schools where children and young adults learn only to drone the Quran and the message of the Brotherhood. Christian schools are often poles of excellence in an otherwise blighted educational landscape, particularly in inner-city neighborhoods. They are schools that teach more than how to recite a sacred book by heart. They teach not only the full range of sciences and humanities, but also about a God who created reason and told humankind to let reason prevail.

This is a contest that Christians have every chance of winning. The belief system of the Muslim Brotherhood stems from a very narrow, Arab culture; that, it seems to me, is its weak point. My own country, Somalia, has always been Muslim, but it was never Wahabi until the mid-1980s. Previously, for most Somalis, Islam was more a question of tradition and occasional ritual than daily practice. Women frequently went bare-headed and wore Western clothes. But when people feel alienated and lost, when fundamental changes in their society make the world strange and unrecognizable, they can become vulnerable to foreign influences.

Many people who allow themselves to be drawn into Wahabist Muslim groups are looking for spiritual solace and a strong sense of community in a cruel and troubling world. I was one too, as a teenager. What they are getting, though, is a toxic mix of Arab imperialism and a violent, revolutionary cult in the guise of religion. If you suggest to a Somali woman in Whitechapel that she become an Arab, of course she'll reject you. But if you show charity and generosity and help her develop a sense of order and goodness, if you terrify her with the punishments and proximity of the hereafter, and if you are the only religion on the market, then she too may be tempted to join the Muslim Brotherhood, and her children may be indoctrinated and recruited for jihad. This is the successful method used by Hezbollah in Lebanon and increasingly by radical Muslims all over Europe.

Religious belief gives you companionship in adversity, the security of fixed rules, and the tempting feeling of self-surrender and submission. I remember the comfort of that feeling. Islam frightens you into submitting. I remember that fear too. The churches should do all in their power to win this battle for the souls of humans in search of a compassionate God, who now find that a fierce Allah is closer to hand.

The critical question is this: Does the United States have Christian networks comparable in their strength to that of the Roman Catholic Church that can be used today to combat the next phase of the expansion of fundamentalist Islam into America itself?

I am not a Christian and have no plans to convert. But I am intrigued by religious institutions and the role they play in socializing young people. So on a few occasions since coming to the United States I have accepted invitations to go to church. When I was a Muslim, of course, I used to go to the mosque. Although both churches and mosques are religious institutions, I soon learned that they are as different as day and night.

A mosque is an island of gender apartheid. As a girl in Nairobi I used to go to the beautiful mosque at the city center, where I had to use the obscure entrance at the back of the building. I slipped in quickly with all the other girls and went up the narrow staircase that led to the female-only prayer hall. This hall was a far cry from the men's hall, with its calligraphic decorations, marble pillars, and curved ceilings with miniature domes. The women's prayer hall was painted in a dull off-white color, and its floors were covered with plain mats and carpets.

Once we got to our modest hall we did our ablutions. (In those days, unlike now, female worshippers had the choice of veiling in the mosque and then removing their veil after prayer. Due to the strict social control and the popularity of the orthodox-minded, however, that is no longer an option.) Then we lined up in rows. Electronic speakers carried the voice of the imam to our room. We prostrated ourselves. After the formal prayer of many bows we sat down for the supplications. We responded "Amen" to every plea that the imam made to Allah. On Fridays and during Ramadan there were sermons in Arabic to which we quietly listened. At the end of the prayer and sermon we slipped out of the mosque as quietly as we went in.

The contrast with the churches I have attended in America could not be more complete. Men and women, children and adults, people of all races intermingle. Their attire is no different from what they might wear on the streets. There are no ablutions. The members of the congregation take their places on long wooden benches. Once in a while people stand up to thank God or to pray, and some kneel down with their heads bowed and their hands clasped together. The sermon is in English, accessible and easy to follow. The central message is one of love.

Before I continue I want to make it very clear, and with the greatest possible emphasis, that not all American Protestant churches are so laudable. Watching some charismatic preachers on television, I have heard overt animosity toward science, rants about the horrors of abortion, and celebrations of the ignorant superstitions of "creationism." I have seen "faith healings" and people "talking in tongues." Unfortunately such freak-show churches are growing in popularity. They are not the kind of allies I would wish to have.

The churches I am referring to are the mainstream, moderate denominations who emphasize personal responsibility and repudiate the notion that faith and reason are in some kind of conflict. These churches are already well established in America and dedicate part of their time and resources to educational and poverty-relief projects. Some of them are already involved with the new and resettled groups from Africa and elsewhere.

Unlike the Islamists, these moderate churches do not offer spiritual guidance but only practical help. I think they should do both. They need to step up to the challenge of providing new Muslim immigrants with the concept of a God who is a symbol of love, tolerance, rationality, and patriotism. They need to organize, to map the Muslim communities and start a tireless campaign to convince Muslims that a constitution of freedom is preferable to a constitution of submission, that life's challenges can best be overcome with the traditional Christian values of hard work, individual responsibility, frugality, tolerance, and moderation.

Some readers may still be skeptical that the clash of civilizations can be won through religious competition. But I know it can work because I have seen it with my own eyes.

The asylum-seeker center in Lunteren where I lived when I first went to the Netherlands was on the outskirts of the small, close-knit town of Ede. Dutch people from the town's many Protestant churches came by frequently to offer language classes and many other kinds of assistance. They welcomed refugee families into their homes. They didn't do this for other immigrants, but the word *asylum* has a strong, almost spiritual pull to it, suggesting suffering in a way that the word *guest worker* does not. So the Moroccan and Turkish guest-worker community of Ede was left to its own devices.

Ede's refugees had Dutch classes, sports groups, help with their kids. Whole congregations helped them out in all kinds of administrative and practical ways, small and large. A few refugee families actually converted to Christianity and were absorbed into the local churches, and it was soon apparent that these people were far more successful than their counterparts in the immigrant zones. Mostly, however, the volunteers would take into their fold only the Christian immigrants but respect the refugees' faith and not attempt to proselytize. Many refugees later moved on to Holland's big cities, as I did, retaining the memory of the goodness and kindness of the many Dutch people who had helped us in the country. I would be willing to bet that those people, and their children, have been subsequently far less receptive to the hateful message of the jihadi Muslims.

The contrast between our experience as asylum seekers and that of Ede's swelling population of guest workers was revealing. The guest workers did not receive the tireless individual help that we refugees did, because their community of voluntary migrants was seen as set apart. Community leaders, usually imams, received grants from the Dutch government to set up community centers, where the jihadis lectured people on the West's "crusade" against Islam. In other words, the country paid for its own undermining. As a result Ede was the little Dutch town where CNN cameras, who happened to be filming in an immigrant community on September 11, 2001, showed young Muslim kids cheering for the hijackers who brought down the Twin Towers.

But that was only one face of Ede.

When I became a member of the Dutch Parliament the government was sending home asylum seekers whose refugee status had been rejected. In the big cities, Rotterdam and Amsterdam, it was common to meet Dutch-born children of Moroccan origin who could barely speak the language properly even after years of schooling; in contrast, many rejected asylum seekers who had lived in small towns like Ede were completely integrated, sometimes after just three or four years. Whole congregations would defend "their" asylum seekers and try to prevent them from being deported. They would say, "They are part of our community, their children were born here, they are assimilated."

Thanks to the Christian churches who had taken such care of them, this was true. There is a lesson here not just for the Netherlands, and not just for Europe, but for all of the West, America included.

The *Miyé* and the *Magaalo*

In many ways my life has been a matter of time travel: I have traversed the centuries between clan culture and the modern, liberal societies of the West. But my grandmother, Ibaado, the daughter of Hassan, the son of Ali, and the grandson of Seed, also traversed centuries. She moved from an ancient nomadic culture to a more contemporary one, to which she never became reconciled. In a sense it has been the work of my lifetime to put my grandmother's ghost to rest.

As soon as I could speak I learned to call Grandma by her formal title, *Ayeeyo*. It was never just *you*; I had at all times to employ the word *Grandmother* to show respect. She was fearsome in policing this, as in most other matters. And she did not appreciate curiosity.

When Grandmother taught me how to milk goats and make fires, and cursed me for failing in these tasks, I would sometimes find the courage to ask her how old she was when she made her first fire and who taught her to milk. When she lamented that sending me to school was a sinful and terrible mistake, I would ask her if there were schools in her time. Questions about her life met with verbal and sometimes physical punishment. "The end of times is nigh!" she would scream. "You disrespectful child, you have the audacity to question me? May the forefathers shorten your life! Why do you want to know my age? Would you like me dead? Am I in the way, perhaps?" Her voice would rise from a hiss to a screech and fall back to a hiss. She would pace around the room with her robe tucked under one arm and loom over me like a hawk over her prey. Then she would use her free hand and grab me by my hair or ear. I learned to duck. As I grew taller and less able to wriggle past her I learned to edge over to the door when Grandmother's anger rose.

"Ayeeyo, Ayeeyo, forgive me, forgive me, please," I would bleat. But my grandmother was teaching me judgment and circumspection. I learned to hold my tongue.

Then, in times of her choosing, she would start talking about herself. These moments were arbitrary; we did not see them coming. She occasionally told us stories of hardships she had encountered, droughts or epidemics. But I gleaned most of my information about her life, and most other subjects of interest, when I eavesdropped on her conversations with one of our female relatives, or when she scolded Ma, in whispers, about Ma's choices and practices that Grandma disapproved of. That's how I learned about the tensions between her and my grandfather, how she had dealt with her feelings about his other wives, and her most difficult dilemma of all: year after year bearing daughters instead of another son.

That was the hardest burden of all. Grandma used expressions like "I swear by my only child," meaning her only son. Although her daughters had always looked after her, she completely dismissed them. To me she would say, "If you were *my* daughter you would shape up or I would personally bury you deep in the ground, in the way that is reserved only for those who bring shame." The only values that she cherished were nomad values. The only traits of character that counted were nomad characteristics.

It was true: my grandma had a temper and a strong will. Always. She ignored my father's wishes and circumcised Haweya and me; when Ma confronted her, she threw the worst tantrum ever and threatened to leave, turning the tables so that Ma had to beg her to stay.

Grandma was thirteen when her father married her off to Artan, the son of Umar, who was the son of Ahmed, who was the son of Samakaab. But it is only through a complex calculation of seasons, droughts, epidemics, and other stories orally transmitted from her parents and relatives that her true age at marriage could be estimated. A bride price was paid to her father: she-camels, goats, sheep, bushels of rice, gold coins, and an oath to resolve potential conflicts between the two clans in discussion instead of combat. An animal was slaughtered; meat and camel milk were served during the feast; poetry was recitals and a rhythmic dancing to drums followed; and the next day the groom departed with his purchase, his child bride.

My grandmother's mother had died young. Her father had remarried, and his new wife, who may not have been much older than my grandmother, did not get on well with his daughter. The solution was to marry her off.

My grandmother tried at first to escape her new husband. She packed a few things—a *guntiino* cloth, her knife for making mats, perhaps a little food—filled her gourd with water, and set off across the desert to find her father's hut. I do not know how many days her journey took. According to her, she won everyone's admiration for finding her way back to her father's home unharmed: she had not been eaten by wild animals, had survived hunger and thirst, and was not raped by the vagabond camel boys who roamed the desert. But her father and her clan were also angry with her, for she had set a terrible example to all the other potential brides of her age and dishonored the family.

It was resolved that my grandmother should be permitted to rest for a day or two and would then be returned to her lawful husband. But before the agreed-upon time had passed a delegation of searchers arrived, led by her husband. They were well received, fed and watered, and offered profuse apologies. Then they set off for the second and last time with my grandmother.

"Two seasons later, I gave birth to your aunt Hawo," she would tell us. Did she mean two dry seasons, or a dry season followed by a rainy season? Who knew? Her method of measuring time was extremely unreliable, as in northern Somalia it sometimes does not rain for very long stretches of time.

Aunt Hawa was, of course, a girl. This was bad news for my grandmother, but she was young and her husband was willing to give her the benefit of the doubt: she would soon bear him sons. But only one of her sons survived infancy. After she had borne him eight daughters and only one son, my grandfather finally married again, for he needed more sons. His new wife gave him three sons in succession.

Overcome with shame and anger, Grandma packed her bags and left, never to return. My grandfather died a year or so later, and Grandmother always made it clear that he died because he could not cope without her. The new wife was foolish. She could not help him navigate the desert by smelling the air and analyzing old trails. She bore him sons but had no idea how to keep order in his camp, how to receive the elders from his subclan and others; she was always late with meals, and her sons were undisciplined.

Under Grandma's hard hand, her husband's caravan had run smoothly and was much admired and much envied. That was thanks to her sacrifices, her endurance, diligence, hard work, and honor. Her husband's decision to take another wife was a shock to her, an insult, an expression of ingratitude on his part. All the talk about nobility did not deter Grandma from bolting a second and final time from her husband and his estate.

The very fact that she could actually leave and not be recaptured was a sign that things had changed. It is on this point that I always found Grandma's resentment of modernity odd. She claimed to hate every part of it: the arrival of the white man, the technology and superior weapons he used to oppress the free and proud Somalis, the decay of our nomad culture and loss of roots. She seemed to forget that she had voluntarily *left* her world because she felt betrayed by her husband and shamed by her cowife's success in bearing sons. And she seemed to forget that the reason she *could* leave, and survive, was that her daughters were, to some extent, able to make a living in those modernizing societies that she so hated.

Even as she taught us the old lessons, she herself knew, I think, that they were not, perhaps had never been, truly valid. She taught us that our husbands would be our rulers, but that if we were good wives they would make us their queens. If we could navigate the desert by listening to the wind our husbands would come to rely on us. If we could make *muqmad*—dried meat cut into the tiniest beads, cooked in oil for hours, and mixed with dates—that did not rot even in the hottest sun, then they would honor us forever.

But we had a refrigerator.

There is a Las Vegas moment in every culture, when the electricity goes on. It represents exactly what the real Las Vegas means in the West: it is a space where you can throw off the fetters of traditional morality and values, where you can gamble and fornicate. You can indulge yourself in secret, and then sneak home to respectability. This

Las Vegas of big neon lights and modern temptations that appears in every culture is something the elders and preservers of morality cannot police, because its power lies outside their understanding. This contact with modernity is a death blow to their ancient culture and the old ways of life.

Culture is accumulated human experience, an anatomy of obstacles and techniques for overcoming them. Traditional culture breaks down once that first contact with modernity is made. For next comes the radio, the TV, and the washing machine; then a rush of neon lights, cell phones, and new roads, all of which usurp the stories of the grandmothers and the elders, stories that used to hold communities together.

When my grandmother left the nomadic life of her clan and moved to the city, the history book that was inside her, the archive of poetry and folk knowledge, the museum of skills, was rendered in one stroke almost irrelevant to her life as well as to ours.

As she learned, modernity is not a controlled zone that you can visit and then leave, then return and ask for forgiveness. Modernity is a permanent state that replaces your former outlook. You can try to fight it, but it is irresistible. It sucks in your young.

It is painful to transition from a premodern society to the contemporary world. But although assimilation can be postponed, it must happen one day. Postponing it only creates difficulty, for those who have failed to make the transition cannot continue to live a purely traditional life. That old world is lost.

The West is full of academic departments, commentators, intellectuals who write about diversity and respect for minority cultures. They have an entrenched interest—endowed university chairs, subsidized publications—so minorities who are stuck somewhere between their original way of life and civilization are literally a source of income for these commentators and prophets of diversity. Unfortunately, celebrating and preserving their traditional cultures cannot recreate the dreamworld of the traditional utopia; all that happens is that the minorities are kept outside of the boundaries of civilization even longer, the recipients of condescension and false compassion.

When I speak of assimilation, I mean assimilation into civilization. Aboriginals, Afghanis, Somalis, Arabs, Native Americans—all these non-Western groups have to make that transition to modernity. When I was a child in Somalia, we called this the difference between *Miyé* and *Magaalo*. If you live in the rural, traditional *Miyé*, life is predictable: it revolves around definite roles for men and women, mostly dedicated to subsistence, getting and cooking food, bearing and raising children, and religious rituals. Community trumps individual urges, vices, passions, and aspirations. Year after year all days resemble each other. Life in the *Miyé* is disrupted by natural disasters, droughts, wars, and conquests, but these are matters you deal with in the old, ancestral ways. They are part of the cosmic plan that we all just accept, *Inshallah*.

The biggest disrupter of the *Miyé* is the *Magaalo,* the city. Whether that urbanization comes to the countryside, or the people of the *Miyé* move to the city, the advent of the *Magaalo* is inevitable and irreparable. This is a tide of history that my grandmother understood could not be stopped, that was sweeping along her and her own family, including me.

Those individuals from the *Miyé* who either instinctively or rationally understand that their traditional order of life is doomed make the transition to modernity, and they thrive there. Those who resist or move back and forth—one inch forward, one inch back, borrowing parts of modernity but not all of it—are sooner or later confronted with reality. They are only prolonging their pain. Learning the language of modern society, learning hygiene, adopting a modern code of sexual and social conduct—only after individuals have mastered those skills can they thrive in the real world.

Prevailing wisdom in the West seems to be that immigrants can thrive only if they stick with their own. It reminds me of my work as an interpreter in Holland. A typical dialogue would be with a social worker trying to find accommodations for a Somali client. The client would cling to the idea of finding a home with separate areas for men and women. After a while the social worker would say that such accommodations cannot be found: Holland does not have houses built like that. "If you really want it, you will have to have a lot of money and have it made on your own," she would say (and I would translate). "Even that will be difficult because you must then meet the city's building requirements." There would be tension in the room;

the conversation would get angry. The client would accuse the social worker of not respecting his wishes, his culture; he would claim (and I would translate) that he was being abandoned, treated with a lack of respect, ill-served.

This idea that immigrants need to maintain group cohesion promotes the perception of these people as victim groups requiring special treatment. If people *should* conform to their ancestral culture, it therefore follows that they should also be *helped* to maintain it, with their own schools, government-subsidized community groups, and even their own system of legal arbitration.

In the real world, equal respect for all cultures doesn't translate into a rich mosaic of colorful and proud peoples interacting peacefully while maintaining a delightful diversity of food and craftwork. It translates into closed pockets of oppression, ignorance, and abuse.

This is one of my grandmother's stories.

Once upon a time there was a man, Saleh the wrestler. He was of such-and-such a clan and subclan. Each week he would challenge another star wrestler from this or that subclan. The challenged man, poor fellow, had to accept or he would never find a wife from a good clan. But if Saleh defeated him, he still would not find a wife from a good clan. Saleh challenged and defeated so many men that good families would now send their firstborn sons far away to avoid meeting the challenge.

Saleh was great at wrestling, but he was not content with that: he boasted also of his talent for poetry. One day a poet named Burhaan from the Dhulbahante clan invited Saleh the wrestler to meet him in the arena of words instead of the arena of muscles. This caused a huge sensation. What would Saleh do now? If he accepted, ooohhh, he would have to defeat Burhaan or forever be taunted as a fool, a man who knew neither his place nor his calling. If he rejected the challenge, he would be dismissed as a bundle of muscles with no brain. But if he won, he would be Godlike. He could then claim strength of body above all other, and also strength of wit.

Saleh accepted the challenge. Burhaan orated his poem. (Grandma would quote it to us; she knew every word of it. Although sadly I have forgotten it, I remember the flash of her eyes as she declaimed the sonorous words.)

Saleh could not come up with an equivalent poem. He was forever discredited.

The moral of this story is that every person has his place. Know your place, and even if it is lofty, stick to that place. Venturing further, into another man's domain, is foolhardy; boasting that you can match his achievements is an invitation to your downfall.

But I couldn't resist asking Grandma what would happen if a wrestler decided to challenge a poet to fight in the arena of muscles.

"Foolish girl," Grandma told me. "A poet is verse-ready: he will of course reject such a stupid proposal with his intelligence."

And so it was that I learned that poets were very smart people, and that words have a power that can break through many other kinds of force.

Letter to My Unborn Daughter

Dear Child,

Let me start by telling you about my encounter with a brave and remarkable woman named Oriana Fallaci. I met her on a Friday afternoon in Manhattan early in May 2006. She had spoken and written much about the threat of radical Islam, and she got in touch with me through a mutual friend, insisting that I visit her. At the time I knew only that she had forcefully condemned the theology of totalitarianism.

When I rang the bell and the door opened, I was let in by an extremely fragile woman. Small, very thin, and pale, she greeted me by saying, "Darling, I don't have long to live, but it is wonderful that you're visiting me. I have cancer." As she walked up a narrow flight of stairs she continued to speak. "The Muslims could not beat me. Mussolini's fascists could not beat me." She talked to me about an incident in Latin America, when, following an burst of gunfire, she was lumped together with dead bodies and someone accidentally discovered her in a morgue. She told me about the lawsuit against her that was filed by the Italian public prosecutor in a bid to silence her criticism of Islam. "All those evil forces could not beat me. But cancer, cancer, the cancer that's eating my brain . . ." Her flow of words fell away.

In her living room Oriana insisted that we drink champagne to celebrate that I had come to see her. "And you're so young," she said. I offered to get the bottle and to open it, but she said, "No, I can still do this, I have to do this." When I saw how much her hands trembled and how tiny she was in proportion to the large bottle, I insisted on helping her. "No," she said again. "I still want to do this, because I'm able to." Then she began to speak again. And as fragile as her body was, her spirit was so strong and resilient. I listened.

After she had recounted her life journey through Italy, the Middle East, and now in the United States, she arrived at the subject that brought our own paths together: the threat of Islam. But instantly she changed the subject. "You must have a child," she said. "I only regret one thing in my life, and that is that I do not have children. I wanted a baby, I tried to have one, but I tried too late, and I failed. Darling," she almost pleaded with me, "it hurts to be alone. Life is lonely. It must be, sometimes. Still, I would very much have liked to have a child. I would have liked to pass on life. I want for you what I wanted for myself and failed to get. I want you to start thinking about having a child of your own before it is too late. Time flies, and one day you will come to regret that you postponed it."

She handed me copies of her books, in Italian. She had other life lessons to tell me, I knew, but she was visibly exhausted. Twice she said, "Darling, don't let life pass you by." She refused to let me say good-bye and invited me to visit her again. I wanted to. Her fierce eyes and sharp cheekbones and her sense of resolution reminded me of my fearsome aunt Khadija. But four months later, on the morning of September 15, 2006, I was behind my desk at the office of the American Enterprise Institute in Washington when I heard on the radio that Oriana was gone. I remember her telling me, "Darling, when the cancer kills me, many will celebrate." I belong to those who mourn her loss.

Dear child, she inspired me to have you. In the short time I was with her Oriana told me that she had miscarried, and months later I read her *Letter to a Child Never Born*. Her message to me was dual: that motherhood is a choice and that love between a woman and a man is a hoax. I agree and disagree with Oriana. Motherhood for women in my circumstances is indeed a choice, but it is not a choice for many others. And love between a man and a woman is not a hoax.

First, motherhood. Your great-grandmother had little choice about being a mother, maybe none. She was about thirteen when she was given away to an older man. She conceived at fourteen. When she was sixteen, she gave birth to twins. She was always proud to tell us that she did it alone, under a tree, cut the umbilical cords herself and returned home that evening, not only with the babies but also with her count of sheep and goats. The only thing that marred what could have been a moment of exceptional joy and pride was that she showed up with two girls instead of two boys.

In her life there was little to choose. The seasons chose for her. It barely rained, so she and her family moved from waterhole to waterhole. Sometimes wild animals attacked them, sometimes enemy tribes. Animals and men vied for the green pastures and oases, for scraps of food and shelter. My grandmother's life oscillated between periods of subsistence that were considered luxurious and periods of malnutrition and famine. All this was punctuated by epidemics. She used to tell us of the seasons of *duumo*, or malaria, an epidemic spread by the mosquitoes that suck the blood of their victims and leave parasites behind. Mothers woke up and found their babies dead after their little bodies had been wracked by fever all night long. Wailing, the women would run to the next hut to ask for help, only to find that another child had died there and two more in the next hut. On and on, death spread over miles of huts. Young men, children, women—many people became sick, feverish, and in a matter of weeks or days passed away.

My grandmother told these stories along with stories of other women getting pregnant and giving birth to more children, of their suffering and dying, of being overtaken by circumstances, being pushed into marriage, war, or worse. It seemed to me like a senseless cycle of pain, discomfort, and death.

In the letter to her unborn baby Oriana Fallaci, that brave, unfazed, and unabashed woman, admits fear. Not fear of pain, suffering, or even death but fear of her child. She worries that her baby may accuse her of bringing him or her into a world of violence, death, pain, and misery. For Oriana life is an effort, a war that is renewed each day, and its moments of joy are brief parentheses for which one pays a cruel price.

My child, the world was always full of fear, full of pain and suffering. Every day there are reports of accidents, bankruptcies, wars and starvation, the threat of nuclear bombs, the rise of dictatorships, mass exoduses of boys and girls, men and women from battle-torn states, whole villages that now carry the status "displaced" because of natural and man-made disasters. There is not only news of destruction but also the threat of more miseries to come: shortages of water in the near future will threaten the lives of millions of people, and rising sea levels could inundate whole cities.

Yet I want you to come into this world.

I think back to my grandmother's life and I am filled with optimism for you. Grandmother was never sure how old she was, but we estimated that she probably made it to eighty-nine. When she died, her children and grandchildren surrounded her. For her too life was an effort. It had moments of joy, sometimes long stretches of joy, but when she was rearing me I do not remember a day when she did not mention death.

My mother, your grandmother, had it a little better than her mother did. She conceived me in a city. I was not born under a tree, and she did not cut the umbilical cord herself; she gave birth to me in a hospital, with a doctor and nurses. But I came too soon. The doctor, nurses, and relatives in attendance were all convinced that I would die, for I weighed no more than 3.3 pounds. Mother had no strategy other than to lay me on her belly, wrap the hospital bed sheets around us both, and rub my back and croon to me. Morning after morning, night after night, my little heart kept beating and I cried—my only signs of life. She wanted me. Unlike Oriana, she did not ponder the complexities of what life would present to me, what it would mean to be born into violence, corruption, torture, and anarchy, countless diseases and upheaval. Mother just wanted me to live, whatever life brought.

My mother went on to conceive child after child. She miscarried and conceived and gave birth and lost children and conceived again. Whenever she and my father were reunited, my mother conceived. The last child was stillborn. Mohammed was his name. He would have been your youngest uncle, born in 1979.

This history of conceptions and miscarriages is very important for me to know. It is the experiences of your foremothers that give me the confidence to take a chance on having you. In that chain of four generations of women—I am counting you as the fourth—I see a profound advancement in the quality of life and also the potential for continued improvement.

I now live in Oriana's world, the world of science, where they take pictures of you in the womb when you are just a seed, "a transparent egg, suspended in the womb that looks like any mammal." Women visit a doctor every two weeks for examinations, and when two months are completed the doctor says, "It's a very delicate transition." I read Oriana's words and grapple with the irony. Your grandmother would say, "With all the science and education and the knowledge that the infidel amasses, they do not grasp that every part of life is a delicate transition!" But that is what knowledge brings. As the third generation from that woman in the bushes, I have been exposed to too much of it to be nonchalant about conceiving you. I have to think, like Oriana, about whether or not you want to be born. Do you want to come into a world of violence and fraud and corruption? Do you want life?

The other choice, as Oriana pointed out, is nothingness and silence. Do you prefer nothingness? To stay where you are, in the silence that is not death, because you have not been alive?

That beautiful frail woman held my hand in her apartment and said, "Let your child come." She knew. She had worked out for herself an answer that appealed to me strongly. When she conceived, almost everyone around her advised her to have an abortion, but she refused. She wanted her baby.

Oriana told me the story of how her community rejected her unborn child: the man who fathered her child, her doctor and nurse, her pharmacist, her boss, her best friend. They all said to her, "Get rid of your baby. Abort. Think of your career." A single woman who decided to have a baby was considered irresponsible. The father of her child offered to pay for half the abortion (only half because, after all, the conception was partially her fault too).

My community would not agree with Oriana's. My doctor is a gay man. I went to him and asked him if he could freeze my eggs or embryos. He said he could, but advised against it. Because I was thirty-seven, he said, "Just have the baby. You are a healthy woman. You are strong. I see no reason for you to take such drastic measures." He never once mentioned the disadvantages to the child of having a single parent. My boss, who is really like an adopted father, would support any decision I made if I were pregnant with you. I could never imagine him persuading me to have you removed. My best friends, my colleagues—no one would stand in my way.

I have struggled with whether to have you on my own, as Oriana tried to, or to marry your father. As she says, having a child is a personal choice. I agree. It's not only a personal choice; it's a very selfish choice. I want to have you for me, for *my* delight, to enrich my existence. I want to know what it is to love unconditionally and be loved back that way. As I carry you in my womb I want to know what it is to "feel the needles of anxiety pierce my soul, each alternating with a flush of joy," as she described the early stages of her pregnancy. I want to feel you grow inside me as another life. I want to hold you. I want to give you life. I want you. And I want you for me.

What shall I give you in return? First I shall teach you how to choose. Sometimes too many options make the mind reel, and sometimes they paralyze us in fear. You, if you make it, will live, unlike your foremothers, in a reality of too many options. And learning to choose is often harder than having only one or no choice at all.

Education—the thrill and pain and exercise of learning—will be available to you in ways it was not to your grandmothers: preschool and kindergarten, elementary and high school, college and university, summer camps and student exchange programs, internships and alumni conferences. You will learn to read and write, to count and clap, to develop your skills at making friends and compromising with rivals; you will have a choice of ballet, painting, classical music, pop, athletics, team sports; you will read Shakespeare in tiny, clever, illustrated children's books and listen to Mozart while you're still in my belly. You will be born in a world of gadgets, and gadgets you shall have—to calculate, to navigate, to call and message and read and listen to music with.

You will have me, your father, your nanny, your teachers, and an extended family of adults all cheering you on. You will learn to assemble and reassemble your priorities with each year that comes. But above all you will have to learn to choose from all the options that we give you.

My education was very different from the one that awaits you. In my school we were required to wear a white shirt and a green skirt, white socks and black shoes, a green cardigan and a green tie with the school emblem. My tie was always askew, my top button always unbuttoned, and my cardigan always getting lost. My high school years were a constant battle with authority.

My mother dictated to me what to wear, when to play (almost never), what to read, and whom to befriend. She did not allow me to make friends with girls, much less boys, from any other community. She banned reading novels and listening to music; asking her if I might go to the cinema made my mother scream and threaten me with physical punishment. The idea of my having a boyfriend made my mother cringe and curse uncontrollably.

Nonetheless I had non-Muslim, Kenyan friends along with my friends from India and Yemen. I read everything I could, and did it practically under her nose. I just tucked the pages of my novels in the midst of the Quran, the only book she allowed. I sneaked out to my friends' homes and listened to their music and watched their movies. I even managed to have a boyfriend. (And this was in the days when there were no cell phones, text messages, or e-mail.)

My dear child, as you grow and make that transition from girl-hood to womanhood your body will change. You'll grow breasts and hips, and your lips will become full. You will become an object of desire for boys, and you will desire them. This was a frightening pros-pect for my mother; I am sure every parent feels a protective twinge at the idea of their child having sex. I am fortunate to have lived in different cultures and to have learned that openness about sexuality is preferable to repression. All cultures that have repressed sexuality attain the opposite of what they seek: sexual diseases spread faster, and unwanted pregnancies increase. Abortions attempted in secret often kill the mother too.

Instead of denying the reality of sexuality, Europeans and Ameri-cans teach their children, as soon as they are old enough to raise the subject, everything they need to know about their bodies: that sex is a source of pleasure, that you can choose when and whom you want to have sex with, all the contraceptives that are available to you, how you can protect yourself against diseases. Then you take the responsi-bility for your own sexuality and for the risk of bringing a child into the world when you're not ready. You take responsibility for avoiding being infected with a disease, as well as for not infecting others. Such openness encourages responsibility and choice based on information and reason and not mystification of intercourse.

So, unlike my mother, I shall not chase away your boyfriends.

My dear child, I shall aspire to give you the freedoms that I did not have. Instead of the rote learning and strict punishments of my childhood, my authority and that of your school will be more relaxed; it will be geared toward training you to make choices, to take responsibility for the outcome of those choices and to learn from the mistakes that you make. This may give you the sometimes dangerous sense that perfection is attainable: the perfect toy, the perfect best friend, the perfect boyfriend, the perfect home, the perfect community, the perfect country. Such constant inspiration to innovate, to improve, and to progress is in many ways healthy. But, my child, there is no such thing as perfection. The quest for it leads only to frustration and a vulnerability to utopian ideas. At such times reflect on what happened and what continues to happen to the societies of your grandmothers, where the tribe is fixated upon the theologian's promise of paradise.

Living in America you'll be exposed to a stronger promise of the perfect society. You will hear of many isms: socialism and communism and all sorts of cults and collectivisms. The perfection they promise usually comes at the price of mass suffering and death.

Challenging authority, playing cat-and-mouse with the teachers, having secret agreements with the other kids, and keeping my parents and teachers in the dark—these all provided me with a great deal of entertainment. I wonder if giving you too much freedom will suck the spice out of life. What if, in giving you too much, I take away something vital from your life? What if I curb your sense of adventure? You will be born in an America of many *post*s: post–civil rights, postfeminism, post–cold war. You will take so much for granted. Decades ago Oriana had to justify the fact that she wanted to be a single mother. Now there is no such hindrance. What will you fight for? What will you fight against?

My dear child, I do not worry about the bleakness of life. I worry about the bleakness of having no challenges in life. In Holland, for example, I lived in a laboratory of a society, where almost all the challenges in life had been erased. We were taken care of from the cradle to the grave. We debated on euthanasia, a movement that started by defending the right of terminal patients to end their lives and then morphed into a movement that defended the right of anyone to be helped by a doctor if he was tired of life. And this demand of a right to be assisted with suicide when you are tired of life had to be subsidized by the state. To my astonishment, some of the active members of that right were in their twenties and thirties. They had been protected from life, exposed to too little challenge; every day was the same for them. They had nothing to fight for. They convinced themselves that the world was a nasty crucible and declared themselves tired of life.

I fear that you might become tired of life, and I cannot think of how to prevent that, except perhaps to remind you of the hard lives of your forefathers and foremothers so that you can appreciate what you have. That is your challenge and the challenge of your peers: not only how to keep the freedoms you have, but how to share that freedom with those who don't have it.

Beware of being brainwashed, my child. Allah and his agents played a big part in my childhood. A man named Boqol Sawm tried to terrify us into being devout. He droned into our ears that we were all headed to hell for sinning. In hell we would be burned in hungry flames, dipped in cooking oil, made whole again and broiled from head to toe. Each time we perished, Allah would remake us, give us back our bodies and skins ever more smooth and sensitive. Then he would give his angels orders to start burning us again. These horrors would go on and on until Allah was satisfied that we had been justly punished.

I came to value the struggle to elude all forms of authority as part of the spice of my life. I have kept the great lessons of duty and perseverance that my mother and grandmother taught, as well as the passion for learning that some of my teachers in high school instilled in me. I was inspired by my father's resistance to state authority when he opposed the Somali dictatorship from 1969 to 1990. But I resisted his authority to decide for me when and whom to marry. Now, of course, I shall worry about your finding the right person. But unlike my father, I will let you pick your mate. And if I think he is wrong for you, I will swallow my judgment, however hard that may be, and defer to you.

My child, love between you and me is unconditional. Unknowingly, we may hurt one another, disapprove of each other's choices, friends, and tastes, but whatever happens, you can depend on me. No matter what your age, your sorrows will be my sorrows, your happiness my joy. Love between a man and a woman is not a hoax, as Oriana stated, but it is conditional. It is contingent on chemistry, compatibility, temperament, lifestyle, even income, but if you fall in love and it's mutual, then it's a very powerful force. Love between a man and a woman can be generous, and should be generous. Unfortunately, my dear child, you will hear of many love stories where the basic desire is to possess one another, to change one another, to control one another. It's precisely these things that kill affection and passion. Steer clear of those, if you can.

There are three values I would like to share with you from my journey of freedom, and one pitfall to avoid.

The first one, I am sure, will be drilled into you in your American school. It is the value of responsibility. I have made a lot of mistakes, but I strive to take responsibility for my actions. I am impulsive and impatient and sometimes I agree to things I don't want to do and can't do. But when I find a moment to think about my actions or inactions I find that most of the time I am the only one to blame.

Related to responsibility is duty. How boring, you might think. Duty: what a tedious four-letter word. There are things in life that are not exciting, that are not fun, that are not fair and do not feel right. But we must do them. Whenever I could, I have supported my family. I did it knowing they would not support me in return, and I rarely enjoyed the tasks. But those tasks gave me a personal reward, a sense of pride and accomplishment. Duty might seem selfless, altruistic, but the outcome, at least for me, has been a selfish pleasure.

The third value is that of critical thinking. I learned about it at the University of Leiden. My professors there gave us the works of different men and women to read. They called those works theories, ideas that could be right or wrong. Our main task for five years was to sort the good ideas from the bad ones, not only to learn to refute the theories of others but to come up with better ones ourselves. The process was to teach us to think and to recognize thoughts, even big complicated ones, as the product of the human mind. There was nothing divine in Leiden except the human faculty of reason. I was very fortunate to have gone to university, to have been exposed to the exercise of critical thinking. If you are lucky, you shall be educated in this valuable skill too. But beware of zealots of any flavor. Beware of proselytizers of religious utopias. And beware of professors who confuse teaching students how to think with teaching them what to think.

Many people in your life will tell you of all the emotional pitfalls that lie waiting for a young a girl to tumble into. Let me touch on one: the trap of resentment. It is probably the worst mental prison in the world. It is the inability to let go of anger and the perceived or real injustices we suffer. Some people let one or two, or maybe ten unpleasant experiences poison the rest of their lives. They let their anger ferment and rot their personality. They end up seeing themselves as victims of their parents, teachers, their peers and preachers.

People always ask me if I am angry at my mother or father, at the Quran teacher who fractured my skull, at the Dutch politician who tried to take away my citizenship, at any number of people who have slighted me or gone out of their way to hurt and humiliate me. I am not. I know that my parents loved me unconditionally in their own way. I know that those who seek to hurt and humiliate me want to trap me in a prison of anger and resentment and there is no point in rewarding them with success.

I have discovered life for what it is: a gift from nature. For those who believe in a benign God, it is a gift from God. It is a gift we enjoy for just a brief period of time. Some of us get to hang around longer than others, but we all pass. In that brief period it is a tragedy to trap our minds in a toxic cage of bitterness and rage. Such a snare shifts our energies from focusing on how to make the best of our lives to becoming vengeful, apathetic victims of others.

Life holds so much promise for you. Please take it with both your little hands, and live it well. Live, laugh, love, and give back with a broad grin.

I shall not bring you up in the Muslim faith, the faith of your forefathers and foremothers, for I believe it is fatally flawed. I will, however, introduce you to different religions, their founders, and some of their followers. I will bring you up to have faith *in yourself*, in science and your own reason and the force of life. And I will never seek to impose my own beliefs or unbelief on you.

Whenever I rebelled against my mother's values she would blackmail me and even curse me with fearsome Somali maledictions. "I wish you a child that will reject your God the way you have rejected my God!" was one. She told me I would never know how painful that rejection is unless I went through it myself. So I fully expect it will be terrible to accept your independence. But even if it is so, I will try to hide my pain.

At my father's deathbed, I knew that his values and mine would never be reconciled. He could never understand my unbelief. He prayed for me until his last breath. And I could never re-adopt his belief in Allah, in prophets, in holy books, angels, and the hereafter. But our unconditional love for one another, the love between a parent and a child, was so much more powerful than that belief. And the proof was the way we clutched each other's hands at the end. That earthly love is my faith. It is the love I shall always give you.

The AHA Foundation

The Ayaan Hirsi Ali Foundation was set up in 2008 as a charitable organization to help protect and defend the rights of women in the West, especially in the United States, against militant Islam and harmful tribal customs. Its aim is to investigate, inform, and influence against several types of crimes against women including the denial of education for girls, genital mutilation, forced marriage, honor violence, and restrictions on girls' freedom of movement.

The AHA Foundation seeks to raise awareness in America that some of these violent practices against women are increasingly carried out in the United States. The foundation also exists to provide girls and women in distress with information and assistance, by creating a database of people and institutions qualified to deal with cases of maltreatment and abuse.

www.theahafoundation.org

About the Author

Ayaan Hirsi Ali was born in Somalia, raised a Muslim, and spent her childhood and young adulthood in Africa and Saudi Arabia. In 1992 she went to the Netherlands as a refugee, escaping a forced marriage to a distant cousin she had never met. She learned Dutch and worked as an interpreter in abortion clinics and shelters for battered women. After earning her college degree in political science, she worked for the Labor Party. She denounced Islam after the September 11 terrorist attacks and became a member of the Dutch Parliament, fighting for the rights of Muslim women in Europe, the enlightenment of Islam, and security in the West. She went on to work for the American Enterprise Institute in Washington, D.C. She established the Ayaan Hirsi Ali Foundation (www.theahafoundation.org), which aims to combat several types of crimes against women, including female genital mutilation, forced marriages, and honor violence, through education, outreach, and the dissemination of knowledge.

Her book *Infidel* has been a #1 bestseller in Europe, and she continues to receive honors from around the world. She was named one of *Time* magazine's 100 Most Influential People of 2005, one of the *Glamour* Heroes of 2005, and was *Reader's Digest*'s European of the Year. She has also received Norway's Human Rights Service's Bellwether of the Year Award, the Danish Freedom Prize, the Swedish Democracy Prize, the Moral Courage Award for commitment to conflict resolution, ethics, and world citizenship, and the Martin Luther King Jr. Unsung Heroes Award.